MEN'S STUDIES

MEN'S STUDIES
A Selected and Annotated
Interdisciplinary Bibliography

Eugene R. August

1985

Libraries Unlimited, Inc. • Littleton, Colorado

LIBRARIES UNLIMITED, INC.
P.O. Box 263
Littleton, Colorado 80160-0263

Library of Congress Cataloging in Publication Data

August, Eugene R., 1935 -
    Men's studies.

    Includes indexes.
    1. Men--Bibliography. I. Title.
Z7164.M49A84   1985   [HQ1090]   016.3053'1   84-28894
ISBN 0-87287-481-8

Libraries Unlimited Books are bound with Type II nonwoven material that meets and exceeds National Association of State Textbook Administrators' Type II nonwoven material specifications Class A through E.

To the memory of my father

Joseph L. August

TABLE OF CONTENTS _____

ACKNOWLEDGMENTS _____

In compiling this bibliography, I have incurred debts of thanks to many people, only some of whom can be acknowledged here:

Francis M. Lazarus, Dean of the College of Arts and Sciences at the University of Dayton, and R. Alan Kimbrough, Chairperson of the English Department, for encouragement and for a sabbatical leave to work on this project;

the students in my "Modern Men: Images and Reality" courses at the University of Dayton, especially Marlene Acito, Charles Longo, Patricia Hayden, Tracey Howard, James Metter, and Elinor Fraver Mitchell, for insights and bibliographic help;

the library staff of the Roesch Library at the University of Dayton, especially Joanne Maynard, for her skill with inter-library loans; Anita Michel and Robert Montavon for help in obtaining hard-to-get books; and Mary Ann Walker, for her work on computer searches;

James R. Rettig of The University Library, The University of Illinois at Chicago, for his expertise and friendship;

Nancy Buddendeck and Fran Suess, for secretarial help above and beyond the call of duty;

Heather Cameron, Head, Editorial Department, Libraries Unlimited, for her editorial skills; and

Barbara August, my wife of twenty wonderful years, and our sons Bob and Jim, for unfailing support.

INTRODUCTION_____

Neither a fad nor a backlash, men's studies are the logical complement to women's studies and a necessary component of any balanced gender-related scholarship.

Although at one time it was argued that all traditional academic disciplines were "men's studies," the inadequacy of this viewpoint has become increasingly clear. Given the obvious omissions and distortions about females in traditional scholarship, few people would now question the need for women's studies; by the same token, however, many people now recognize that these traditional studies also contained serious omissions and distortions about males. Scholars in the past had been very selective about *which* males were studied and *what* was studied about them. Historians tended to focus upon a minority of males in positions of political and social power while ignoring the lives of the vast majority of males. "Feminist historians rightly point out that until recently most history dealt with men," writes Peter N. Stearns in *Be a Man!* "But it did not deal with ordinary men, nor with the private spheres of male existence." Similarly, fathers have often been overlooked in psychology, sociology, and family studies.

The concept of gender or sex role, moreover, is so recent that it has not had time to permeate academic studies or popular writing. In the past, masculinity was taken as an unquestioned presupposition; few people recognized that social forces, as well as biological ones, profoundly influenced what they thought was "natural" behavior for men. While considerable attention has been given to women's roles, only recently have some scholars begun to regard masculinity as a cultural construct imposed upon a biological given. The result has been an imbalance in our knowledge of the sexes. "Compared with what we know about the identity problems of women," writes Joe L. Dubbert in *A Man's Place: Masculinity in Transition*, "we know relatively little about the American male's struggle with his identity."

Finally, little attention has been paid to the class bias of cultural definitions of masculinity. The male taken as the norm for an entire society was most often a member of the more influential and wealthier classes. The poorer male, faced with an imperfect chance of emulating this cultural norm, frequently was not regarded as a man at all, and thus he was usually beneath the notice of scholars and writers. In defining masculinity, societies and scholars have sometimes exhibited a definite upscale bias: not only women, but poorer and minority males as well, have been regarded as "the other."

Given such limited concepts of masculinity in the past, it is small wonder that many people have questioned the adequacy of traditional studies as "men's studies." Moreover, the gradual emergence of consciousness-raising and men's rights groups has begun to focus attention upon an array of men's issues and concerns, ranging from the treatment of fathers in divorce and custody procedures to male-only military obligations. While lacking the extensive support and acceptance of the women's liberation movement, the men's movement and the issues it raises are not likely to disappear. The time has clearly arrived not only for a new range of scholarship to extend and re-evaluate what we thought we knew about men but also for full-scale discussion of men's social issues and concerns.

This need has been felt both inside and outside academia. At its first national convention in Houston in 1981 the National Congress for Men approved resolutions calling for equal funding of, and attention to, men's studies as well as women's studies. In recent years courses focusing solely on men have sprung up in college curricula across the country, and segments devoted to males have been incorporated into many established women's courses. In 1984 the National Organization for Changing Men established a task group on men's studies and began publishing a men's studies newsletter. The impetus for such innovations was succinctly expressed by Betty Friedan in 1980. "The dialogue has gone on too long in terms of women alone," she wrote in the May issue of *Redbook*. "Let men join women in the center of the second stage" of the modern gender colloquy.

It is precisely this need for greater knowledge about males in modern society that *Men's Studies* addresses.

SCOPE OF THE PRESENT BIBLIOGRAPHY

To prevent an unmanageable sprawl in its contents, *Men's Studies* includes only books written in English or available in English translation. In addition, books were required to meet one or more of the following criteria:

1. The book must be primarily about males as males. That is, it must not be about another topic (such as war or the labor movement), however closely related that subject might be to men's lives.

2. The book must exhibit an awareness of the masculine gender role. It should not contain unquestioned assumptions about the nature of masculinity.

3. The book must demonstrate an awareness of other works in men's studies and women's studies. It should not proceed as if nothing of value has been written on gender-related subjects.

4. The book must make some effort to transcend stereotypes of males and to present them as human beings in all their complexity and contradictions, with their triumphs and failures given equitable treatment.

5. The book must contribute significant insights either into the universal experience of being male or into current conditions shaping men's lives.

6. The book must explore topics or issues of importance to males as males, such as men's rights or vasectomy. It must exhibit an understanding of differing views on the topic when disagreement exists.

Although few books meet all of the above criteria, those included in *Men's Studies* meet one or more of them in some significant fashion.

Men's Studies is designed for a varied audience. It is intended as a guide for students and scholars researching gender-related topics in the emerging men's studies courses, in the already established women's studies programs, and in traditional disciplines. The amount of writing on women and women's concerns is enormous and widely known; the amount of writing on men and men's concerns, while smaller, is considerable but not widely known. The present bibliography is intended to aid those researchers needing to complement or balance women's studies with an equal awareness of men's history, psychology, sexuality, gender roles, public issues, and so on.

For researchers in several areas, the present bibliography provides a long-needed interdisciplinary overview of recent literature about men. Published works in men's studies cover such a wide range of disciplines that important books in one area are too often lost to researchers in another. One goal of the present bibliography is to provide easy access to "hidden literature" for the person largely unfamiliar with work in other disciplines. By doing so, *Men's Studies* should stimulate the intellectual cross-fertilization that is necessary for interdisciplinary studies. It should thus be a welcome addition to the collections of both public and academic libraries.

Finally, it is hoped that *Men's Studies* will be useful for a wider audience of general readers—especially for men seeking greater awareness of men's issues, history, roles, and rights, and for women interested in the other half of the modern gender revolution.

ENTRIES AND ANNOTATIONS

Entries in *Men's Studies* follow *The Chicago Manual of Style*, 13th ed., revised and expanded (Chicago and London: University of Chicago Press, 1982). The author's last name—or, in the case of edited anthologies, the editor's last name—is used to list items alphabetically. The author's name is followed by the book's full title and subtitle, series title, translator or editor, place of publication, publisher, publisher's subdivision or book series, date of publication, and page numbers to the last relevant page. If the book has been reprinted, the place of publication, publisher, and date are given. If the book is available in paperback, the abbreviation "pa." is used.

Considerable effort has been made to locate all reprintings of a book, although it is likely that some omissions occur. Price information for books has been omitted because, given the rapid fluctuations in prices, the entry would most likely consist of price misinformation. The ISBN has also been omitted because, with the information provided here, it will be readily accessible to those who wish it.

The citations note illustrations, including drawings, photographs, art works, graphs, or other visual aids. Appendixes, notes, indexes, and bibliographies are listed. The page numbers of bibliographies are included as a research tool: in this way, *Men's Studies* offers valuable openings into a much larger literature about men than is included here.

Given an audience of interdisciplinary researchers and educated general readers, the annotations in *Men's Studies* have been written for the nonspecialist. This practice enables readers versed in one discipline to comprehend work in another. Specialized jargon has been avoided. Although description of methodology is included where appropriate, no detailed critique of methodology from a specialized viewpoint has been attempted.

Annotations in *Men's Studies* attempt to record the work's major theses and conclusions, as well as its methods of study where appropriate. In cases when the book's relevance to men's studies might not be immediately apparent, the annotation attempts to explain its pertinence. For more controversial books, the annotation often indicates what the range of reader reactions is likely to be. In some cases, the annotation reflects a personal assessment of the book—an assessment with which the reader should feel free to disagree.

A word about some words. In general, an attempt has been made in the annotations to retain the useful distinction between "sex" signifying biological and physiological differences between males and females, and "gender" signifying the culturally defined behavior and attitudes appropriate for males and females. Similarly, "male" and "female" usually designate sexual differences, while "masculine" and "feminine" usually designate gender differences. In practice, however, complete consistency has been impossible: the various authors have themselves been inconsistent, and the meshing of physiological and cultural forces to shape males and females sometimes makes such distinctions impractical.

Similarly, words like "patriarchy," "patriarchal society," "male-oriented society," and similar terms have been avoided whenever possible. Such expressions are often used with extreme looseness; indeed, they have become virtually meaningless terms, usually used as political buzz words rather than descriptive vocabulary. The words "feminist," "women's liberation," and "the women's movement" cover a range of opinions and attitudes that defies exactness, as do the terms "men's liberation" and "the men's movement." Readers should be aware of the leeway of definition in such expressions. The word "feminist," incidentally, is not limited to females; male feminists are included. Moreover, terms like "homosexual," "homosexuality," "gay," and "lesbian" can be imprecise and emotionally charged; every effort has been made to use them exactly and neutrally in the annotations.

The present selection has been made from a list of nearly a thousand items gathered through several methods. Library subject heading searches and database computer searches were made. Often, however, such searches were less than satisfactory because subject headings for men and men's topics have yet to be fully standardized. An obvious problem is the use of "man" for humans in general and for males in particular. (A major desideratum of men's studies is a systematic and less ambiguous listing of subject categories.) Bibliographies in published works about males proved to be the most fruitful and reliable sources for compiling *Men's Studies*. Through its bibliography page listings, the present bibliography provides researchers with perhaps the surest way at present of locating additional sources pertaining to males.

The bibliography includes both scholarly and popular works, and tries to represent fairly both traditional and avant garde views. Inevitably, some worthy books will have been omitted from the bibliography; both authors and readers are asked to be indulgent in such cases.

Books have been listed in the following categories:

Bibliographies. The paucity of book-length bibliographic materials about males will be readily apparent—a further indication of the need for a work like *Men's Studies.* Bibliographies dealing with male-related topics are included under a separate listing in this section. These items are cross-referenced after appropriate sections of *Men's Studies.*

Anthologies. General anthologies pertaining to males have been included; more specialized anthologies have been listed in their appropriate sections of *Men's Studies.*

Men's Awareness. This term has been chosen as more accurately descriptive than "men's consciousness raising" or "men's liberation," although it includes both. Included are those works, usually expounding a definite viewpoint, that examine men's lives and roles in modern society, assessing gains and losses across a broad range of topics. Annotations in this section tend to be longer than those elsewhere in order to convey nuances of thought and argument.

Autobiographies, Biographies, Memoirs. The entries here contain recollections that express in some significant way male experiences in modern life.

Men's Rights. This section includes works that discuss legal discrimination against males. Because of America's male-only military obligations and because most prisoners and most homosexuals are males, books dealing with the rights of soldiers, prisoners, and gays have been included.

Divorce and Custody. Selections here focus upon the particular problems of husbands facing divorce and of fathers seeking child custody.

War and Peace. War—and resistance to war—are closely bound up with male experience and even identity. This section includes a range of items concerning soldiers, careers in the military, the military draft and resistance to it, and the effects of combat upon men.

Men's Issues and Topics. This section is subdivided into five categories, each dealing with a particular area of men's interests, concerns, or controversy: (1) health, with special attention to the prostate; (2) vasectomy; (3) work and play, including careers, unemployment, and sports; (4) crime and violence, including rape, male rape, and domestic violence; and (5) prisons, with special attention to male victimization in prisons.

Women and Men. Books in this section focus upon a number of current male-female topics, including marriage, affectional relationships, two-paycheck households, and sexual equality.

Masculinity. Selections include books on the nature of masculinity and on the masculine gender role or male sex role. Anthropological-sociological and historical studies are given separate subsections. Specialists will readily recognize that the selection represents only a fraction of the total literature pertinent to males, but for the nonspecialist it should provide an introduction to some major themes of the literature. Moreover, no attempt could be made here to include the many controversial books on the nature of aggression because of their number and their often indirect bearing on masculinity.

Psychology. From the extensive literature on the psychology of men, a selection of items has been made with an eye to their pertinence for the nonspecialist reader.

Sexuality. This section includes research studies of male sexuality, as well as books on impotence and sexual dysfunction, sex advice, and sexual health.

Homosexuality. The volume of literature on homosexuality—especially in the past two decades—has been enormous. Fortunately, bibliographic efforts have been praiseworthy. The two-volume *Annotated Bibliography of Homosexuality* compiled by Vern Bullough and others (1976) and William Parker's *Homosexuality: A Selective Bibliography of Over 3,000 Items* (1971) and his *Homosexuality Bibliography: Supplement, 1970-1975* (1976) are excellent for pre-1976 items. Likewise, Martin S. Weinberg and Alan P. Bell's *Homosexuality: An Annotated Bibliography* (1972) offers detailed commentary on many important items. No attempt has been made here to duplicate their efforts. Hence, all items included in this section of *Men's Studies* date from 1976. Tom Horner's *Homosexuality and the Judeo-Christian Tradition: An Annotated Bibliography* (1981) is broader than its title might suggest; it lists 176 books, plus numerous articles and pamphlets, mostly from the seventies. Once again, no effort has been made here to duplicate Horner's work, although some of his titles are listed in *Men's Studies* because of their importance to the general reader. For convenience, books on transsexuality, transvestism, and homophobia have also been included in this section.

Men in Families. The neglect of fathers in past literature is being rectified, as the large selection of books in this category indicates. Books for expectant and new fathers are listed separately, as are books concerning divorced and unmarried fathers and stepfathers. A few titles on men's other family roles are included—as husband, grandfather, and son. Books on fathers and sons, incidentally, are included in the section on fathers.

Single Men. The few titles listed here indicate the scarcity of attention to males who remain unmarried and to widowers.

Male Midlife Transition. This section includes works dealing with the male climacteric, or midlife crisis.

Literature. A selection of fictional works—including novels, plays, poems, and dramas—is listed here. Any such selection necessarily must be highly idiosyncratic, and many readers will mentally supply titles that they would have included. The choices here attempt to reflect the criteria used throughout *Men's Studies* of works that illuminate in some way either male experience or the condition of being male. This section is subdivided into "classic" literature and "modern" literature. The first category includes works from around the world written before 1900; the second includes twentieth-century works, mostly American.

Images of Men. Included here is a potpourri of books dealing with the depiction of males in the arts—including literature, films, and photography.

Minorities. Books in this section concern males in America who are members of racial or ethnic minorities.

Religion. Books that include a religious dimension can be found throughout *Men's Studies*; works here focus primarily on a religious topic or are permeated with a religious viewpoint.

Humor. Given the solemnity with which current gender problems are often discussed, it is gratifying to know that some writers have not lost their sense of humor; the titles included in this section represent a selection of such writers.

BIBLIOGRAPHIES

MEN'S STUDIES BIBLIOGRAPHIES

1. Grady, Kathleen E., Robert Brannon, and Joseph H. Pleck, comps. **The Male Sex Role: A Selected and Annotated Bibliography**. Washington, D.C.: U.S. Department of Health, Education, and Welfare; Rockville, Md.: National Institute of Mental Health, 1979; sold by The Superintendent of Documents, U.S. Government Printing Office, Washington, D.C. 20402. P. x, 196. author index. pa.

This guide to more than 250 items, mostly in the social sciences, groups entries into fourteen major divisions: general; attitudes about men and masculinity; the socialization of masculinity; paid employment; marriage; fatherhood; relationships with women; relationships with men; antisocial behavior; some other traits associated with the male role; mental and physical health and the male role; physical and physiological factors in male behavior; male issues in institutions (military service, athletics); and subcultural, crosscultural, and historical comparisons. Selections have been made from the personal researches of the compilers. Annotations are often evaluative. For "hard" research, a regular pattern (subjects, method, findings, comments) is used, while with more theoretical writings a looser approach is used. According to a note in Pleck's *The Myth of Masculinity* (1981), single copies of this bibliography are available (while supply lasts) free from National Clearinghouse for Mental Health Information, NIMH, 5600 Fishers Lane, Rockville, MD 20857.

2. **Men's Studies Bibliography**. 4th ed. Cambridge, Mass.: Massachusetts Institute of Technology Humanities Library, 1979. P. i, 73. appendix. author index. pa.

This typed bibliography consists of approximately fourteen hundred items, mostly from journals, magazines, and newspapers, contained in the Humanities Studies Collection in the Humanities Studies Library at MIT. The items are divided into eleven categories: socialization—masculinity; mental and physical health; relationships and attitudes toward women; homosexuality; fatherhood and family; employment; sexuality; power, violence, crime, military, sports; other cultures; history, literature; men's liberation movement. Items are not annotated. The appendix consists of a listing of fifty-five books. At the present writing, copies are available for $4.00, prepaid, with checks payable to MIT Libraries. Write Humanities Studies Collection, MIT Humanities Library, Cambridge, MA 02139.

BIBLIOGRAPHIES IN RELATED AREAS

3. Anderson, Martin, and Valerie Bloom, comps. **Conscription: A Select and Annotated Bibliography**. Stanford, Calif.: The Hoover Institution Press, Stanford University, 1976. P. xvii, 453. title and author indexes.

This precisely annotated bibliography lists approximately 1,385 items concerned with the military draft. Books, unpublished manuscripts, articles, pamphlets, reprints, speeches, and government documents are separately categorized. The following subject headings are used: United States history; general history; general works (i.e., more comprehensive works dealing with conscription); all-volunteer armed forces; selective service; universal military training (i.e., conscription applying to all males); National Guard and Reserves; universal national service (i.e., a diversified form of conscription that would force both men and women to perform a variety of public service jobs); economics; law and the Constitution; philosophy (i.e., whether conscription is moral or immoral); conscientious objection; race; England; other foreign countries; miscellanea; and bibliographies.

4. Astin, Helen S., Allison Parelman, and Anne Fisher, comps. **Sex Roles: A Research Bibliography**. Washington, D.C.: Center for Human Services, and Rockville, Md.: National Institute of Mental Health, 1975. P. viii, 362. author and subject indexes. pa.

This fully annotated bibliography of 456 items is divided into five sections: observation and measurement of sex differences, origins of sex differences and sex roles (biological, sociological, attitudes toward sex roles), manifestation of sex roles in institutional settings (e.g., family, work, law, politics), crosscultural overviews and historical accounts of the sexes, and general reviews and position papers on socialization and the development of sex roles. As might be expected, more material on women than on men appears.

5. Bahr, Howard M., ed. **Disaffiliated Man: Essays and Bibliography on Skid Row, Vagrancy, and Outsiders**. Toronto: University of Toronto Press, 1970. P. xiv, 428. name and subject indexes.

This book is concerned with men who have hit rock bottom. Its two main objectives are: first, to provide easy access to an extensive literature from several disciplines on men who are homeless or who are suffering from chronic inebriation and other forms of disaffiliation; second, to enable researchers to relate this literature to the study of general social problems and processes. The bibliography is preceded by five essays exploring different areas of disaffiliation. In "The Sociologist and the Homeless Man" Theodore Caplow explores how skid row research has shaped the historical development of sociology as a discipline. James F. Rooney's essay "Societal Forces and the Unattached Male: An Historical Review" traces the changing nature of skid row and its men in the United States. In "Homelessness, Disaffiliation, and Retreatism" Howard M. Bahr links disaffiliation to retreatism and anomie theory. Felix M. Berardo studies the problems of widowed males in "Survivorship and Social Isolation: The Case of the Aged Widower." In the final essay "Dimensions of Religious Defection" Armand L. Mauss relates religious defection and disaffiliated men. The bibliography, annotated but unnumbered, is divided into twelve sections: skid row and its men; taverns and bars; the law; treatment, punishment, rehabilitation: homelessness; treatment, punishment, rehabilitation: alcoholism; drinking and alcoholism: etiology and patterns; transiency among young persons; journalistic and literary accounts; employment and unemployment; voluntary associations; aging and disaffiliation; and anomie, isolation, and marginality.

6.   Bowker, Lee H., comp. **Prison and Prisoners: A Bibliographic Guide**. San Francisco: R and E Associates, 1978. P. vii, 93. pa.
This bibliography is divided into four sections: (1) books and articles on prison subcultures among incarcerated men, (2) publications on female correctional subcultures, (3) publications on correctional subcultures in institutions for boys, and (4) background materials for the study of prisons and prisoners. (This final section is coauthored by Joy Pollack.) Each section is preceded by an introductory overview. Items are unannotated and unnumbered.

7.   Bullough, Vern L., W. Dorr Legg, Barrett W. Elcano, and James Kepner, comps. **An Annotated Bibliography of Homosexuality**. 2 vols. Garland Reference Library of Social Science, vol. 22. New York: Garland Publishing, 1976. P. xxxvii, 405; P. xii, 468. appendixes. author indexes.
These two volumes contain more than 12,794 items relating to homosexuality. Despite the title, annotations are nonexistent or minimal. In volume I, items are grouped in the following categories: bibliography; general studies; behavioral sciences (anthropology, history, psychology, sociology); education and children; medicine and biology; psychiatry; law and its enforcement; court cases; military; and religion and ethics. In volume II, the categories are: biography and autobiography; studies in literature and the arts; fiction (novels, short stories, drama); poetry; the homophile movement; periodicals (movement and other); and transvestism and transsexualism. Because so much writing about homosexuality has been done under pseudonyms, a list matching pen-names and (where known) identifications at the end of volume II is most useful. (A similar listing in volume I is less clear and full.) Volume I contains an appendix of legal code indexing; volume II includes a brief history of the homophile movement from 1948 to 1960 by Salvatore J. Licata.

8.   Franklin, H. Bruce, comp. **American Prisoners and Ex-Prisoners: Their Writings: An Annotated Bibliography of Published Works, 1798-1981**. Westport, Conn.: Lawrence Hill and Co., 1982. P. vii, 53. pa.
In this bibliography of prison narratives, autobiographical novels, poems, and political writings, the entries are unnumbered but (usually) annotated briefly.

9.   Horner, Tom, comp. **Homosexuality and the Judeo-Christian Tradition: An Annotated Bibliography**. ATLA Bibliography Series, no. 5. Metuchen, N.J., and London: American Theological Library Association, Scarecrow Press, 1981. P. ix, 131.

Spreading a wider net than its title might suggest, this bibliography collects 459 items—books, articles and essays, pamphlets and papers, and bibliographies. If an item makes any connection, even minor, between homosexuality and the Judeo-Christian tradition, it is included. Nearly all items are annotated. The appendixes list biblical references to homosexuality and periodical publications of gay religious organizations.

10. Johnson, Carolyn, John Ferry, and Marjorie Kravitz, comps. **Spouse Abuse: A Selected Bibliography**. National Criminal Justice Reference Service. Washington, D.C.: U.S. Department of Justice, Law Enforcement Assistance Administration, National Institute of Law Enforcement and Criminal Justice, 1978. P. ix, 61. appendixes. index. pa.

This bibliography contains ninety-one annotated items, a few dealing with battered husbands. According to one study, three women are battered for every one male; the battered husband, however, remains largely ignored in the literature and by the social agencies. The appendixes include a list of sources and of resource agencies.

11. Parker, William, comp. **Homosexuality: A Selective Bibliography of Over 3,000 Items**. Metuchen, N.J.: Scarecrow Press, 1971. P. viii, 323. appendix. subject and author indexes.

Parker's unannotated bibliography is divided into fourteen sections: books, pamphlets, theses and dissertations, articles in books, newspaper articles, articles in popular magazines, articles in religious journals, articles in legal journals, court cases involving consenting adults, articles in medical and scientific journals, articles in other specialized journals, articles in homophile publications, literary works, and miscellaneous works—movies, television programs, and phonograph records. An appendix lists state-by-state laws applicable to consenting homosexual acts.

12. Parker, William, comp. **Homosexuality Bibliography: Supplement, 1970-1975**. Metuchen, N.J.: Scarecrow Press, 1977. P. v, 337. appendixes. author and subject indexes.

A supplement to Parker's 1971 bibliography, this listing of 3,136 items follows the same outline and format as its predecessor. The appendixes contain lists of motion pictures and television shows with a homosexual theme, audiovisual materials, and U.S. laws applicable to consensual adult homosexuals as of January 1, 1976.

13. Schlesinger, Benjamin. **The One-Parent Family: Perspectives and Annotated Bibliography**. 4th ed. Toronto: University of Toronto Press, 1978. P. x, 224. appendixes. author index.

Sections of this book are extremely valuable for students of men's studies. The bibliography is preceded by six essays by Schlesinger, the first of which—"Motherless Families: A Review"—points to over one million American single-parent families headed by fathers, explores research done on motherless families in several countries, and comments on common themes, social policies, and needed research on these families. The other essays are: "Fatherless Separated Families," "Divorce and Children: A Review of the Literature," "The Crisis of Widowhood in the Family Circle," "The Unmarried Mother Who Keeps Her Child," and "Single-Parent Adoptions: A Review." The bibliography itself contains 750 annotated items divided into three period sections: 1930-1969, 1970-1974, and 1975-1978. All three sections are subdivided into subject categories. "One-Parent Families" appears in all three sections; "Motherless Families" appears only in the third section. Especially valuable is appendix I which contains a selected and annotated bibliography prepared by Parents Without Partners of sixty-two books for children and teens on single-parent families, death of a parent, divorce, and so on. Books portraying a positive father-child relationship are keyed. Appendix II contains a list of publishers' addresses.

14. Sell, Kenneth D., comp. **Divorce in the 70s: A Subject Bibliography**. Phoenix, Ariz.: Oryx Press, 1981. P. viii, 191. author, geographic, and subject indexes.

Among the pertinent subjects in this bibliography of 4,760 items are alimony and maintenance, child custody, father absence, one-parent families, father custody, stepfathers, male alimony, and joint custody.

15. Stineman, Esther, comp., with Catherine Loeb. **Women's Studies: A Recommended Core Bibliography**. Littleton, Colo.: Libraries Unlimited, 1979. P. 670. author, title, and subject indexes.

Clearly, this is the place to turn for information on women's topics. Among its 1,748 fully annotated items are many of interest to students of men's studies.

16. Suvak, Daniel, comp. **Memoirs of American Prisons: An Annotated Bibliography**. Metuchen, N.J.: Scarecrow Press, 1979. P. viii, 227. name-title index and prison index.

This bibliography, containing nearly eight hundred annotated items, includes memoirs from criminals, prisoners of conscience, and military prisoners. The vast majority of the writers are male.

17. Weinberg, Martin S., and Alan P. Bell, comps. **Homosexuality: An Annotated Bibliography**. New York: Harper and Row, 1972. P. xiii, 550. author and subject indexes.

A fully annotated guide to 1,265 items on homosexuality, mostly from the social sciences. Items are grouped in the following categories: physiological considerations (etiology, treatments), psychological considerations (etiology, assessments, treatments), and sociological considerations, which include the homosexual community: social and demographic aspects; homosexuality in history, non-Western societies, and special settings; societal attitudes toward homosexuality; and homosexuality and the law. Other bibliographies and dictionaries are listed in a final section. The bibliography excludes belles lettres (biographies, autobiographies, literary works) and items from popular magazines and from newspapers.

18. Young, Ian, comp. **The Male Homosexual in Literature: A Bibliography**. 2d ed. Metuchen, N.J.: Scarecrow Press, 1982. P. x, 350. appendixes. title index and title index of gay literary anthologies.

In addition to listing more than 4,282 works of fiction, drama, poetry, and autobiography in which male homosexuality is a theme or in which male homosexual characters appear, this bibliography contains five essays: a short history of the gay novel, the poetry of male love, some notes on gay publishing (all by the compiler), homosexuality in drama (by Graham Jackson), and gay literature and censorship (by Rictor Norton).

ANTHOLOGIES _____

19. Bradley, Mike, Lonnie Danchik, Marty Fager, and Tom Wodetzki. **Unbecoming Men: A Men's Consciousness-Raising Group Writes on Oppression and Themselves.** Washington, N.J.: Times Change Press, 1971. P. 64. illustrations. pa.

This collection of twelve brief personal essays was compiled by four members of a men's consciousness-raising group. The unsigned articles recall episodes—mostly painful ones—illustrating what growing up male in white middle-class America can be like. One writer recalls how odd he was made to feel when he and a male friend arrived at a party populated by couples only. Another recounts his inability to live easily with small children. A third remembers the awkwardness of being a boy who was not interested in sports. Other essays deal with such matters as men's feeling of isolation amid the togetherness of women involved in the women's liberation movement, the phoniness of "being popular," and the guilt which religions have attached to masturbation. The final essay, written collectively by the four men, describes their consciousness-raising group, warts and all.

20. Bucher, Glenn R., ed. **Straight/White/Male.** Philadelphia: Fortress Press, 1976. P. x, 149. notes. pa.

This collection of ten essays and dialogues by six authors castigates straight white males for the oppression of blacks, women, and homosexuals. While Bucher laments the insensitivity of heterosexual Caucasian male oppressors, other contributors manage to lay most of the world's evils at their door. Readers are advised to expect not an equitable assessment of men's lives and experiences, but an inundation of heated accusations, sweeping generalizations, and racist and sexist stereotyping of white males.

21. Cooke, Chris, and others, eds. **The Men's Survival Resource Book: On Being a Man in Today's World.** Minneapolis, Minn.: M.S.R.B. Press, 1978. P. xii, 195. illustrations. bibliographies after several chapters. pa.

A potpourri of articles, self-evaluation quizzes, and lists of resources (mostly in the Minneapolis-St. Paul area), this handbook contains chapters dealing with career and play, health, birth control, sexuality, legal matters related to marriage dissolution, fathers and parenting, men and violence, and education and personal growth. Aimed at readers interested in men's liberation issues, the contents include a play by Daniel Rudman dramatizing the relationship between a man and his penis, and essays on such topics as stress as a man-killer, circumcision, the prostate gland, testicular self-examination, venereal disease, vasectomy, masturbation, homosexuality, noncustodial parenting, and assertiveness training for nontraditional males.

22. David, Deborah S., and Robert Brannon, eds. **The Forty-Nine Percent Majority: The Male Sex Role.** Reading, Mass.: Addison-Wesley Publishing Co., 1976. P. xiv, 338. notes. bibliography, 331-34 and after several essays. pa.

Widely used in college courses, this anthology contains thirty-eight essays or excerpts by thirty-six authors. The lengthy introduction by Brannon, "The Male Sex Role: Our Culture's Blueprint of Manhood, and What It's Done for Us Lately," defines four principal components of the role, which are the subjects of the first four chapters. Chapter 1 contains essays on the stigma of anything feminine, while those in chapter 2 explore the requirements of success and status. The essays in chapter 3 examine the "manly air of toughness, confidence, and self reliance"; those in chapter 4 deal with "the aura of aggression, violence, and daring." Two additional chapters are concerned with learning the male role and changing it. Among the selections are Gregory K. Lehne's original essay on homophobia among men, Robert Gould's "Measuring Masculinity by the Size of a Paycheck," James Thurber's famous short story "The Secret Life of Walter Mitty," Ruth E. Hartley's classic essay "Sex-Role Pressures and the Socialization of the Male Child," Julius Lester's hilarious "Being a Boy," Andrea S. Hayman's informative "Legal Challenges to Discrimination Against Men," and Lois Gould's thought-provoking "X: A Fabulous Child's Story."

23. Filene, Peter, ed. **Men in the Middle: Coping with the Problems of Work and Family in the Lives of Middle-Aged Men.** Englewood Cliffs, N.J.: Prentice-Hall, 1981. P. xi, 193. illustrations. notes. pa.

In this collection of autobiographical essays, eight men try to answer the questions "Where Do We Come From, Who Are We, Where Are We Going?"—to borrow the title of a Gauguin painting which fascinates one of the men. The contributors— Harry C. Boyte, Paul B. Fiddleman, Peter Filene, Robert Hahn, Tom Kreilkamp, Lawrence Rubin, Arn Strasser, Steve Turner—are "men in the middle," i.e., from the middle class, at midlife. Bright, well-educated, radicalized by the civil rights movement of the sixties, sensitized by the women's movement of the seventies, they await fuller men's liberation. Having imbibed the work ethic as youths, all confront problems of balancing career and family. Highlights include Fiddleman's humorous account of how he made it over the hump of turning forty, Filene's lyrical and anguished retelling of career successes and marital failures, and Kreilkamp's incisive view of how his own liberation sometimes baffles his wife. "Why should women be allowed to shuck the feminine roles," he wonders, "and men be forced to stay with the masculine roles?" Filene's introduction tells how the book took shape and comments on its themes. In a concluding chapter, he constructs a "conversation" from the contributors' most recent letters updating their stories and commenting on the others' essays.

24.   Firestone, Ross, ed. **A Book of Men: Visions of the Male Experience.**
New York: Stonehill Publishing Co., 1975. P. ix, 324. illustrations.
Reprint. Edinburgh: Mainstream Publishing Co., 1981. Distributed by
State Mutual Book and Periodical Service.

This collection contains over one hundred brief excerpts, poems, and observations
from famous twentieth-century men, mostly creative artists. "Each selection,"
the editor explains, "resonates for me with some sort of truth about what it means
to be male." Items are divided into four categories: sons, lovers, husbands, and
fathers. The men represented include C. G. Jung, Jack Kerouac, Havelock Ellis,
Franz Kafka, Huey P. Newton, August Strindberg, Lenny Bruce, Bertrand Russell,
Dalton Trumbo, and many more. The illustrations are collage engravings by Jim
Herder.

25.   Kriegel, Leonard, ed. **The Myth of American Manhood.** New York: Dell
Publishing Co., Laurel Edition, 1978. P. 412. pa.

This collection of twenty-one selections—essays, short stories, excerpts from
longer works—provides views of American masculinity from Cotton Mather's
idealized portrait of William Bradford to Pete Hamill's "Farewell to Machismo"
(1976). Kriegel's introduction provides historical and cultural perspective, indicating that traditional masculinity is no longer fashionable and will change
irretrievably. Nineteenth-century selections include writings of Melville, Twain,
and Crane, as well as Grant's account of Lee's surrender. Twentieth-century selections include essays on boxing and baseball, Mailer's "The Time of Her Life" and
"The White Negro," and Kriegel's essay on being crippled, "Uncle Tom and Tiny
Tim."

26.   Lewis, Robert A., ed. **Men in Difficult Times: Masculinity Today and
Tomorrow.** Englewood Cliffs, N.J.: Prentice-Hall, 1981. P. xvi, 332.
illustrations. notes. index. bibliographies after some items. pa.

This unusually rich collection contains fifty-five items, including essays, research
summaries, historical analyses, autobiographical accounts, poems, and songs.
The material from numerous contributors is gathered into six sections. Only a
partial summary of contents can be attempted here. In section I, The High Costs
of Traditional Male Roles, items focus on competitiveness, lack of playfulness,
divorce and custody, men in therapy, and midlife decline. In section II, Socialization into Male Sex Roles, authors deal with sports, masculinity in comic strips,
male chauvinism, and inexpressive males. Section III, Feminism and Men Facing
Change, includes discussions of social change and the family, women's changing
(and sometimes conflicting) expectations, the rise and fall of a men's group, and
evolving male sex roles and identities. In section IV, Nurturance By and For Males,
authors tackle the problems of single fathering, grandfatherhood, male teachers
and young children, and removing barriers that make men's closeness with each
other so difficult. Section V, Resources for Change in Males, includes an analysis
of male power and powerlessness, advice on consciousness-raising groups for men,
explorations of how homophobia can be cured, and desiderata for research on black
males. The final section on The New Man includes an essay on shared parenting,
suggestions for moving men towards greater intimacy, and a historical survey of
the male role from preindustrial to postindustrial times.

27. Petras, John W., ed. **Sex: Male/Gender: Masculine: Readings in Male Sexuality**. Port Washington, N.Y.: Alfred Publishing Co., 1975. P. 256. notes. bibliographies after some selections. pa.

Twenty-four previously published items examining the physiology of maleness and the cultural roles of masculinity make up this anthology. Part I, The Individualistic Perspective, includes essays on the biological imperatives of maleness, as well as a nineteenth-century discourse on the hideous effects of masturbation and early twentiety-century views of how the "real boy" ought to behave. In part II, The Socio-Cultural Perspective, the socialization of males is presented. Two comical boyhood memoirs by Julius Lester and Bill Cosby are followed by portraits of executive males and blue-collar working-class men at home. Mirra Komarovsky explores contradictions in the masculine role as experienced by college students. Part III, Masculinity/Feminity, includes Jack O. Balswick and Charles W. Peek on the inexpressive male, Norman Mailer on women's liberation, and Michael Korda on the domestic chauvinist. Part IV, Male Liberation and the New Masculinity, explores new directions for men, including Keith Olstad's "basis for discussion" of brave new men, and essays on breaking away from mainstream American masculine roles.

28. Pleck, Joseph H., and Jack Sawyer, eds. **Men and Masculinity**. The Patterns of Social Behavior Series. Englewood Cliffs, N.J.: Prentice-Hall, Spectrum, 1974. P. viii, 184. bibliography, 175-84. pa.

This collection of thirty-one previously published essays is divided into seven sections. Essays in section I, Growing Up Male, explore how boys are socialized into learning the masculine role; selections include Brian Allen's disturbing short story "A Visit from Uncle Macho," Ruth E. Hartley's classic essay on the socialization of the male child, and Sidney M. Jourard's study of lethal aspects of the male role. Section II, Men and Women, examines relationships between the sexes and sexual problems; Julius Lester's hilarious "Being a Boy" and Sam Julty's discussion of impotence are among the selections. Items in section III, Men and Children, include Robert A. Fein's informative essay "Men and Young Children" examining how men are blocked from the rewards of child nurturing and Kelvin Seifert's discussion of problems encountered by men who work in child care centers. The next section, Men and Men, explores the troubled relationships between men, especially the problem of homophobia as a bar to male friendships. Section V, Men and Work, consists of essays on measuring masculinity by the size of a paycheck (by Robert E. Gould), executives as human beings (by Fernando Bartolomé), and an autobiographical account of a hip homosexual college teacher attempting to work within the system (by Michael Silverstein). Section VI, Men and Society, focuses on machismo in the military and in politics. The final section, Men's Liberation, includes such items as Barbara J. Katz's survey of the men's liberation movement, two accounts of men's groups, Jack Sawyer's brief essay "On Male Liberation," and the Berkeley Men's Center Manifesto. Pleck and Sawyer provide introductions to the volume and to each section.

29. Rubin, Michael, ed. **Men without Masks: Writings from the Journals of Modern Men**. Reading, Mass.: Addison-Wesley Publishing Co., 1980. P. xx, 312. pa.

This anthology contains samplings from the diaries of thirty men of the late-nineteenth and twentieth centuries. Selections are divided into six categories: sons; idealists; lovers, husbands, fathers; working men; explorers; and aging, old, and dying men. A gold mine of insights into modern men's experiences, selections range from the journals of anguished sons (e.g., Richard Meinhertzhagen, Franz Kafka, and editor Rubin) to idealistic World War I soldiers killed in their youth (Otto Braun and Alan Seeger). Readers can glimpse the love lives of photographer Edward Weston and musician Ned Rorem, as well as the joys and trials of father-hood as experienced by David Steinberg and Josh Greenfield. Other selections portray the triumphs and trials of work—as well as the costs of unemployment. Explorers include those like Richard E. Byrd and Tobias Schneebaum who explore new lands, and those like Thomas Merton and Howard Nemerov who explore strange regions of the soul. Doing so has not been considered "masculine," Rubin notes in the introduction, praising those who look behind the mask of masculinity to the human reality. "Though the women's movement has done much to break down myths and stereotypes about women in the interests of their complexity," he writes, "it does not often recognize a similar complexity in men."

30.   Snodgrass, Jon, ed. **For Men against Sexism: A Book of Readings**. Albion, Calif.: Times Change Press, 1977. P. 238. notes. bibliography, 234-38. pa.

This collection of thirty-two radical items draws heavily upon Marxist feminist thought. Essays in part I, Women's Oppression, adhere to the party line that all men are oppressors and thus a humane consideration of male concerns and male issues is an impertinence. Male victims in modern society get short shrift in these discussions; the existence of male rape victims, e.g., is denied as rape is defined as "a crime of violence against women." Leonard Schein argues that "All Men are Misogynists," and John Stoltenberg calls for *"a total repudiation of masculinity"* (emphasis his). While homosexual relationships are exalted, heterosexual male bonding is excoriated as a conspiracy of the "oppressors." Likewise, the men's liberation movement is denounced for focusing on the "oppressor's" problems. The shorter part II, Gay, Class, and Racial Oppression, explores issues of homosexuals, blue-collar work, and third world men. Polemics throughout the volume resound with vituperation, finger-pointing, revolutionary rhetoric, and wholesale denunciations of capitalism, patriarchal society, and men.

31.   Sutherland, Alistair, and Patrick Anderson, eds. **Eros: An Anthology of Male Friendship**. London: Anthony Blount, 1961. P. 433. Reprint. New York: Citadel Press, 1963.

The selections in this anthology illustrate the range of male friendships from the nonsexual to the homoerotic to the homosexual. To illustrate the graduated spectrum in male-male relationships, the editors have deliberately cast a wide net. Historically, selections cover biblical times, ancient Greece and Rome, the Dark and Middle Ages in Europe, and the Renaissance through modern times in the Western world. A chapter of accounts from "exotic" lands and a chapter of selections describing life at English boys' schools close the book. The authors include Plato, Virgil, Petronius, Michelangelo, Montaigne, Shakespeare, Tennyson, Verlaine, Gide, Proust, and D. H. Lawrence.

Cross references:

305.   Solomon, Kenneth, and Norman B. Levy, eds. **Men in Transition: Theory and Therapy**.

MEN'S AWARENESS
Consciousness Raising, Men's Liberation _____

32. Avedon, Burt. **Ah, Men! What Do Men Want? A Panorama of the Male in
     Crisis—His Past Problems, Present Uncertainties, Future Goals.** New York:
     A and W Publishers, 1980. P. 213. illustrations. notes.

For this potpourri of opinions on men in crisis, Avedon interviewed twenty well-
known people—seventeen men (e.g., Art Buchwald, Bruce Jenner, Ashley Montagu,
Gore Vidal) and three women (Helen Gurley Brown, Gael Greene, Elizabeth
Janeway). Their views appear in chapters on gender roles, sports, work, sex,
feelings, homophobia, men's liberation, and related topics.

33. Barbeau, Clayton C. **Delivering the Male: Out of the Tough-guy Trap
     into a Better Marriage.** Minneapolis, Minn.: Winston Press, 1982. P. 136.
     notes. bibliography, 133-36. pa.

A readable and sensitive attempt to extricate men from the pitfalls of outmoded
masculine roles, this book opens with a personal note celebrating the role played
by Barbeau's late wife Myra in effecting his liberation. A psychotherapist with a
Catholic Christian perspective, Barbeau argues that many men are now in a more
acute identity crisis than are women. Part of the problem is that the older masculine roles no longer deliver on their promises. Drawing upon writers like Marc
Fasteau and Herb Goldberg, Barbeau enumerates the penalties that accompany
more traditional male lifestyles. Although the hostility toward men that marked
the women's movement of the early seventies has tempered itself, men must change
constructively to avert future crises with women. Barbeau points to the dehumanizing effects that careers often have upon men and how in modern America public
success often means private failure. He applauds those men who have the courage
to choose simpler, more satisfying lives. A final chapter noting the widespread
passivity among American men urges a more passionate approach to positive growth
through role changes.

34. Bednarik, Karl. **The Male in Crisis.** Translated by Helen Sebba. New York:
     Alfred A. Knopf, 1970. P. xi, 194, xiv. notes. index. Reprint. Westport,
     Conn.: Greenwood Press, 1981. Originally published as *Die Krise des
     Mannes* (Vienna: Fritz Molden Verlag, 1968).

Bednarik sees males in crisis because modern bureaucratic and technological society
prevents their being naturally active and autonomous. Evidence of crisis can be

found in the "impotent anger" of alienated male violence and in the "absurdist revolt" of beats, hippies, hooligans, and other disaffected males. Although he favors equal rights for women, Bednarik sees women's roles as fundamentally different from men's. Men are, he feels, women's natural defenders and protectors. The crisis of modern Eros results from the commercialization—and hence depersonalization—of sex which allows aggression to contaminate sexual relations. Because male aggressiveness can no longer find legitimate expression in warfare (modern war has made heroism impossible and would result in catastrophic annihilation), conscious control must continually rechannel aggression into constructive or relatively harmless outlets. Because the state has undermined the authority of the father, the male need for exercising authority and autonomy can be recovered only by democratic processes that work upwards from the grassroots.

35.   Bell, Donald H. **Being a Man: The Paradox of Masculinity**. Lexington, Mass.: Lewis Publishing Co., 1982. P. ix, 158. notes. Reprint. New York: Harcourt Brace Jovanovich, 1984. pa.

Drawing upon his own experiences and those of men whom he interviewed, Bell explores the paradox of modern masculinity, caught between older traditions and newer lifestyles. In the first three chapters, Bell and his interviewees—all upper middle-class white men—describe their relationships with their fathers, their lack of close male friends beyond the school years, and their teen boy-girl relationships. Chapters 4 and 5 tell how their marriages became casualties of the gender conflict of the seventies, and how they coped with "beginning again" after divorce. Chapter 6 deals with work experiences, including unemployment and the tensions arising between a working wife and a nonworking husband. The experiences of fatherhood—including being present at birth, and being a divorced father—are explored in chapter 7, while the final chapter draws conclusions about the present and raises questions about what lies ahead for men.

36.   Bertels, Frank. **The First Book on Male Liberation and Sex Equality**. Miami, Fla.: Brun Press, 1981. P. 415. illustrations. pa.

This is definitely not the first book on male liberation and sex equality; it may be, however, the most embarrassing one. Indiscriminately mixing valid points with sexist clichés, Bertels harangues women in general and "women's lib" in particular. He reserves praise for "old-fashioned females," whom he labels "OFF's." Apparently unaware of the men's movement, the author calls for men to awake and organize. In a format designed "for the 'television age' of non-book readers," the text is interrupted by cartoons, sample bumper stickers, unidentified newspaper clippings, and other matter. Intended as a manifesto of men's liberation, the book will strike many readers as a travesty of it.

37.   Brenton, Myron. **The American Male**. New York: Coward-McCann, 1966. P. 252. notes. index. Reprint. Greenwich, Conn.: Fawcett Book Group, Crest, 1967. pa.

One of the earliest, fullest, and most discerning analyses of the masculinity crisis, Brenton's *The American Male* retains its relevance in the eighties. "At the present time in his history, the American male is subject to an unprecedented number of pressures and tensions," the author writes, underlining his thesis: "Their effect is needlessly deleterious, because he's still trapped by the beliefs and value systems of the past." Brenton states and explores most of the themes that later writers on men's issues would reiterate, including the attention given to women's concerns and the inattention to men's concerns; the seemingly active man who uses activity to mask his passivity in decision making and leadership; the new demands placed upon men to be emotionally closer, to interchange roles with women, and to be a sexual superstar; the binds in which traditional roles place today's men; the "myth" of the good old days of patriarchy when men ruled supreme (Brenton argues convincingly that women privately had great resources for wielding power in patriarchal societies); the father absence which results when males are unprepared by society to assume parental roles; and the "momism" and permissiveness which result from father absence. Brenton closes with a chapter pointing out new ways to manliness. He cautions men to avoid the breadwinner trap, the overspecialization which renders a man vulnerable to adversity and change, the fallacy that being woman's equal means a loss of manliness, and the "myth" that women are morally superior and that real men are destructively aggressive. Conversely, men need to recognize that masculinity can be expressed in personally and socially constructive ways. Especially welcome is Brenton's ability to discuss gender issues candidly without hostility toward either men or women.

38. Carlson, Dale. **Boys Have Feelings Too: Growing Up Male for Boys.** New York: Atheneum, 1980. P. 167. illustrations. bibliography, 167.
A boy's guide to male liberation, this book will interest adults as well, especially parents. In language addressed to teenage boys, Carlson warns that the "privilege" of being male in America carries a price tag: males must repress feelings, constantly prove their masculinity, never say "no" to pressures, enter areas of study which lead to moneymaking jobs, be responsible for supporting their wives and children, and die early as a result of these demands. Discussing what happens to males in the parental home, in school, after high school, and on the job, the author does not blink at the radical implications of her message. Males must reject the pressures to "succeed," for such pressures only make men into society's scapegoat, i.e., someone to be blamed for everyone else's problems. Carlson reviews religious and historical views of males, the use of men as canon fodder in wars, and the rise of the men's movement in the United States. "The truth is that male liberation is a very simple idea," Carlson concludes. "A man can be a man without being treated like a work slave, a replaceable robot with no human rights or feelings, a sacrifice on the altars of economic security, or an animal on a battlefield."

39. Dolan, Edward F., Jr. **Be Your Own Man: A Step-by-Step Guide to Thinking and Acting Independently.** Englewood Cliffs, N.J.: Prentice-Hall, 1984. P. ix, 146. index. pa.
This self-help guide is aimed at general male readers and touches on such matters as achieving independence, working and the family, guilt, judgments, and interpersonal relationships.

40. Doyle, James A. **The Male Experience.** Dubuque, Iowa: Wm. C. Brown, Co., 1983. P. xiv, 321. illustrations. notes. name and subject indexes. bibliographies after each chapter. pa.
For the informed general reader, Doyle lucidly surveys recent topics concerning men. Distinguishing between public sex role and private gender identity, he discusses recent changes in the male role, taking a "feminist approach." Part I examines the male from several disciplinary perspectives. Doyle offers an overview

of historical definitions of masculinity, of biological information about males, of anthropological studies about men in different cultures, of sociological views of how males are socialized, and of psychological theories of male development. Part II examines elements of the male sex role, specifically the "antifeminine" element, the significance of aggressive behaviors, the sexual component of the role, and the demand for male self-reliance. In part III Doyle's examination of men's issues is limited to discussions of homosexuality and power in male-female relationships. (Some readers will be disappointed that several issues important to activist men—male longevity and health, military obligations, divorce and custody practices, legal requirements upon men as breadwinners, and so on—are ignored or given short shrift.) A final chapter finds little evidence that the men's movement and men's liberation are about to become matters of national concern, however significant they may be to individuals or smaller groups of men.

41. Editors of *Look*. **The Decline of the American Male**. New York: Random House, 1958. P. 66. illustrations.

This exercise in pop sociology indicates the kind of criticism and advice which the American man heard in the fifties. The three essays in the book depict him as henpecked, passive, tired, anxious, and impotent; the Robert Osborn cartoons caricature him as ludicrous. J. Robert Moskin in "Why Do Women Dominate Him?" blames women: as wives, they place too many demands on husbands and drive them to early graves. George B. Leonard, Jr., in "Why Is He Afraid to Be Different?" depicts the American male as obsessed with conformity to group standards. In "Why Does He Work So Hard?" William Attwood answers—the puritan work ethic, the social expectations of being always busy, the pressure of public opinion, the need to keep up a standard of living, the pushing by wives, the love of action for its own sake, and ambition. The book's view of men makes it easier to understand such subsequent phenomena as dropouts, countercultures, and the flight from commitment of many American males.

42. Farrell, Warren. **The Liberated Man: Beyond Masculinity: Freeing Men and Their Relationships with Women**. New York: Random House, 1974. P. xxxii, 381. notes. index. bibliographies, 359-66. Reprint. New York: Bantam Books, 1975. pa.

One of the earliest, fullest, and most influential statements about men's liberation, Farrell's book reflects his commitment to applying the insights of the women's movement to men's condition. Part I, Beyond Masculinity, argues the case for men's liberation by pointing to the constrictive nature of traditional masculinity as seen in such matters as value systems, socialization, advertising images of men, Super Bowl football, war, gangs, religion, and absentee fathers. Farrell offers suggestions for effecting men's liberation, including day-care centers, flexible work schedules, pay for homemakers, altering schoolbook images of the sexes, and a program of men's liberation goals. In part II Farrell cites twenty-one ways in which women's liberation abets men's liberation. He explores current stereotypes of women and suggests how men's attitudes and behaviors can be changed. Part III includes exchanges from consciousness-raising groups and points the way toward human liberation. In addition to a bibliography of study resources on various topics, the book contains a bibliography on starting a child-care center.

43. Fasteau, Marc Feigen. **The Male Machine**. New York: McGraw-Hill Book
     Co., 1974. P. xv, 227. notes. Reprint. New York: Dell Publishing Co.,
     Delta, 1975. pa.

In this widely read critique influenced by feminist thought, Fasteau touches upon
nearly all the major dissatifactions with the traditional masculine role: the stereotyped ideal of the male as a cool and efficient machine, the lack of friendships
among adult men, the confusion of sex and violence, the obsession with sexual
technique, the denigration of women as inferiors, the failure of fathers as caring
parents, sports as a training ground for competition, the cutthroat nature of
success-oriented careers, and the mystique of violence. Fasteau also explores how
the cult of toughness affected U.S. foreign policy and the Watergate imbroglio.
In a final chapter he offers the ideal of androgyny, which he sees as creating not a
unisex sameness but a greater range of behaviors for both men and women. The
book contains an introduction by Gloria Steinem.

44. Gilder, George F. **Sexual Suicide**. New York: Quadrangle/New York Times
     Book Co., 1973. P. xi, 308. notes. index. bibliography, 287-94. Reprint.
     New York: Bantam Books, 1975. pa.

In Gilder's conservative vision, modern sexual liberation has become a form of
sexual suicide. Most individuals, he argues, attain their fullest humanity within
carefully defined gender roles, which are neither infinitely malleable nor immune
from careless social and political tampering. Modern civilization exists because
males, whose sexual needs are briefly satisfied, have adapted to the long-term
rhythms of women's sexuality, procreativity, and child nurturing. But this adaptation is endangered: if the man's contribution as the family's prime provider is
undermined, he will quickly recognize that his domestic role is inferior to his wife's,
and he will abandon family responsibilities to find masculine affirmation in antisocial forms of male bonding. Defending the male role of primary breadwinner,
Gilder criticizes women's liberationists, the advocates of open marriage, gay liberationists, *Playboy* philosophers, equal rights advocates, pornographers, sexologists,
prophets of androgyny, and social planners who intrude into family autonomy.
He accuses women's liberationists of having appropriated the civil rights machinery
for which blacks fought; he argues that job quotas and equal pay for women
will benefit only the well-to-do whose greater incomes will enable a two-paycheck
marriage to work. Meanwhile, working-class and poorer males will be increasingly
unable to support their families, their upward mobility having been blocked by the
affluent women who have taken over the jobs the men were striving for. Thus,
poorer families will suffer more because of their demoralized (and often defecting)
males.

45. Goldberg, Herb. **The Hazards of Being Male: Surviving the Myth of Mascu-
     line Privilege**. Plainview, N.Y.: Nash Publishing, 1976. P. 200. notes. index.
     Reprint. New York: New American Library, Signet, 1977. pa.

An enormously influential book, *The Hazards of Being Male* attempts to debunk
the idea that males are a favored sex, "a notion that is clung to despite the fact
that every critical statistic in the area of longevity, disease, suicide, crime, accidents,
child emotional disorders, alcoholism, and drug addiction shows a dispropor-
tionately higher male rate." Starting from the premise that American men must
unlock themselves from old, destructive patterns of life, Goldberg explores at
length the negative aspects of being male in America. He argues that most men live

in harness, drudging out their lives at onerous jobs and struggling to reconcile the conflicting demands of their roles as breadwinners-husbands-fathers. Most men's lives begin and end in a series of impossible binds, which Goldberg describes tellingly. Although sympathetic to the women's movement, he warns men against expecting it to liberate men; without undue intellectualization, men themselves must cultivate spontaneity, close male friendships, and the ability to regard women as equals. Significantly, he rejects guilt as a means of motivating men to change; he deplores the stereotyping that occurs in some feminist writings of males as oppressors. The book's conclusions are supported by the author's experiences as a clinical psychologist and by his researches into the male condition. A powerful expostulation, *The Hazards of Being Male* has changed, and is still changing, many men's lives.

46.   Goldberg, Herb. **The New Male: From Self-Destruction to Self-Care**. New York: William Morrow and Co., 1979. P. 321. notes. index. Reprint. New York: New American Library, Signet, 1980. pa.

In this energetic exhortation, Goldberg sees the modern male in crisis, and offers advice on how to replace his self-destructive tendencies with positive changes which will include self-care, spontaneity, and personal fulfillment. The book's first section, analyzing the present male dilemma, depicts modern American men as card-board Goliaths, compulsively proving their masculinity, running from failure, and facing midlife burnout. In section II, Goldberg explores how different kinds of women can place men in difficult binds. Especially interesting is his account of the Actor-Reactor syndrome, in which the man's role as the initiating and responsible partner inevitably leads to accusations that he is an oppressor and exploiter. Conversely, Goldberg also analyzes the binds which men can place women in by their conflicting demands upon women. In section III, he explores men's reactions to the women's movement, discussing how men's timid responses can result in their getting the worst of both sides of the liberation crunch. He castigates the willingness of present society to accept and perpetuate negative and sexist stereotypes of men; he advises men that the women's movement can save their lives—but only if men stop reacting with guilt-laden accommodation and start refashioning their lives to meet their own needs. The final section offers advice to help men emerge from the restrictions of past gender roles. It urges men to become aware of anti-male sexist vocabulary, learn to feed themselves, cultivate buddyships, avoid "earth mother" women, and "custom-make" their own lives.

47.   Goldberg, Steven. **The Inevitability of Patriarchy**. New York: William Morrow and Co., 1973. P. 256. appendix. notes. index. pa.

Goldberg argues that anthropological and biological considerations point to the inevitability of patriarchal leadership, male dominance, and male attainment of high-status nonmaternal roles. Patriarchy is universal in world history; no evidence exists of any matriarchal societies, except in myth. Male dominance (the feeling that men are and should be in charge of concerns outside the family) is likewise universal. Hormonal differences between males and females give most men an edge on aggression (i.e., initiative, taking the lead), providing them with an advantage in striving for high-status positions outside the family. Different cultures may define different roles as high status, but whatever the definitions males will strive and succeed in attaining these roles. Men do not seek to oppress women; they simply follow their natural bent to take the lead, a decision usually concurred in by women. Goldberg insists he is not arguing the superiority of one sex to the other, simply the differences. He takes issue with feminists from John Stuart Mill (*On the Subjection of Women*) to Kate Millett (*Sexual Politics*) who argue that cultural, not physiological, factors create male dominance. Cultural socialization, Goldberg says, simply follows biology's lead, guiding girls away from aggressive activities and boys toward them. Equal rights doctrines would only force women to compete with men on men's terms—and women would lose. In later chapters, Goldberg argues (with admittedly less assurance) that physiological differences affect cognitive aptitudes, performance, and genius—again giving the male an edge over the female. Goldberg argues that males are naturally less nurturant, suffer from "womb envy," and are destined for eternal restlessness. "Males are expendable and females are not; that alone would have been reason enough for nature to select males to serve the protective function." Even if one disagrees, Goldberg provides a forceful argument for considering biological and anthropological evidence in assessing gender roles.

48. Goodman, Andrew, and Patricia Walby. **A Book about Men**. London: Quartet Books, 1975. P. 167. notes.

"The thesis of this book is that men need liberating as well as women," Goodman and Walby note in their introduction. The authors, each writing alternate chapters, touch informally on a variety of topics, including male bonding, the macho mystique, sex fantasies, and the "daily crucifixion" of work for most men. At times, the authors depict men as privileged oppressors, at other times as victims of a malevolent social order. "The subject matter is extensive," the authors write, "and we are aware that we have made too many generalizations and skated over large areas of controversy, but the subject is in its infancy and hitherto undefined."

49. Gordon, John. **The Myth of the Monstrous Male, and Other Feminist Fables**. New York: Playboy Press, 1982. P. xv, 253. bibliography, 251-53.

In this lively polemic, Gordon takes issue with some current trends of militant feminism. Describing himself as a feminist who supports equal rights and opportunities, Gordon goes on to offer a riposte to such feminists as Susan Brownmiller (*Against Our Will*), Marilyn French (*The Women's Room*), Kate Millett (*Sexual Politics*), Adrienne Rich (*Of Woman Born*), Mary Daly (*Gyn/Ecology*), and Ashley Montagu (*The Natural Superiority of Women*). He contends that the women's liberation movement has become sexually repressive, linking itself to the antisex elements of earlier women's movements. He regards the men-are-oppressors stereotypes of some modern feminists as variants of the men-are-sexual-beasts stereotypes of older feminists. In the past, he argues, women pretended to be asexual creatures; they granted sex to the hungry male only in exchange for marriage (which included the male's commitment to lifetime financial support). The recent women's movement, which initially promised to liberate women from hypocritical bargaining, is now becoming reluctant to surrender the power such bargaining confers on women. "As for men," Gordon concludes, "their need right now is not for the much-vaunted right to cry, but simply for the capacity to get very damned angry at what is being said about them as a sex, and at the everywhere-manifest consequences of the propaganda." Recent information indicates that this book is now available from Bioenergetics Press, Madison, Wis.

50. Greene, Thayer A. **Modern Man in Search of Manhood.** New York: Association Press, 1967. P. 128. illustrations. notes.

"Being a man has never been easy," Thayer begins, adding that the job is more difficult now than ever before. A college chaplain, parish minister, and psychotherapist, Greene notes that, although much has been written about men, less has been written for them or to them. Addressing himself primarily to young men between eighteen and thirty, he explores the changing roles of men in modern society. Although both biology and culture contribute to sexual identity, the female's menstruation provides definite and regular affirmation of her femininity. Males, on the other hand, must constantly prove their masculine identity. Exploring conflicting images of masculinity contained in our culture, Greene feels that men can easily be trapped between roles and their real selves. Homophobia and the need to repress feelings—even anger and aggression, which are "inappropriate" for the Christian gentleman—hamper men in their efforts to discover and nurture their "feminine" qualities. The penultimate chapter stresses the need to find the authentic self in solitude; the final chapter summarizes the book concisely.

51. Herzig, Alison Cragin, and Jane Lawrence Mali. **Oh, Boy! Babies!** Boston: Little, Brown and Co., 1980. P. 106. illustrations. pa.

In 1978 an urban boys' school offered an elective minicourse in infant care which would include real infants. Ten boys signed up for the class. Through text, and photographs by Katrina Thomas, *Oh, Boy! Babies!* tells what happened during the next six weeks as the boys learned to handle, dress, diaper, feed, bathe, and play safely with the infants brought to school. At first unsure of themselves, the boys quickly gained confidence and looked forward to the babies' appearance each Wednesday. ("Hi, Freddy," calls one boy to an arriving infant, "Remember me? I'm the one you peed on.") Enthusiastic and resourceful, the boys ingeniously coped with a roomful of squalling, crawling babies. They also became greatly attached to the infants and to the idea of caring for them. The book, as Dr. Benjamin Spock writes, "reveals in touching form ... how human beings eventually turn into parents." Hilarious and heartwarming, *Oh, Boy! Babies!* is a book which many readers will feel is very special.

52. Hoch, Paul. **White Hero, Black Beast: Racism, Sexism and the Mask of Masculinity.** London: Pluto Press, 1979. P. 191. notes. index. pa.

This examination of masculinity goes well beyond the narrower limits suggested by its title. In part I an intriguing critique of feminists and male liberationists notes their failure to raise questions about *why* men behave as they do: males, as well as females, are shaped by historical and cultural forces beyond their control. Examining different facets of masculinity, Hoch explores theories of manhood as a social ritual and as a defense mechanism against impotence and homosexuality. A fascinating chapter containing allusions to folk art from classical myth to *Star Wars* outlines the white hero-black beast myth which depicts males as conquering some savage aspects of themselves. The racial implications of this account are significant. Drawing upon Freud's *Totem and Taboo*, Hoch examines masculinity as a mask hiding patricidal impulses and incestuous desires. Part II examines the fall from classless into class society; it traces alternating versions of puritan and playboy through Western history from Roman times to the present, culminating in the rise of manly individualism in a production and consumption society. Despite the book's "pious hope" ending which promises vague renewal through a new socialist order, Hoch's often dazzling perceptions repeatedly point to areas of needed investigation in men's studies. Equally important, his spirit of inquiry—neither guilt-ridden nor chauvinistic—demonstrates a refreshing and vitalizing approach to men's studies.

53. Karsk, Roger, and Bill Thomas. **Working with Men's Groups: Exploration in Awareness**. Columbia, Md.: New Community Press, 1979. P. ix, 126. appendix. bibliographies after each chapter. pa.

A useful tool for leaders or facilitators of men's groups, this book is aimed at men seeking to enhance personal awareness about alternatives for growth and change. The authors are not interested in examining men's alleged sexism or guilt; instead, they focus on the great unexplored territory of men's feelings about themselves, the sources of men's anger, male sexuality, and parenting. Formats for group sessions are provided, including materials needed, the amount of time allotted, desirable group size, objectives of the session, and procedures. Suggestions for outside reading and audiovisual materials are also included. An appendix lists national, specialized, and local support groups for men. Recent information indicates that this book is now distributed by BDR Learning Products, Inc., P.O. Box 3356, Annapolis, MD 21403.

54. Kaye, Harvey E. **Male Survival: Masculinity without Myth**. New York: Grosset and Dunlap, 1974. P. 213. index.

Writing in popular style, Kaye examines the crisis of modern masculinity. A practicing psychiatrist and psychoanalyst, he discusses genially and forthrightly various aspects of the masculine mystique—the Superman syndrome, the Neanderthal ideal, the sexual athlete, the heroic imperative, the achiever complex, the playboy in paradise, the dominance drive, and the myth of male superiority. After explaining the biological, psychological, and societal components of masculinity, Kaye delves into the workaday world of the average man. He discusses the performance pressues being put upon heterosexual men and views with some reservation the homosexual "alternative" now being offered to them. Reviewing attacks upon the family and the demands for success placed upon men, Kaye offers a modest critique of some of the more extreme views expounded by women's liberationists. Changing male roles will not be easy, Kaye believes, but the possibility of improving conditions for many men makes the effort worthwhile.

55. Kilgore, James E. **The Intimate Male**. Nashville, Tenn.: Abingdon Press, 1984. P. 144. pa.

Within a religious context, Kilgore explores the value of intimacy for men in the eighties. Noting a fear of intimacy as "feminine," Kilgore examines the male need for self-acceptance and sharing. Stressing the importance of male closeness with wives and children, he discusses his concept of God as loving father and a boy's need for male models who verbalize their love. He argues that male chauvinism is often the result of mothers who teach their sons that other women want to lean on them. In discussing the continuing need for intimacy throughout the life cycle, Kilgore advises men not to repress their little-boy spontaneity.

56. Kriegel, Leonard. **On Men and Manhood**. New York: Hawthorn Books, 1979. P. x, 206. notes. bibliography, 201-206.

Crippled by disease when he was a boy, Kriegel learned early the virtues of courage and endurance, the virtues of old-fashioned manhood. In this prose-poem of recollections and observations, Kriegel hymns the positive values of traditional masculinity as embodied in American literature (especially Hemingway), sports, and certain screen images (John Wayne in *Stagecoach*, Marlon Brando in *The Men*). Kriegel has little patience with male liberationists who denigrate this masculinity or with the current drive toward androgyny, which he equates with unisexuality. Kriegel also discusses the gay rights movement and the new black masculinity. Knowing that his views are not trendy, Kriegel concludes with a chapter significantly entitled "Waiting."

57. Lyon, Harold C., Jr., with Gabriel Saul Heilig. **Tenderness Is Strength: From Machismo to Manhood**. New York: Harper and Row, 1977. P. xii, 270. index.

"This book is a statement in behalf of men's liberation," Lyon writes. Fearful that women's liberationists may exalt the macho hardness that has been a male ideal, he concludes: "The best thing that could happen to women's liberation would be men's liberation." For Lyon, toughness may have been a virtue at one time in history when most men had to be protectors and enduring laborers, but at present it represents a block to self-growth and a lethal trap for many men and some women. The author sees tenderness and strength less as opposites than as complements or as a continuum. Lyon gathers up numerous strands of thought upon such matters as hypermasculinity, homophobia, diet, meditation, the courage to fear, laughter, fatherhood, brotherhood, and the need for tenderness at birth and at death. He occasionally refers to his experiences as a wartime child (told by his soldier father to be "the man of the house"), a West Point cadet, a Ranger-paratrooper Army officer, government official, teacher, university administrator, divorced and remarried husband-father, and therapist. Gabriel Saul Heilig contributes a chapter on his spiritual odyssey from confused striving to inner enlightenment. The foreword is by John Denver.

58. Mailer, Norman. **The Prisoner of Sex**. Boston: Little, Brown and Co., 1971. P. 240. notes. Reprint. New York: New American Library, Signet, 1971. pa.

Oddly reminiscent of Virginia Woolf's *A Room of One's Own* in its third-person ruminations, Mailer's *Prisoner of Sex* reflects upon radical feminism in general and Kate Millett's *Sexual Politics* in particular. In an extended, meandering essay laced with sly wit, Mailer is perhaps at his best dissecting Millett's questionable treatment of the writings of Henry Miller and D. H. Lawrence. As usual, Mailer leaves one wondering how seriously to take him: in the end he endorses women's liberation— so that women can be free to find the right man.

59. Men Against Patriarchy. **Off Their Backs ... and on our own two feet**. Philadelphia: New Society Publishers, 1983. P. 29. pa.

This publication consists of three essays written from male feminist viewpoints. In "More Power Than We Want: Masculine Sexuality and Violence" Bruce Kokopeli and George Lakey trace a sinister connection between "patriarchal" society and violence, suggesting androgyny as the solution. Peter Blood, Alan Tuttle, and George Lakey in "Understanding and Fighting Sexism: A Call to Men" describe how sexism works against both males and females, how male guilt is not the answer, and how change can be effected. Among the solutions are a change from capitalist to socialist economy and communal childrearing instead of the nuclear family's role. "Overcoming Masculine Oppression in Mixed Groups" by Bill Moyer and Alan Tuttle lists suggestions for replacing confrontational tactics with cooperative ones.

60. Miller, Stuart. **Men and Friendship.** Boston: Houghton Mifflin, 1983. P. xvii, 206. bibliography, 199-206.

Rejecting the idea of writing a "cold" study of the much-neglected topic of male friendship, Miller presents a "warm" view, using his own search for male friends as the springboard for larger considerations. Finding himself at midlife with a need for friends, Miller consciously set out to cultivate them but found the process difficult. The partial successes and failures of his early efforts are followed by the achievement of several reasonably satisfying friendships, one of which holds the possibility for greater closeness. Among the diary entries and personal letters, the author defines friendship as involving intimacy and "complicity," that is, a secret you-and-me-against-the-world understanding. He distinguishes between male bonding involving a group of men and friendship involving two individuals. Miller notes that many men put such a low priority on friendship that it has little chance of flourishing in their lives. One of Miller's interviewees even argued that male friendship is no longer needed, wanted, or possible in today's world. To his dismay, Miller found the closest friendships among gay men who were not lovers. Apparently, sexuality is unnecessary to friendship despite the arguments of modern "sexualists." Of the massive social pressures allied against male friendship, certainly the greatest is fear of homosexuality which has reached extraordinary intensity in the twentieth century. In lieu of a conclusion, Miller offers some advice on achieving friendship despite the odds.

61. Naifeh, Steven, and Gregory White Smith. **Why Can't Men Open Up? Overcoming Men's Fear of Intimacy.** New York: Clarkson N. Potter, 1984. P. xii, 193. index. bibliography, 181-93.

Summarizing current views of men's difficulties in feeling and expressing their emotions, the authors explore the dimensions and causes of the problem. In the latter half of this popularly written book, they offer advice for the woman trying to reach intimacy with a closed man. After sketching in their own experiences, the authors stress the cultural roadblocks to male expressiveness, indicating that most males have been carefully taught to hold back emotionally and are penalized when they do not. Hormones are not the problem, but fathers who teach male inexpressiveness often are. Many women also send out mixed signals to men: some women who say they want their man to open up are frightened or repelled when he does. The mystique of the strong, silent male still flourishes in the post-John Wayne era. Men by themselves either cannot or will not transform themselves; women (who are better versed in expressiveness) will have to help them. Practical suggestions for women are provided, a casebook of closed male types is presented, and the authors conclude with personal reflections on what they have learned from their researches and interviews.

62. Nichols, Jack. **Men's Liberation: A New Definition of Masculinity.** 1975. Rev. ed. New York: Penguin Books, 1978, 1980. P. 333. notes. pa.

"In future decades," Nichols writes, "today's male role will be remembered as a straitjacket." Pinpointing the over-reliance upon rationalistic, mechanistic thought as the source of men's problems, Nichols in general extols Eastern philosophy, denigrates Western religion and thought, and urges men toward an androgynous state of mind which will incorporate both "masculine" and "feminine" mental abilities. In brief chapters Nichols explores such topics as the loss of playfulness among men, the exaltation of "masculine" competition and violence, and the deadening effect upon men of a lifetime in the workplace. He praises liberated women, deplores manipulative ladies, and argues that the nuclear family, which restricts men sexually and emotionally, will be radically changed. The term "father," he says, has become synonymous with "financial functionary." Nichols writes movingly of the need for forming close male friendships and for expunging homophobia ffrom modern society. He sees in Walt Whitman's *Leaves of Grass* the noblest expression of American men's liberation.

63. Olson, Ken. **Hey, Man! Open Up and Live!** New York: Fawcett Gold Medal, 1978. P. 251. notes. pa.

In upbeat style, Olson describes why men need to break out of their conditioning. He touches upon such matters as work, emotions, success and failure, the crisis of middle age, retiring, love and sex, and fathering.

64. Olson, Richard P. **Changing Male Roles in Today's World: A Christian Perspective for Men—and the Women Who Care about Them.** Valley Forge, Pa.: Judson Press, 1982. P. 159. appendix. notes. pa.

Olson combines insights from men's awareness writers (especially Farrell and Goldberg) with a biblical Christian viewpoint. The Bible does not endorse macho behavior, and the freeing of men's feelings can bring personal and spiritual gain. Although skeptical of feminist critiques of men as oppressors, Olson garners insights from the women's liberation movement. He finds the Bible less sexist than some critics have argued, and he endorses egalitarian marriages. Men's liberation, he concludes, should be a conversion experience.

65. Pace, Nathaniel. **The Excess Male.** Norfolk, Va.: Donning Co., 1982. P. vii, 102. bibliography, 101. pa.

One presumes that this book is a satire in the vein of Jonathan Swift's "A Modest Proposal." Arguing that most human evils are the result of the roughly 50-50 male-female birth rate, the author modestly proposes that "an artificial control of male births be imposed, to insure that of every ten births, only one would be male." (Exactly how this control would be exercised is not made clear.) The author then explains that most of the world's woes are due to "excess" males. Within geographic locales, there are three classes: the privileged (women and children), the preferential males (leaders, executives, etc.), and the excess males (nine-tenths of the male population). These excess males keep trying to become preferential males but do not succeed; they cause all sorts of problems fighting for the available women. The author praises (ironically, one presumes) war, alcoholism, and crime as great eliminators of excess males. He extols Stalin and the Ayatollah Khomeini;

Hitler, however, muffed his calling by eliminating women and children instead of just young men as a good tyrant should. Despite its deadpan seriousness, *The Excess Male* may be a blistering satire on the modern habit of blaming all the world's evils on men and on the widespread acceptance of abuses visited by society upon them. The author is either insane or insanely comic. Readers should have a jolly time deciding for themselves.

66. Playboy Enterprises. **The Playboy Report on American Men**. Chicago: Playboy Enterprises, 1979. P. 59. pa.

This survey explores the values, attitudes, and goals of American males between the ages of eighteen and forty-nine. Between December 6, 1976, and January 12, 1977, 1,990 men were interviewed extensively on four hundred "items." The survey was conducted for Playboy Enterprises by Louis Harris and Associates; analysis and interpretation of key data were made by William Simon and Patricia Y. Miller. Harris calls the sampling "representative." The survey discloses a rich diversity of male opinion, fairly evenly divided among four groups—traditionalists, conventionals, contemporaries, and innovators. Areas touched upon in the survey include basic values, family, love and sex, marriage and children, the outer man's appearance, religion and psychotherapy, attitudes toward drugs, money and possessions, work, politics, and lesiure. The survey found that most men are hardly playboys in their values and attitudes. Nearly 85 percent rated family life as very important for a satisfied life, while only 49 percent rated sex as similarly important. Married men had the highest levels of satisfaction with their sex lives, and three out of four men considered sexual fidelity as very important for a successful marriage. Although 82 percent of the men believed in a Supreme Being, only 41 percent said religion was personally significant for them. Although work is important to men, most rated it below health, love, peace of mind, and family life as very important for a happy, satisfied life. In these and other areas too often subjected to impresionistic speculations, the Playboy survey offers hard information about American men's attitudes and values.

67. Reynaud, Emmanuel. **Holy Virility**: **The Social Construction of Masculinity**. Translated by Ros Schwartz. London: Pluto Press, 1983. P. vi, 119. notes. pa. Originally published as *La Sainte Virilité* (Paris: Editions Syros, 1981).

A French male feminist, Reynaud explores familiar radical themes—men are a class of powerful oppressors (although they pay dearly for their alleged power), women are an oppressed class whose roles are shaped for them entirely by men (Reynaud never examines women's part in socializing children), and men use sex to confirm their power over women (although Reynaud has some interesting stories about females raping males). Some readers will find the book a stirring piece of consciousness raising, others a ludicrous collection of sexist clichés about men.

68. Ruitenbeek, Henrik M. **The Male Myth**. New York: Dell Publishing Co., 1967. P. 223. illustration. notes. pa.

In 1967 Ruitenbeek was analyzing the crisis of American men in terms that will strike many readers as still pertinent. The author sees men in an identity crisis, needing to evolve a new definition of masculinity in the face of economic and social changes. While modern technology has created a world in which men as providers are no longer essential and in which men are often alienated from their jobs, seeking masculine identity through work is perilous. Emancipated women, moreover, can support themselves if need be. But, Ruitenbeek argues, the father's family role is crucial; father absence can hamper the development of both male and female children. The increasing abdication of males from families may be due to an awareness that home life costs them more than it offers in satisfactions. Widespread homophobia hampers father-son relationships. The demands that men provide sexual satisfaction to women may be causing an increase in impotency (or the reporting of it). This impotency in some cases may be an expression of hostility toward an aggressive woman by humiliating her and refusing to satisfy her. Widespread passivity and homosexuality may also be negative reactions to hostility between the sexes. "For the future," Ruitenbeek writes, "the male faces this final question: Can he develop a new concept of his social role and adequate psychological support to confirm him in his conviction of his identity as a male?" While offering some modest suggestions (e.g., men must resist depersonalization, must accept family responsibilities, and must insist upon integration into family life), Ruitenbeek concludes: "We must not fool ourselves that the problems of contemporary American men can be solved by prescription; they only can be solved ultimately in the renewal of man and the rediscovery of his sense of dignity."

69.   Sadker, David. **Being a Man: A Unit of Instructional Activities on Male Role Stereotyping**. Resource Center on Sex Roles in Education. National Foundation for the Improvement of Education. Washington, D.C.: U.S. Department of Health, Education, and Welfare, 1977. P. v, 64. illustrations. bibliography, 63-4. pa.

A "must" for high school teachers, this government publication is enlightening for other readers as well. In a brief rationale, Sadker writes: "With so many women now striving for political, economic, and psychological equality with men, one might conclude that men enjoy a special and privileged place in our society, and that their roles and behaviors should be emulated. Such an assumption would be both misleading and simplistic." Section I, Background for Teachers, enumerates five "lessons" of the male stereotype—stifle it (repress emotions), choose your occupation (from the following list only), money makes the man, winning at any cost, and acting tough. Then, eight "costs" of living out this stereotype are discussed: early pressures on boys, barriers between men, barriers between men and women, the separation of fathers from families, being locked into a job, being locked out of leisure activities and a satisfying retirement, physical disability and early death, and social and political machismo which endangers everyone. Section II presents a series of learning activities designed to counteract stereotyped ideas about male behavior and attitudes. Sadker avoids some controversial issues which might well be of interest to students, e.g., whether a male-only draft is sexist, who pays for dates, and so on. The bibliography lists works on female role stereotyping. The publication is offered for sale by the Superintendent of Documents, U.S. Government Printing Office, Washington, DC 20402; stock number 017-080-01777-6.

70.   Schenk, Roy U. **The Other Side of the Coin: Causes and Consequences of Men's Oppression**. Madison, Wis.: Bioenergetics Press, 1982. P. 256. appendixes. notes. pa.

Arguing that men as well as women suffer oppression in modern society, Schenk locates the source of men's anger against women in socialization which depicts women as spiritually superior to men. Often fostered by mothers and female teachers, the idea of male moral inferiority is internalized by men, leading them to become cannon fodder in wartime, providers for females in the family, and pursuers of females for sex. By encouraging male guilt for female benefits, women help to create male anger against them. Schenk has little patience with male feminists who perpetuate ideas of male oppression and guilt. He attacks the selective equality preached by militant feminists, that is, equality only to the point where it benefits women without inconveniencing them. Reducing male anger and violence against females requires reducing female violence against men's psyches. Schenk finds evidence of the belief in female spiritual superiority in American laws and customs, sees little hope for genuine equality in the sex bias of most feminists, and argues that only a recognition of men's oppression can lead to a more harmonious relationship between the sexes.

71.   Shostak, Arthur B., and Gary McLouth, with Lynn Seng. **Men and Abortion: Lessons, Losses, and Love.** New York: Praeger Publishers, 1984. P. xx, 334. appendixes. notes. name and subject indexes.

Each year approximately 1,360,000 men are involved in an abortion experience, with 600,000 of them designated as "waiting room men" who utilize abortion clinics. Moved by their personal experiences and dismayed by the almost total lack of information about men in abortion situations, the authors have generated a study based upon responses from one thousand such "waiting room men," research, and extended interviews with some of the men, clinical counselors, abortion activitists, and others. Written in readable prose for the general reader, *Men and Abortion* demonstrates that, contrary to popular belief, many men are profoundly affected by abortion—indeed, they are haunted by it. Despite fears of militant feminists, most men do not want to control abortion decisions, although they do want to share in the decision-making. Many men, however, also feel that women are in control of contraception and that men therefore are not responsible for it. On the day of the abortion, men at clinics are usually ignored by an overworked staff; the men are left to face their stress alone and unaided. The authors explore the views of "waiting room men" who regard abortion as immoral, repeaters (those who have been through more than one abortion), black males, prochoice and antiabortion activists, and counselors of males in abortion clinics. The legal implications of abortion are starkly depicted: the man has no rights in the matter at all, while he is still obliged to support a child born to him—even though he wishes to have the fetus aborted and agrees to pay for the procedure. The pros and cons of spousal prenotification laws are reviewed. The final chapters provide suggestions for preventing or easing the trauma of abortion—before conception, on "clinic day," and afterwards. The eight appendixes include such matters as an evaluation of the study's methodology by Joan Z. Spade, a look at men whose wives have undergone mastectomy, a copy of the questionnaire, and a list of the thirty cooperating clinics. (Because of deadlines, this entry was prepared from partially corrected proofs of *Men and Abortion*.)

72.   Skjei, Eric, and Richard Rabkin. **The Male Ordeal: Role Crisis in a Changing World.** New York: G. P. Putnam's Sons, 1981. P. 247. notes. bibliography, 246-47.

This book explores the negative effects of recent changes in women's roles upon men. Focusing on "male sex-role transition stress," i.e., the difficulties men are experiencing as concepts of masculinity shift in modern society, the book draws upon interviews with thirty-one persons (twenty-seven males, four females). Skjei and Rabkin found that men, far from being gender imperialists, were often sensitive and vulnerable to women's changes, and that men were often needlessly hurt by "the new misandry" or anti-male hostility of some feminists. The authors accuse these ideologies of a "repressive radicalization" which attempts to defeat men as an enemy rather than enlist them as allies in the women's cause. This "reverse sexism," which desires to punish men for alleged oppression of women, threatens to alienate the sexes at a time when each sex must include the other in its quest for selfhood. In speaking with interviewees, the authors found men were more committed to monogamy than is usually believed, that they were neither gypsies nor tyrants in family life, and that they believed firmly in the value of being actively involved parents. The men were divided, however, on whether the two-career family can work. Men, Skjei and Rabkin conclude, need "to reclaim a sense of masculine dignity and pride, but to do so without making assumptions of any kind about women and their roles."

73.   Steinmann, Anne, and David J. Fox. **The Male Dilemma: How to Survive the Sexual Revolution**. New York: Jason Aronson, 1974. P. xv, 324. appendixes. notes. index.

Assessing the conflict between men and women in the late sixties and early seventies, the authors attempt to redress the imbalance of writings stressing women's issues and changes with a view which includes men's needs and changes. They address themselves to general readers, both male and female, hoping to provide greater understanding to effect positive changes. In their research, the authors find contradictions in what men want for themselves and what they believe women want from them; women exhibit similar conflicts. Moreover, communication between the sexes is often limited and thus misunderstood. Assessing sex roles in history, the authors see modern men as having to surrender privileges without a clear-cut idea of the gains such surrender could bring. Women, on the other hand, are uncertain whether they really "want it all." The results of these confusions are increasing hostility in marriage and children caught in ambivalent attitudes. The authors assess the biological and cultural sources of differences between the sexes, indicating that only toward the end of the life cycle does equality become a more easily achievable goal. Nevertheless, social norms are too restrictive for both males and females. Without advocating unisex childrearing, the authors offer a number of practical suggestions. In a final chapter, the authors suggest social changes to lessen misunderstanding and hostility between men and women. The appendixes provide details of the authors' research "inventories" of masculine and feminine behavior.

74.   Thornburg, Hershel D. **Punt, Pop: A Male Sex Role Manual**. Tucson, Ariz.: H.E.L.P. Books, 1977. P. 156. illustrations. notes. index. pa.

Stressing the need for men to change their attitudes, Thornburg has designed a self-help manual for male consciousness raising. Complete with quizzes to chart the reader's views, the book examines such matters as the breadwinner role, discrimination against women in employment, images of women in advertising, sex stereotyping in sports, and fathering. Some readers may find the book a helpful exercise in nonsexist training; others may regard it as simplistic and condescending to men.

75.   Tolson, Andrew. **The Limits of Masculinity: Male Identity and the Liberated Woman.** New York: Harper and Row, 1979. P. 158. index. bibliography, 147-52. pa. Originally published London: Tavistock, 1977.

Tolson provides a view of men's awareness in Britain as it has been shaped by feminist and socialist thought. After the initial chapter traces the influence of the women's liberation movement upon men, Tolson explores the socialization of boys by the family, the school, and the peer group. Chapter three examines men at work in a capitalist-patriarchal society. Employing excerpts from interviews, Tolson stresses the alienating effect of labor on working-class men, the frustrations involved in middle-class masculinity, and the contradictions in "progressive" men trying to reconcile their liberalism with traditional notions of masculinity. A final chapter recounts the experiences of Tolson's male consciousness-raising group: having accepted the ideas that men are a class of oppressors and that patriarchal society always works to men's advantage, the group had reached a dead end which rendered it politically immobile. Readers will have to decide whether Tolson's Marxist-feminist ideology clarifies or clouds his view of men and masculinity.

76.   Vilar, Esther. **The Manipulated Man.** Rev. ed. Translated by Eva Borneman and Ursula Bender. New York: Farrar, Straus and Giroux, 1972. P. 184. Originally published as *Der dressierte Mann* (N.p.: Abelard-Schuman, 1972).

Standing militant feminism on its head, Vilar argues that women have conspired successfully to enslave men: "Women let men work for them, think for them, and take on their responsibilities—in fact, they exploit them." From infancy males are trained by women to be dependent upon females. Men are conditioned to believe that supporting a woman is "masculine," that being taken care of is "feminine." Women have successfully used sex as a reward to manipulate males into supporting females; most women, according to Vilar, are not primarily interested in men sexually or personally but rather financially. Deliberately outrageous, Vilar's book is designed to provoke strong and divergent responses. Is it a hilarious put-on? a refreshing corrective? a misogynist diatribe? an eye-opening piece of consciousness raising? a cynical exposé of women's parasitism? an ironic exposé of men's gullibility? In this never-a-dull-moment polemic, the penultimate chapter—in which Vilar dissects the American women's liberation movement—makes for especially heady reading.

Cross references:

156.   Julty, Sam. **Men's Bodies, Men's Selves.**

219.   Marine, Gene. **A Male Guide to Women's Liberaton.**

240.   Franklin, Clyde W., II. **The Changing Definition of Masculinity.**

304. Skovholt, Thomas M., Paul G. Schauble, and Richard Davis, eds. **Counseling Men.**

305. Solomon, Kenneth, and Norman B. Levy, eds. **Men in Transition: Theory and Therapy.**

579. Berman, Edgar. **The Compleat Chauvinist: A Survival Guide for the Bedeviled Male.**

588. Mead, Shepherd. **Free the Male Man!**

AUTOBIOGRAPHICAL
AND BIOGRAPHICAL ACCOUNTS_____

77. Bouton, Jim. **Ball Four, Plus Ball Five**. Rev. ed. New York: Stein and Day, 1981. P. xix, 457. illustrations. appendixes. pa. (*Ball Four*, 1970, ed. Leonard Shecter.)

It is difficult to know why this account of Bouton's experiences as a professional baseball player aroused such hostility around the big leagues in 1970, but part of the reason may be its less than flattering look at baseball machismo. In this account, baseball "heroes" are depicted, warts and all, in an ironic narrative that often stresses their puerility. This latest edition of *Ball Four* contains information about Bouton's former team mates, the death of his editor and friend Leonard Shecter, Bouton's comeback in baseball, and his divorce and remarriage.

78. Brown, Claude. **Manchild in the Promised Land**. New York: Macmillan Co., 1965. P. 415. Reprint. New York: New American Library, Signet, 1971. pa.

Brown's harsh account of growing up in Harlem contains numerous insights into black machismo and what it does to both males and females. Throughout this story of fist fights, paternal beatings, crime, drugs, prostitution, and correctional institutions, Brown weaves the theme of the black boy's need to be seen as a "bad nigger." To be a man, a boy must fight; even his parents will force him to. In correctional facilities, the boy suspected of being gay must be consistently vicious or be degraded. On the streets, males are required to fight over money, women, and manhood. Especially in chapter 10 Brown outlines the code of black masculinity that could lead males to be cruel to women, to each other, and to themselves.

79. Clary, Mike. **Daddy's Home**. New York: Seaview Books, 1982. P. ix, 230.

When reporter Mike Clary and his wife Lillian Buchanan (a Ph.D. in counseling) had their first child, they decided that she would continue working outside the home and that he would be the "housespouse" raising their child through its first two years of life. In *Daddy's Home* Clary recounts, with a journalist's eye for telling details, his life as a "mother"—the rewards and the frustrations, as well as the feeling of being an outsider among the men who worked and the women who mothered. Nurturing his infant daughter, however, was an experience that Clary clearly would regret having missed. Talking to a college sociology class, he tells the students: "But as long as men are denied the chance to be househusbands—because it's considered unmasculine—they are being discriminated against as surely as are women refused entry to the top levels of business."

80. Covington, Jim. **Confessions of a Single Father.** New York: Pilgrim Press, 1982. P. viii, 181.

In a compelling narrative, Covington recalls his alcoholic father and dominating mother, his early marriage, his preparation for the ministry, and the births of his daughter and son. Then came the social upheaval of the sixties. Covington's religious faith evaporated, his marriage disintegrated, and he found himself a single parent with custody of two children. The troubles and triumphs of this new role are interspersed with reflections on manhood in recent years.

81. Diamond, Jed. **Inside Out: Becoming My Own Man.** San Rafael, Calif.: Fifth Wave Press, 1983. P. 184. illustration. bibliography, 182-83. pa.

Set amid California's swinging scene, Diamond's vivid and frank autobiographical account depicts his father-absent childhood and his dependence upon media definitions of manhood. He describes disconcerting experiences with an open marriage, women liberationists, encounter groups, Synanon, Transactional Analysis, and LSD. Divorce, the breakup of other relationships, his role as a single parent, help from men's groups and men's awareness writings (particularly Herb Goldberg's), coming to terms with his parents, and a new relationship mark Diamond's odyssey to discover himself as a man.

82. Gibson, E. Lawrence. **Get Off My Ship: Ensign Berg vs. the U.S. Navy.** New York: Avon Books, 1978. P. x, 385. illustrations. appendixes. index. bibliography, 369-77. pa.

Closely following the hearings in which Ensign Vernon E. Berg III contested his discharge from the Navy as a homosexual, this book provides insights into the workings of military justice and into military thinking about homosexuality. The illustrations of various participants in the hearings, including the author, are by Berg himself, and five appendixes provide additional information. Amid the tangle of legal issues looms the fact that, as one district court judge lamented, the U.S. Supreme Court has "been reversing any court that suggested that the Constitution applied to servicemen."

83. Greenburg, Dan. **Scoring: A Sexual Memoir.** Garden City, N.Y.: Doubleday and Co., 1972. P. 223.

Frank and funny, Greenburg recounts his sexual misadventures as a young man driven by the imperative to score.

84. Kafka, Franz. **Letter to His Father/Brief an Der Vater.** Translated by Ernest Kaiser and Eithne Wilkins. New York: Schocken Books, 1953. P. 127. pa.

Written in November 1919, this angry and anguished letter to his father from the thirty-six-year-old Kafka crystallizes in vivid detail a classic antagonism between father and son. "You asked me recently why I maintain that I am afraid of you" is the famous opening sentence, and the rest of the letter explains why—in terms of the father's insensitivity, his sarcastic belittling of his son, his oppressive intellectual and physical presence, his boasting, his crudeness, his displays of temper, and his aversion to the son's writings. Kafka also laments his "saintly" mother's failure to side sufficiently with him against the father, the roles of his sisters in the family conflicts, and the warping of his experiences of Judaism because of the father's behavior. As a result of this antagonism in the home, Kafka insists he has been rendered incapable of career or marriage. Characteristically, in the penultimate paragraph, Kafka imagines his father's "reply" to the letter—and a disconcertingly convincing reply it is. The Schocken edition includes both German text and English translation, as well as a brief publisher's note providing background.

85.   Kantrowitz, Arnie. **Under the Rainbow: Growing Up Gay**. New York: William Morrow and Co., 1977. P. 255.

Kantrowitz's family was a "Freudian classic," complete with castrating Jewish mother and hapless father. His head filled with film fantasies, Kantrowitz goes off to college in Newark, discovers his gayness, becomes a college teacher, comes out, and evolves into a gay activist in Greenwich Village. Told with humor and verve, Kantrowitz's story carries the reader through the gay awakening of the seventies.

86.   Kopay, David, and Perry Deane Young. **The David Kopay Story: An Extraordinary Self-Relevation**. New York: Arbor House, 1977. P. xii, 247. illustrations. Reprint. New York: Bantam Books, 1977. pa.

A professional football player, Kopay created shockwaves in 1975 by publicly revealing his homosexuality. His story includes such details as the sexual repressiveness of his Catholic upbringing, his initial awareness of being homosexual, and the anguish of being a closet gay in a sport that prides itself on hypermasculinity. The book contains numerous insights into the relationship between sports and sexual identity.

87.   Martin, Albert. **One Man, Hurt**. New York: Macmillan Co., 1975. P. 278. Reprint. New York: Ballantine Books, 1976. pa.

This pain-filled retelling of a marital breakup reads like a powerful novel. At age forty-three, Albert Martin (a pseudonym) is a successful family provider, a caring father of four sons, an enlightened Catholic, and a loving husband—right up to the moment on February 5, 1972, when his wife Jean tells him that she no longer loves him and wants a divorce. After months of painful marriage counseling and negotiations, Albert—and probably Jean too—only partly understand her reasons for wanting to leave. Although vaguely involved with a local minister and belatedly rebelling against her perfectionist mother, Jean seems rather to be motivated principally by the current adulation of self-fulfillment. According to Martin, marriage counseling itself, which exalts finding the self above salvaging the marriage, is part of the problem. Eventually, the divorce proceedings are less agonizing than the marital rift which preceded them and the emotional void which follows them. The story of marital collapse may be a familiar one these days, but Martin records a husband's experiences of the ordeal with unusual eloquence and drama.

88. McGrady, Mike. **The Kitchen Sink Papers: My Life as a Househusband.** Garden City, N.Y.: Doubleday and Co., 1975. P. 185. Reprint. New York: New American Library, Signet, 1976. pa.

At age forty, newspaper columnist Mike McGrady reversed roles for a year with his wife Corinne, who was starting her own business. He became the homemaker and full-time parent to their three children; she became responsible for paying the bills. With an eye for comic details and a knack for hilarious narrative, McGrady charts the reactions of friends and relatives, his successes and failures as a househusband, and his wife's exhilarations and exhaustions as a businessperson. At year's end, the McGradys became a two-career family, complete with family contract for sharing household chores and bill-paying responsibilities.

89. McKuen, Rod. **Finding My Father: One Man's Search for Identity.** New York: Coward, McCann and Geoghegan, 1976, and Los Angeles: Cheval Books, 1976. P. 253. illustrations. appendixes.

This moving autobiography by the well-known actor-composer-poet is haunted by his search for the father he never knew.

90. Meggyesy, Dave. **Out of Their League.** Berkeley, Calif.: Ramparts Press, 1970. P. 263. illustrations.

Meggyesy depicts his life as a football player with emphasis on negative aspects of the game, including its dehumanizing impact, brutality, injuries, fraud, under-the-table payments, painkillers, drugs, racism, and sexism.

91. Nichols, Beverley. **Father Figure.** New York: Simon and Schuster, 1972. P. 215. illustrations. Reprint. New York: Pocket Books, 1973. pa.

This memoir at times approaches hysteria as it describes how Nichols on three occasions plotted to murder his maddening, alcoholic father. The scene is Edwardian and postwar England; the principal characters are Nichols's domineering and drunken father, his long-suffering mother, and Nichols himself—sensitive, precocious, and already leaning toward homosexuality. Although Nichols's hatred for his father is everywhere manifest in the book, the memoir itself may have the reverse effect of increasing readers' sympathies for the elder Nichols. The son's self-pity is extravagant, the "saintly" mother often appears to be a whining non-entity, and the fact that immediately after her death the father gave up drinking speaks volumes.

92. Painter, Hal. **Mark, I Love You.** New York: Simon and Schuster, 1967. P. 224. appendix. illustrations.

When his wife and daughter were killed in an automobile accident, Hal Painter left his son Mark temporarily in the custody of his in-laws, Dwight and Margaret Bannister of Iowa. A little more than a year later when Hal was about to remarry, he tried to reclaim his son. The rigidly conventional Bannisters, however, loathed Hal's mildly unconventional lifestyle and refused to yield Mark. Those who believe a father has legal right to custody of his child need to read on. The Iowa Supreme Court reversed a lower court decision to return Mark to his father, exhibiting fears that the Painter household "would be unstable, unconventional, arty, Bohemian, and probably intellectually stimulating." (The appendix contains the full text of the court's ruling.) Despite a nationwide storm of protest, the U.S. Supreme Court refused to consider the case. At the close of this moving account of frustration and love, Painter had lost custody of his son.

93. Richards, Renée, with John Ames. **Second Serve: The Renée Richards Story**. New York: Stein and Day, 1983. P. 373. illustrations.

This frank autobiography recounts the transformation of Richard Raskind into Renée Richards, the well-known tennis player and doctor. Fraught with perils to a young boy's sexual identity, the Raskind household included a domineering and man-hating mother, an ineffectual and absent father, and an older sister who alternated between attacking Richard and dressing him in her clothing. Eventually, Richard discovered a female personality (whom he named Renée) emerging within himself. The explicit narrative follows the struggle between Richard and Renée for ascendancy, the sex change operation which settled the matter, and Renée's trials and triumphs on the tennis courts. Aside from other interests, the book offers a textbook case of how *not* to raise a male child.

94. Seabrook, Jeremy. **Mother and Son**. New York: Pantheon Books, 1980. P. 191. Originally published London: Victor Gollancz, 1980.

"This book is about the haunted and obsessive relationship with my mother which, for more than thirty years, was the most total and only real experience of my life." Thus begins Seabrook's account of growing up during the forties in Great Britain with a dominating, man-hating mother, a twin brother who seemed more of an opposite than a sibling, and a father who was alienated, ostracized, disliked, and belittled—and who eventually deserted. Seabrook notes the psychosexual damage he sustained. An episode of transvestism and crushes on other boys hint of impending homosexuality, but the book ends abruptly with nothing certain determined.

95. Sifford, Darrell. **Father and Son**. Philadelphia, Pa.: Westminster Press, Bridgebooks, 1982. P. 270.

A newspaper columnist, Sifford describes his midlife crisis, his decision to divorce his wife of twenty-two years, and the ensuing estrangement from his two sons. Despite some near tragedies, Sifford reconstructs a new life, remarries, and slowly achieves reconciliation with his sons.

96. Stafford, Linley M. **One Man's Family: A Single Father and His Children**. New York: Random House, 1978. P. 181.

A writer with a gift for narrative, Stafford recounts how he came to have custody of a teenage son and daughter. The idea was not his. After the divorce Stafford's ex-wife had custody of the children, but at age eleven their son tearfully begged his father to let him live in the father's cramped Manhattan apartment. Stafford describes how nearly everybody he knew discouraged the idea, his own misgivings about it, his broaching the subject to his ex-wife (although hurt, she maturely put the boy's needs ahead of her own feelings), the father and son's first disastrous weeks together, and their eventual success as a two-party family. The unsettling process began anew, however, when Stafford's daughter announced to him that she too wanted to live with him and her brother. Not content merely to record events, Stafford recreates his experiences for the reader. *One Man's Family* is as vivid and poignant as a good novel. Accompanying the story are Stafford's pithy reflections on contemporary society—especially its attitudes toward fathers. In the final chapter the author hails the new breed of fathers who are determined to fight for a place in their children's lives. Many readers will find *One Man's Family* the quintessential "good read."

97. Steinberg, David. **fatherjournal: Five Years of Awakening to Fatherhood.** Albion, Calif.: Times Change Press, 1977. P. 91. illustrations. pa. Reprint. New York: Monthly Review Press, 1977. pa.

Dedicated "to all the fathers who have been taught to turn away from their children, and the growing number of fathers who are turning back," this series of diary entries begins with the birth of David and Susan's child, Dylan Joshua, on April 1, 1971. Steinberg records his responses to fathering as he and Susan both work part-time, as he becomes a full-time worker and she becomes a full-time parent, and then as they reverse roles with her working full-time and his becoming a househusband. In poems, songs, and photographs, Steinberg records his deep love for Dylan, but other entries record his moments of anger, frustration, and burnout. "Fathering is something I do well after all," Steinberg writes. "It's not a marketable skill, but it's an important one to me."

98. Waller, Leslie. **Hide in Plain Sight.** New York: Delacorte Press, 1976. P. 275. Reprint. New York: Dell Publishing Co., 1980. pa.

Can government bureaucrats kidnap a father's children and keep their whereabouts unknown to him for eight years? Of course they can, as this fascinating retelling of the Tom Leonhard case demonstrates. When law enforcement agents wanted to convict some Mafia bosses in Buffalo, they offered mobster Paddy Calabrese protection, including a new life and identity, for his testimony against the Mafia kingpins. The offer extended to Paddy's wife, Rochelle, and her four children. The problem was, however, that Rochelle's two oldest children were from a previous marriage. When she and Paddy disappeared with them, her ex-husband Tom Leonhard had no idea where they had gone. All he knew was that they were in the company of a man whose life was in danger from the Mafia. But none of the law enforcment people apparently gave two thoughts to Leonhard's plight; in their zeal to convict some Mafia kingpins, robbing a father of his children was a mere triviality. For eight years Leonhard and his new wife fought a legal battle to recover knowlege of the children's whereabouts. Eventually, he won his case, but at the close of this account he had not yet received an adequate apology from the U.S. government. The author notes that similar cases of separating fathers from their children have already occurred.

99. Wright, Richard. **Black Boy: A Record of Childhood and Youth.** New York and Evanston: Harper and Row, 1945. P. 285. pa.

Wright's wrenching account of his early years in the South reveals how poverty and racism can foster a cruel, embittered concept of masculinity in the humiliated black "boy." Wright's childhood was warped by many things, including the absence of strong male models and the superabundance of domineering female authority figures. Threatened also by a white world which denied his status as a man, Wright as "black boy" had to battle and connive relentlessly to maintain a modicum of masculine integrity.

Cross references:

23. Filene, Peter, ed. **Men in the Middle: Coping with the Problems of Work and Family in the Lives of Middle-aged Men.**

29. Rubin, Michael, ed. **Men without Masks: Writings from the Journals of Modern Men.**

35. Bell, Donald. **Being a Man: The Paradox of Masculinity.**

521. Gosse, Edmund. **Father and Son: A Study of Two Temperaments.**

MEN'S RIGHTS_____

100. Chambers, David L. **Making Fathers Pay: The Enforcement of Child Support**. Chicago and London: University of Chicago Press, 1979. P. xiv, 365. illustrations. appendix. notes. index. bibliography, 359-62.

Chambers covers the procedures used in three Michigan counties to force divorced fathers to pay alimony and child support. He examines the treatment of men by the courts, a public agency named Friend of the Court, and the jails. Fathers' rights advocates will find plenty to outrage them in what is reported, but the book depicts a situation producing more than enough misery and hardship for everybody involved—fathers, mothers, and children. The methodological appendix is by Terry K. Adams.

101. Doyle, R. F. **The Rape of the Male**. St. Paul, Minn.: Poor Richard's Press, 1976. P. vii, 286. illustrations. notes. bibliography, 279-86. pa.

The founder of Men's Rights Association, Doyle here takes angry aim at favoritism toward women in American society, especially in the divorce courts. Doyle criticizes no-fault divorce laws which permit automatic granting of custody to women and support payments to men, without any real enforcement of noncustodial visitation rights. "Upon dissolution of marriage, men's functions continue to be enforced," Doyle writes, "yet no judge has ever ordered a woman to cook, clean, and sew for her ex-husband; and damned seldom for an existing one." Ex-husbands are jailed if they cannot meet support payments, perhaps the only surviving example of imprisonment for debt. Courts routinely presume males guilty until proven innocent: "'orders to show cause why the accused should *not* be held in contempt of court' are a subterfuge, applied almost exclusively to males." Doyle illustrates his arguments with horror stories gleaned from years of counseling divorced men and from his own experiences with the courts. As Doyle himself admits, "This is not a chivalrous book." Present information indicates that this book can be obtained from Poor Richard's Press, P.O. Box 189, Lake Forest, MN 55025, and from World Wide Book Service, 544 Madison Square Station, New York, NY 10010.

102. Kanowitz, Leo. **Equal Rights: The Male Stake**. Albuquerque: University of New Mexico Press, 1981. P. viii, 197. appendix. notes. case and subject indexes. pa.

One purpose of this book is to demonstrate that men as well as women have been historically victimized by social gender discrimination and by sexist legal decisions. "By contrast, a casual glance at the treatment males have received at the hands of the law solely because they are males suggests that they have paid an awesome price for other advantages they have presumably enjoyed over females in our society," Kanowitz writes. "Whether one talks of the male's unique obligation of compulsory military service, his primary duty for spousal and child support, his lack of the same kinds of protective labor legislation that have traditionally been enjoyed by women, or the statutory or judicial preference in child custody disputes that has long been accorded to mothers vis-à-vis fathers of minor children, sex discrimination against males in statutes and judicial decisions has been widespread and severe." Kanowitz argues that men's interests coincide with those of women seeking equal rights under the law; he deplores the anti-male attitude of some feminists. In a series of essays, Kanowitz examines such matters as "benign" sex discrimination (which he finds not so benign at all), Social Security benefits favoring women, alimony decisions, "protective" laws which are not extended to males, equal pay and overtime restrictions, the New Mexico Equal Rights Amendment, the military draft, the national campaign for the ERA during the 1970s, and prospects for future adoption of such an amendment. Particularly disturbing is the evidence presented to demonstrate the almost total inability of the Supreme Court to recognize the extent and effects of anti-male discrimination in the past. Although the book is somewhat disjointed because it is made up in part of materials published over an eight-year period, readers can watch Kanowitz evolving from a male feminist who in 1972 accepted the fashionable idea of males as an oppressor class to a genuine equal rights advocate who in 1980 recognizes the impact which anti-male bias has had on men. A postscript on recent Supreme Court decisions concerning statutory rape laws and the male-only draft leaves little doubt that men have a long way to go before achieving equality in the courts.

103.   Katz, Sanford N., and Monroe L. Inker, eds. **Fathers, Husbands and Lovers: Legal Rights and Responsibilities.** Chicago: American Bar Association Press, 1982. P. v, 318. notes. pa.

Ten essays plus an introduction originally published in *Family Law Quarterly* explore several aspects of law relating to males, including medical tests to determine paternity more accurately (and hence child support obligations), the complications arising from "test tuby baby" situations, the impact of *Stanley v. Illinois* on securing the rights of unwed fathers, the impact of *Roe v. Wade* on paternal support (if the woman and her doctor have the right to decide on abortion or birth, why should the father be responsible for supporting a child he may not want?), a historical survey of laws regulating father's rights and obligations, laws concerning wife-battering (no laws concerning husband-battering are discussed), and changing alimony and property decisions. A few of the writers are sympathetic to men's rights, but others—like the editors—convey the impression that males are a privileged class who deserve to be punished by the law.

104.   Rivkin, Robert S. **GI Rights and Army Justice: The Draftee's Guide to Military Life and Law.** New York: Grove Press, 1970. P. xxii, 383. appendixes. notes. index.

Regarding the draftee or reluctant enlistee as a member of an oppressed minority, Rivkin depicts the realities of power and law in the army as a system of coercion producing a travesty of justice. From the time of induction to discharge, the soldier can expect harassment, low pay, maltreatment, and questionable legal practices. The military mind, the author argues, believes that humiliation plus fear equals obedience, revels in an antidemocratic caste system, glorifies killing, and likes to try its own cases. The ordinary soldier can expect little redress for many abuses he suffers. Exercising First Amendment rights of free speech, for example, can be hazardous for the GI, and rights of privacy can be easily violated. Nevertheless, Rivkin spells out what the soldier's rights are and explains how he can best protect himself legally, including methods of filing complaints and bringing charges. The abuse of servicemen in stockades is described, including an account of the Presidio 27. The final chapter debunks a series of military "myths" (e.g., discipline in combat will disappear in the absence of terror in training) and argues for a more humane and equitable system of military justice. Appendix A contains resolutions of the National Conference on GI Rights for reform of the military legal system. Appendix B lists GI newspapers, coffeehouses, counseling organizations, and lawyer referral services.

105. Rivkin, Robert S., and Barton F. Stichman. **The Rights of Military Person-
      nel: The Basic ACLU Guide for Military Personnel.** Rev. ed. New York:
      Avon Books, Discus, 1977. P. 158. appendix. notes. pa. Originally pub-
      lished as *The Rights of Servicemen* (New York: Avon Books, 1972.
      Reprint. New York: Richard W. Baron, 1973).

"The military services are still unnecessarily oppressive," the authors state, "but no longer are they immune from public scrutiny and civilian court review of their lawless actions." Taking a less than enthusiastic view of military law and practice, the authors use a question-and-answer approach to review such matters as the military law and the court-martial system, Article 15 (which authorizes a commanding officer to impose nonjudicial punishment upon any member of his command for minor offenses), the soldier's rights during interrogation, AWOL and desertion, the right to privacy (apparently more honored in the breach than in the observance), First Amendment rights of freedom of expression, conscientious objectors, the right to disobey illegal orders, getting out of the military, and filing complaints against military superiors. The appendix includes a worldwide list of agencies that provide in-service counseling, counseling to upgrade discharges, lawyer referrals, and Veterans Administration counseling.

106. Rudovsky, David. **The Rights of Prisoners: The Basic ACLU Guide to a
      Prisoner's Rights.** An American Civil Liberties Union Handbook. New
      York: Richard W. Baron, 1973. P. 129. appendixes. notes. bibliography,
      127-28.

Painting a dismal picture of prisoners' rights, Rudovsky argues that the courts' hands-off policy regarding prisons guarantees almost total control of them by prison officials. In question-and-answer format, he touches briefly upon such matters as due process in prison disciplinary matters, freedom from cruel and unusual punishment, problems of censorship in prisons, prisoners' rights to free communication and access to the courts, questions of religious and racial discrimination in prison policies, political rights of prisoners, questions of privacy and personal appearance, and rights to medical care and protection from physical or sexual abuse. The author also discusses pretrial confinement ("The jails are an unmitigated disgrace"), parole, and procedures for remedies of prisoners' complaints. Prisoners' rights are both scarce and arbitrary: Rudovsky advises the reader that "this guide offers no assurances that your rights will be respected."

107. Sherrill, Robert. **Military Justice Is to Justice as Military Music Is to Music.** New York: Harper and Row, 1970. P. 235. index. Reprint. Rev. ed. New York: Harper and Row, 1971. pa.

While American women are exempt from compulsory military service, American men still face the possibility of conscription. And once he is in service, the American man "may anticipate not only the possibility of giving up his life but also the certainty of giving up his liberties." This book indicates what men can expect from military courts because both Congress and the Supreme Court have consistently refused to extend constitutional rights to soldiers. Sherrill intersperses his history of military law with accounts of specific cases of miscarriage of justice, atrocities in military stockades, and cruel and unusual punishment meted out by the military. He concludes: "Justice is too important to be left to the military. If military justice is corrupt—and it is—sooner or later it will corrupt civilian justice."

108. Stoddard, Thomas B., E. Carrington Boggan, Marilyn G. Haft, Charles Lister, and John P. Rupp. **The Rights of Gay People.** Rev. ed. New York: Bantam Books, 1983. P. xii, 194. appendixes. notes. bibliography, 167-70. pa.

Using a question-and-answer format, this book surveys gay rights in such areas as freedom of speech and assembly, employment, armed services, security clearance, immigration and naturalization, and housing and public accommodations. Separate chapters cover the gay family, gays and criminal law, and the rights of transvestites and transsexuals. The appendixes include state-by-state criminal statutes relating to consensual homosexual acts between adults, antidiscrimination laws of Minneapolis and East Lansing, executive orders of the governors of California and Pennsylvania concerning sexual minorities, a selective list of gay organizations, and ACLU state affiliates. This book is the revised edition of *The Basic ACLU Guide to a Gay Person's Rights.*

109. Weitzman, Leonore J. **The Marriage Contract: Spouses, Lovers, and the Law.** New York: Free Press, 1981. P. xxiii, 536. appendix. notes. index. pa.

In exhaustive detail, Weitzman examines the legal implications of marriage and cohabiting, focusing on traditional obligations (the husband must support the wife, the wife must provide domestic service and child care), as well as the discrepancies between the law's view of marriage and social reality. Weitzman argues the case for "intimate contracts" between couples to insure a more equitable distribution of powers and obligations. The author's feminist slant stresses the disadvantages to women in the traditional view of marriage and sometimes downplays or overlooks the disadvantages to men. This latter topic badly needs to be examined by men's rights advocates, but until it is Weitzman's book will be indispensable.

110.   Wishard, William R., and Laurie Wishard. **Men's Rights: A Handbook for the 80's.** San Francisco: Cragmont Publications, 1980. P. 264. appendix. index. bibliography, 259-60.

"This book is pro-men; it is not anti-women or anti-family," the authors explain. In informal and lively language, the Wishards—father and daughter—begin with the idea that, with the qualified success of women's rights in the courts, the time has come to balance the scales by considering men's rights. Most of their discussion concerns family law: marriage as a blank contract, the legal obligations of cohabitation arrangements, the father's well-defined responsibility to support his children and his less-well-defined rights as a parent, the father's lack of rights in abortion cases, and the slightly expanding rights of unmarried fathers. The Wishards devote much space to discussing the legal ins and outs of separation, divorce, custody (including the benefits and drawbacks of joint custody), spousal support (as, traditionally, a form of discrimination against men), child support, visitation, and related matters. The authors also discuss the less-noticed matter of reverse sex discrimination in employment opportunities and on the job—how it occurs and what has been and can be done to nullify it. Only a brief mention is made of men's unequal military obligations. The appendix contains a short list of men's rights organizations.

Cross references:

71.   Shostak, Arthur B., and Gary McLouth, with Lynn Seng. **Men and Abortion: Lessons, Losses, and Love.**

82.   Gibson, E. Lawrence. **Get Off My Ship: Ensign Berg vs. the U.S. Navy.**

92.   Painter, Hal. **Mark, I Love You.**

98.   Waller, Leslie. **Hide in Plain Sight.**

466.   Silver, Gerald A., and Myrna Silver. **Weekend Fathers.**

468.   Beer, William R. **Househusbands: Men and Housework in American Families.**

See section on Divorce and Custody.

DIVORCE AND CUSTODY_____

111. Athearn, Forden. **How to Divorce Your Wife: The Man's Side of Divorce.**
Garden City, N.Y.: Doubleday and Co., 1976. P. 167. appendixes. index.
Like its title, the book is abrupt and direct. A West Coast divorce attorney, Athearn
provides a how-to guide to the legal and emotional pitfalls of divorce—including
such topics as what to do *before* telling your wife you want a divorce, the foolish
and destructive reactions of some men whose wives file for divorce, the grounds for
divorce, the trial, alimony, custody, child support, visitation, property division,
and handling lawyers. Appendix A contains state-by-state divorce information;
appendix B is a glossary of legal terms.

112. Cassidy, Robert. **What Every Man Should Know about Divorce.** Washington, D.C.: New Republic Books, 1977. P. ix, 247. appendixes. index.
bibliography, 190-96.
A veteran of the divorce wars, Cassidy offers advice to avoid the pitfalls of marital
separation and to encourage growth amid the pain. He focuses upon the emotional
turmoil which the divorcing man will face. Horror stories about what divorce courts
have done lead into Cassidy's advice about fighting back. He offers information
about finding an attorney, how the courts work, custody, visitation, children's
reactions, and starting a new life. The appendixes include a state-by-state guide to
divorce laws and a listing of divorce reform groups. The foreword is by Mel
Krantzler.

113. Doppler, George F. **American Needs Total Divorce Reform—Now!** New
York: Vantage Press, 1973. P. 125.
This denunciation of the American judicial system's handling of divorce focuses
on men's concerns. Dealing primarily with divorce and custody proceedings in
Pennsylvania, Doppler points to abuses in other states and issues a call for reform.
He touches upon such matters as discrimination against men in the courts, how the
law rewards wives for ending a marriage, how attorneys profit from marital breakup but not from reconciliation, the inequities involved in child support, how
alimony and separate maintenance are forms of legalized extortion, the abuse of
fathers' visitation rights by ex-wives, and the imbalance of property settlements.
The author argues for mandatory counseling for separating couples, includes a
petition to the United Nations for equal rights for fathers, and lists men's divorce

organizations around the country. Doppler writes not as a dispassionate observer but as a militant activist for reform.

114.   Epstein, Joseph. **Divorced in America: Marriage in an Age of Possibility.** New York: E.P. Dutton and Co., 1974. P. 339. Reprint. New York: Penguin Books, 1981. pa.

"The book you are about to read," Epstein writes in his preface, "is by a divorced man whose bias is on behalf on the nuclear family, a man who, despite all its flaws, really cannot imagine any other arrangement being any better. God, as the sages suspected, must love a good joke." Epstein regards divorce as a painful joke, as this ironic narrative reveals. Interspersed with ghastly scenes from a divorce, the book reviews the toll upon marriage taken by sexual liberation, female emancipation, and "growth" philosophies. Epstein provides a quick history of divorce and delves into the improbabilities of alimony. He concludes that divorce brings at least as much bondage as a bad marriage, that those who boost "creative divorce" are full of hot air, and that the nuclear family is really the only option for men and women. Throughout the book, Epstein provides a vivid account of divorce from a male viewpoint.

115.   Franks, Maurice R. **How to Avoid Alimony.** New York: Saturday Review Press/E.P. Dutton and Co., 1975. P. xiv, 173. notes. index. Reprint. New York: New American Library, Signet, 1976. pa.

Gleefully dedicated to the author's ex-wife and her attorney (who failed to get Franks to pay alimony), this book offers strategies for avoiding wife maintenance after divorce. Franks's principal tactic is to remove the divorce case from the state courts (which regularly discriminate against males) to the federal courts where such issues as equal rights and slavery can be raised. In this day of working wives, Franks argues that wife support is sexist and a form of peonage, and he cites constitutional and legal support for his view. An attorney, Franks opposes no-fault divorce as too broad a definition, as actually encouraging divorce, as permitting courts to exercise traditional bias against males, and as allowing the wife who is at fault to soak her husband for property and maintenance. In snappy prose, Franks also offers suggestions about how to find the right kind of lawyer, how to lower unreasonable child support payments, what to do if your ex-wife has a live-in lover, how men in divorce cases can take advantage of an ERA, and why premarital contracts are expedient.

116.   Franks, Maurice R. **Winning Custody.** Englewood Cliffs, N.J.: Prentice-Hall, 1983. P. 192. notes. index. pa.

In this "no-holds-barred guide for fathers" Franks provides jargon-free advice on the problems and strategies of winning custody. He estimates costs, offers suggestions for finding a good lawyer, and warns the father to prepare for war. He discusses means of impressing judges favorably, and he explains the legal factors which will influence a custody decision. Attacking no-fault divorce and the "tender years" mentality, Franks goes beyond courtroom practice to discuss the possibilities of taperecording telephone conversations and of hiring detectives. In later chapters he provides advice for fathers seeking to change custody or to enforce visitation rights. One chapter is devoted to Franks's formulas for determining how much child support both mothers and fathers ought to pay. Suing malpracticing lawyers and removing bad judges are also explored. The penultimate chapter contains Franks's suggestions about what divorce and custody law ought to be, and the final chapter offers advice to divorced fathers who are thinking of remarriage.

117.　Goldstein, Joseph, Anna Freud, and Albert J. Solnit. **Beyond the Best Interests of the Child.** Rev. ed. New York: Free Press, 1979. P. xiv, 203. notes. index. pa.

First published in 1973, this book became a center of controversy. Applying psychoanalytic theory and learning to law cases, the authors attempt to discover "the least detrimental alternative" in placing a child after a family breakup. They argue that the child, whose sense of time is different from an adult's, needs continuity with a "psychological" parent; therefore, long delays in settling cases, joint custody, and disruptive visitations from a noncustodial parent are harmful to the child. In legal matters, the child—not just the parents—should be legally represented. In an epilogue added to the latest edition the authors attempt to answer objections raised by the first publication. The book's most controversial suggestions still involve visitation from a noncustodial parent: the authors argue that the custodial parent, not the courts, should determine whether visitation is beneficial to the child. Because most noncustodial parents are fathers, the book's guidelines seem especially inimical to them. The discussion ignores the question of whether noncustodial parents without visitation rights must still provide child support, and critics of the book argue that the authors have underestimated the value to the child of having contact with two parents, even when they are separated and somewhat hostile to each other.

118.　Kerpelman, Leonard. **Divorce: A Guide for Men.** South Bend, Ind.: Icarus Press, 1983. P. xi, 292. index.

Convinced that the judicial system is prejudiced against males in divorce cases, attorney Kerpelman provides hardnosed advice for men contemplating divorce. Speaking bluntly, he says that anything less than militancy in conducting his case will insure the man's defeat. Finding a good attorney is difficult: Kerpelman has a low opinion of most lawyers' willingness and ability to handle the man's case. Judges are even worse: most are "male chauvinists," i.e., they believe that women should be protected and supported by males and are automatically more suited for parenting than men. Kerpelman tells the male reader that to win his case he needs the support of a competent and active fathers' group; if he cannot find such a group, he had better start one. Drawing upon the experience of a Maryland Father's United for Equal Rights group with which he is associated, the author tells of its founding by Dr. Paul Hanson and of how it evolved tactics to pressure judges who regularly handed down blatantly anti-male decisions. Mr. Nice Guy will invariably lose, Kerpelman argues, advising men to be tough, angry, and militant—but never violent—throughout the divorce experience.

119.　Kiefer, Louis. **How to Win Custody.** New York: Simon and Schuster, Cornerstone Library, 1982. P. xi, 308. appendixes. index. pa.

A divorced attorney who obtained custody of his children "not because of the legal system but in spite of it," Kiefer writes primarily for fathers (the traditional underdogs in custody cases), although his advice is useful for either parent and the book includes a chapter for noncustodial mothers. Kiefer's legal knowledge provides an unusually detailed account of the custodial tug of war, his courtroom experiences enable him to cite numerous (often hair-raising) cases, and his writing skills produce clear, jargon-free prose. Kiefer has few illusions about the legal system, his advice is both practical and blunt ("trust no one"), and his thorough coverage explores not only the usual topics (how to locate a good lawyer) but such less-familiar ones as how to nullify your spouse's "dirty tricks," making phone taps and taping conversations, the legalities of absconding with children, and how to locate "kidnapped" children. The six appendixes include a sample joint custody agreement, a sample sole custody agreement, a list of deposition questions, questions for cross-examining a psychiatrist, and the texts of the Uniform Child Custody Jurisdiction Act and the Parental Kidnapping Prevention Act of 1980.

120. Metz, Charles V. **Divorce and Custody for Men: A Guide and Primer Designed Exclusively to Help Men Win Just Settlements.** Garden City, N.Y.: Doubleday and Co., 1968. P. xvii, 147.

Metz's primer is designed to jolt about-to-be divorced men out of their complacency; they must be prepared to fight viciously if they hope to win even the semblance of a just settlement. Loss of income, property, and children are among the prices men pay for their ignorance of divorce law and practice, which are strongly biased in women's favor. Get mad, be prepared, file first, and fight to win, Metz advises. He takes a dim view of alimony, social workers, judges, attorneys, and visitation practices, arguing that men must organize to effect changes in divorce law and procedures.

121. Morgenbesser, Mel, and Nadine Nehls. **Joint Custody: An Alternative for Divorcing Families.** Chicago: Nelson-Hall, 1981. P. vii, 168. illustrations. index. bibliography, 151-61.

Calmly and equitably, the authors provide a history of child custody and a definition of current joint custody. After describing the effects of divorce upon children, they argue the benefits—and potential drawbacks—of joint custody. Also included are advice on how to achieve joint custody, sample joint custody agreements, interviews with parents sharing custody, and an overview of research on the topic.

122. Ricci, Isolina. **Mom's House/Dad's House: Making Shared Custody Work.** New York: Macmillan Co., 1980. P. xv, 270. illustrations. appendixes. notes. index. bibliography, 264-66, and throughout notes. pa.

Indicating that single-parent custody often does not work well, Ricci offers an extensive list of suggestions for separated couples to turn two houses into two homes for their children. She considers myriad complications that can arise, offers practical solutions, and in the process makes a case for shared custody as often preferable to single-parent custody.

123. Roman, Mel, and William Haddad, with Susan Manso. **The Disposable Parent: The Case for Joint Custody.** New York: Holt, Rinehart and Winston, 1978. P. 215. notes. index. Reprint. New York: Penguin Books, 1979. pa.

The disposable parent, Roman and Haddad argue, is usually the father. With divorce, child custody goes to the mother in over 90 percent of contemporary cases. After an introduction describing their own cases and those of other men, the authors in chapter 1 explore the legal history of custody, concentrating upon the reversal in England and America from nineteenth-century practice (which regularly awarded custody to the father) to twentieth-century practice (which does just the opposite). In chapter 2 the authors argue that the present method of splitting the family between custodial and noncustodial parents does not work, while chapter 3 is devoted to what little is known about fathers and fathering, as well as the stereotypes that underlie many studies. Chapters 4 and 5 reply to arguments against joint custody and cite evidence for its feasibility. In chapter 6 the authors show why joint custody is seldom considered. In particular, they point to feminist ambivalence on the subject: while recognizing that single parenthood places a heavy burden on women, some feminists have been reluctant to surrender the principal stronghold of female power, and some are guilty of reverse sexism, believing that men do not care about or cannot handle parenting. In the final chapter, the authors make suggestions for creating a social climate in which joint custody can work better.

124.   Vail, Lauren O. **Divorce: The Man's Complete Guide to Winning**. New York: Simon and Schuster, Sovereign Books, 1979. P. viii, 280. appendixes. notes. index. bibliography, 246-51.

"Definitely pro men" but not "against women," Vail's book takes a dim view of the legal system of domestic relations in the United States. Vail sees men victimized by their ignorance of the law, the bias against men in the courts, and the nice-guy psychology which makes men vulnerable to manipulation. Arguing that men must pursue their cases aggressively, Vail offers hardnosed advice on such matters as preliminary dos and don'ts of divorce; finding a good lawyer; the grounds and proofs needed for divorce; what to expect of the legal system; support, property, and custody agreements; preparing for trial; and how to survive psychologically during and after the divorce. A clinical psychologist (not a lawyer), Vail avoids legal jargon in his writing. The four appendixes contain advice on how to do your own legal research, a list of helpful readings, a list of men's rights organizations, and a glossary of legal terms.

125.   Victor, Ira, and Win Ann Winkler. **Fathers and Custody**. New York: Hawthorn Books, 1977. P. xiii, 209. appendixes. notes. index. bibliography, 193-201.

"There is overwhelming evidence," the authors write, "that prejudice exists against fathers in a custody situation." This book considers the growing phenomenon of fathers with child custody, the difficulties they encounter in obtaining it, and the problems they face once they have it. After presenting case histories to demonstrate that a representative father does not exist, the authors explain why more men are seeking custody than in the past. One reason is that the "feminine" bride who valued motherhood sometimes becomes the "feminist" wife who deplores it. Discussing the women who "drop out" of marriage and fathers who "cop out" of custody hassles, the authors observe that the principal victims in these situations are often the children. Despite changing attitudes, fathers seeking custody have an uphill battle. In discussing the ambiguous impact of the men's movement, the authors review the division in its ranks between militants pushing for men's equal rights and male feminists reiterating feminist accusations against men. The hostility of the women's movement toward awarding custody to fathers, except when the mother agrees to give it up, is also noted. The authors examine the increase of kidnapping among divorced parents, help for fathers with custody, and visitation problems. Despite the doomsaying of some authorities, joint custody and full custody for fathers can—and often does—work, the authors argue. In concluding chapters, they look briefly at dating, remarriage, and step-parenting, as well as the emerging parental consciousness. The appendixes list divorced fathers' groups, single-parent and child-help groups, and legal advice referral groups.

126.   Woody, Robert Henley. **Getting Custody: Winning the Last Battle of the Marital War.** New York: Macmillan Co., 1978. P. xii, 179. appendixes. index. bibliography, 172-73.

A clinical psychologist specializing in marriage problems, Woody offers legal suggestions and psychological advice (mostly to fathers) for waging and surviving custodial battles.

Cross references:

14.   Sell, Kenneth D., comp. **Divorce in the 70s: A Subject Bibliography.**

87.   Martin, Albert. **One Man, Hurt.**

512.   Corman, Avery. **Kramer Versus Kramer.**

See section on Divorced and Single Fathers.

See section on Men's Rights.

WAR AND PEACE
The Military, The Draft,
Resistance, Combat_____

127. Anderson, Martin, ed. **Registration and the Draft: Proceedings of the Hoover-Rochester Conference on the All-Volunteer Force.** Stanford, Calif.: Hoover Institution Press, Stanford University, 1982. P. xi, 417. notes. index.

This volume contains twenty-six presentations (papers, summaries, rebuttals, discussions) from the Hoover-Rochester Conference on the All-Volunteer Force held during December 13-14, 1979. The legality and advisability of national service are considered, as well as numerous issues connected with it. Significantly, the issue of inequity to males is never raised.

128. Barker, A. J. **Prisoners of War.** New York: Universe Books, 1975. P. 249. illustrations. appendixes. index. bibliography, 236-42. Originally published as *Behind Barbed Wire* (London: Batsford, 1974).

The fate of men captured during war has always been miserable and precarious, but in the twentieth century the numbers of military prisoners and the barbarities visited upon them have risen alarmingly. (In World War II alone, an estimated six to ten million men perished in prison camps.) Even those who survive and are repatriated can often expect lifelong aftereffects from their ordeal. Without sensationalizing, Barker provides a historical overview of military prisoners, and he describes the shock of capture and the first ordeals of prison life. He then explores numerous facets of military prison life, the effects of indoctrination, and the results of repatriation. A concluding chapter offers a code for survival in prison camps. One appendix discusses the 1949 Geneva Convention rules of prisoner treatment, the other the roles of "protective powers" and humanitarian agencies in alleviating the prisoner's lot. A useful bibliography is included.

129. Bradley, Jeff. **A Young Person's Guide to Military Service.** Harvard and Boston: The Harvard Common Press, 1983. P. xiv, 175. notes. index. bibliography, 167-70. pa.

Impartially examining the advantages and disadvantages of military service, Bradley provides high school students (and to some extent college students) with balanced information to help them assess military life intelligently. He supplies questions which young people need to ask about themselves to see if they can fit comfortably into the military. Each branch of service (Army, Navy, Air Force, Marine Corps,

National Guard, and Coast Guard) is described in such matters as a brief history, length of service hitches, what basic training is like, location of facilities, sample job opportunities, advanced training, bonuses, and a list of available jobs. Basic requirements for admission to the services are detailed. Discussion of becoming an officer includes information on the military academies, ROTC programs, and officer candidate schools. Bradley tells how to bargain with recruiters; he explores the difficulties of leaving military service before one's hitch has been served. Separate chapters on women and blacks in the military precede a final discussion of the male-only draft, draft counseling, and conscientious objector status.

130. Bressler, Marion A., and Leo A. Bressler, eds. **Country, Conscience, and Conscription: Can They Be Reconciled?** Inquiry into Crucial American Problems. Englewood Cliffs, N.J.: Prentice-Hall, 1970. P. iv, 121. notes. bibliography, 116-21. pa.

This selection of twenty-nine essays and excerpts covers the pros and cons of the military draft, the reasons why some men oppose it, and what alternatives to it exist. Included is an abridged version of Margaret Mead's "The Case for Drafting All Boys—and Girls," originally published in *Redbook* (September, 1966).

131. Friedman, Leon. **The Wise Minority**. New York: Dial Press, 1971. P. xvii, 228. appendixes. notes. index.

"We are a nation of ... *conscientious* lawbreakers," writes Friedman in this study which places resistance to military draft into the historical context of American civil disobedience. Discussion covers such matters as the intellectual background for conscientious lawbreaking, the Whiskey Rebellion, the Alien and Sedition Acts, abolitionists, labor and farm revolts, minority groups, as well as resistance to the draft from the Civil War to the Vietnam War. The author concludes: "Draft resistance is nothing new in American history."

132. Gaylin, Willard. **In the Service of Their Country: War Resisters in Prison.** New York: Viking Press, 1970. P. vi, 344.

A psychoanalyst, Gaylin explores the effects of prisons upon conscientious objectors during the Vietnam War, offering critical reflections upon a society which perpetrates such dehumanization upon its young men.

133. Goldman, Peter, and Tony Fuller, with Richard Manning, Stryker McGuire, Wally McNamee, and Vern E. Smith. **Charlie Company: What Vietnam Did to Us.** New York: William Morrow and Co., A Newsweek Book, 1983. P. 358. illustrations. appendixes. index. bibliography, 351.

This emotionally powerful account of sixty-five men from Charlie Company tells how they were swept up at the age of eighteen or nineteen, placed amid the carnage of the Vietnam War, and then returned home to face indifference or hostility from a nation that wanted to forget them. The authors also include accounts of those men who were killed in Vietnam. A final section of the book tells of a reunion of the men in 1981. Expanded from a *Newsweek* special report, *Charlie Company* provides vivid evidence of what Vietnam and its aftermath did to the men who served there.

134. Gray, J. Glenn. **The Warriors: Reflections on Men in Battle**. 3d ed. New York: Harper and Row, Torchbooks, 1970. P. xxiv, 242. pa.

In this classic series of reflections on men and war, Gray draws upon his experiences as a soldier in World War II to consider the appeals of war, love as an ally and foe of war, the soldier's relation to death, images of the enemy, the ache of guilt, and the future of war. First published in 1959, the book contains an introduction by Hannah Arendt (1967) and a new foreword by Gray (1970).

135. Habenstreit, Barbara. **Men against War**. Garden City, N.Y.: Doubleday and Co., 1973. P. iv, 210. index. bibliography, 203-4.

"There has never been a war when no one came," Habenstreit notes, "but in every war some men have always stood up against their governments and refused to serve." This survey aimed primarily at high school readers focuses upon pacificists who rejected all violence, opponents of particular wars, and draft resisters in American history. Beginning with the Shakers and Quakers in colonial times, Habenstreit follows chronologically the Revolutionary War, the Mexican War, the antidraft riots during the Civil War, the war hysteria and persecutions of World War I, the nonresistant methods of the civil rights movement, and opposition to the Vietnam War. Among the men touched upon are David Low Dodge, Noah Worcester, William Ladd, William Lloyd Garrison, Henry David Thoreau, James Russell Lowell, Samuel J. May, Elihu Burritt, George C. Beckwith, the unlikely combination of Clarence Darrow and William Jennings Bryan (who were both temporarily disciples of Russia's Leo Tolstoy), Oswald Garrison Villard, Norman Thomas, Roger Baldwin, Eugene V. Debs, Martin Luther King, and Philip and Daniel Berrigan. The "men" against war include some women too, notably Angelina and Sarah Grimké, Jane Addams, and Fanny Garrison Villard. Habenstreit also notes the existence of peace organizations in American history, the influence of such foreigners as Gandhi, and the many unknown men who stood their ground, often at great personal cost, against violence and war.

136. Helmer, John. **Bringing the War Home: The American Soldier in Vietnam and After**. New York: Free Press, 1974. P. xv, 346. illustrations. appendixes. notes. index.

Characterizing Vietnam soldiers as "the poor man's army," Helmer uses a questionnaire and interviews to assess the impact of the war upon working-class veterans. He has selected ninety subjects, divided evenly into three groups: members of the Veterans of Foreign Wars (straights), drug users (addicts), and members of Vietnam Veterans Against the War (radicals). Helmer describes how these men enlisted or were inducted into military service, their experiences in Vietnam, and their homecomings. He notes the tendency of the military to equate combat suitability with masculinity. Frequently, he compares and contrasts his findings with those in *The American Soldier* by Samuel A. Stouffer and others. Drawing upon Marxist class-consciousness theories, the author describes the alienation and rebellion among veterans; he suggests why the American working class failed to mobilize against Vietnam-era injustices. The appendixes include additional information about Vietnam veterans, the survey questionnaire, and the interview questions.

137. Hicken, Victor. **The American Fighting Man**. New York: Macmillan Co., 1969. P. ix, 496. illustrations. notes. bibliography, 457-74.

Although sometimes critical, Hicken's readable study remains a tribute to the American soldiers, sailors, and marines who fought from pre-Revolutionary days to the Vietnam conflict. Rather than presenting a chronological survey, Hicken analyzes the representative American fighting man, exploring his motives for participation in various wars. After recording how the American soldier has been viewed by allies and enemy, Hicken constructs a composite picture of the "average" soldier, and analyzes his character. Hicken shows him amid the hardships of combat and the horrors of enemy prisons, as well as in the role of victor occupying another country. The all-American soldier represents a bewildering variety of ethnic and racial groups, and despite his universal love of griping, he has demonstrated enormous *esprit* and awesome courage. (For a somewhat less enthusiastic view of the American fighting man, readers should see John Laffin's *Americans in Battle*.)

138.   Just, Ward. **Military Men**. New York: Alfred A. Knopf, 1970. P. 259.
       appendix. bibliography, 255-56.
At the height of anti-Vietnam feeling in the U.S., Just surveyed the military establishment and found defensive men and institutions. Occasionally, he also found the strong link between the military and machismo, as when a wounded sergeant explains why he returned to the infantry: "Oh, maybe I wanted my masculinity back."

139.   Kasinsky, Renée G. **Refugees from Militarism: Draft-Age Americans in Canada**. New Brunswick, N.J.: Transaction Books, 1976. P. 301. appendixes. notes. index. Reprint. Littlefield, N.J.: Adams Quality Paperbacks, 1978. pa.
Drawing upon six years (1969-1975) as a participant observer, more than six hundred questionnaire responses, and thirty in-depth interviews, Kasinsky depicts events which led thousands of young American males to leave the United States for Canada during the Vietnam era.

140.   Keegan, John. **The Face of Battle**. New York: Viking Press, 1976. P. 354.
       illustrations. index. bibliography, 337-43. Reprint. New York: Penguin Books, 1983. pa.
A highly acclaimed book, *The Face of Battle* attempts to recreate what combat is like from the viewpoint of the ordinary fighting man. Citing the limitations of traditional military history with its "decisive battle" mentality and set-piece language, Keegan tries to answer questions seldom raised in these accounts. He shifts his focus away from the generals and their strategy to such matters as the motivations for the men to engage in battle, the conditions under which the men in the ranks fought, how they were wounded and were treated, how they died, how prisoners were taken, the relationship between junior officers and fighting men, and the use of compulsion to get men to hold their ground. With these and similar concerns in mind, Keegan describes three famous battles: Agincourt (October 25, 1415), Waterloo (June 18, 1815), and The Somme (July 1, 1916). In a final chapter he concludes—perhaps too sanguinely—that the young men who are increasingly unwilling to be forced into warfare have already spelled the doom of battle as a historical event.

141. Klein, Robert. **Wounded Men, Broken Promises**. New York: Macmillan
      Co., 1981. P. xv, 278.
In this account of "how the Veterans Administration betrays yesterday's heroes,"
Klein reports horror stories of red tape, insensitivity, medical bungling, and psychiatric mistreatment. For young men contemplating a military stint, Klein offers
sobering food for thought.

142. Laffin, John. **Americans in Battle**. New York: Crown Publishers, 1973.
      P. x, 213. illustrations. index. bibliography, 195-204.
Viewing the American fighting man with an admiring but critical eye, Laffin finds
him generous, charitable, resourceful, but possessing a "rowdy strain" which makes
him oversexed, given to drink and drugs, and lacking in discipline. The author traces
the history of the ordinary American soldier from the Revolution to Vietnam,
finding the United States a war-loving nation. (This book is intended as something
of a corrective to Victor Hicken's *The American Fighting Man*.)

143. O'Sullivan, John, and Alan M. Meckler. **The Draft and Its Enemies: A
      Documentary History**. Urbana: University of Illinois Press, 1974. P. xx,
      280. notes. index. bibliography, 281-85.
Utilizing pertinent documents, the authors plot the stormy history of conscription
from colonial times to the 1970s. The account raises questions about the legal and
political legitimacy of the military draft in a democracy; certainly, such conscription goes against the grain of American ideals of free choice and individualism. The
preface is by Russell F. Weigley; the introduction is by Senator Mark O. Hatfield
who describes the draft as "inherently inequitable, inefficient, and unjust—a form
of involuntary servitude striking at the heart of the principles which have made
this country strong, vital, and creative." Whatever one's views on America's male-
only military obligation, this book is essential reading.

144. Starr, Paul, with James F. Henry and Raymond P. Bonner. **The Discarded
      Army: Veterans after Vietnam**. The Nader Report on Vietnam Veterans
      and the Veterans Administration. New York: Charterhouse, 1973. P. xiii,
      304. notes. index.
Based upon considerable research, this study of veterans after the Vietnam conflict
examines such problems as VA hospitals, drug treatment programs, "bad" discharges, veteran unemployment, and education. The introduction by Ralph Nader
indicates that the Veterans Administration is central to the men's postwar
problems.

145. Stouffer, Samuel A., and others. Vol. 1: **The American Soldier: Adjust-
      ment during Army Life**. Vol. 2: **The American Soldier: Combat and Its
      Aftermath**. Vol. 3: **Experiments on Mass Communications**. Vol. 4:
      Measurement and Prediction. Studies in Social Psychology in World War
      II. Princeton, N.J.: Princeton University Press, 1949-1950. P. ix, 600;
      676; x, 346; x, 758. illustrations. appendixes. notes. indexes.
The result of massive studies conducted over a four-year period by the Research
Branch of the Army's Information and Education Division, these four volumes pro-
vide an enormous body of information about American fighting men during World

War II. General readers are likely to be most interested in the first two volumes. After exploring the differences between the "old" army of World War I and the "new" army of the 1940s, volume I examines how men adjusted to the authoritarian nature of the military, its sharply defined class system, and other elements of army life. The authors explore such matters as social mobility in the army, job assignment and job satisfaction, attitudes toward leadership and social control, and the soldiers' orientation toward the war. A separate chapter is devoted to Negro soldiers. Volume II utilizes responses from 12,295 men to explore such matters as the soldiers' attitudes toward combat before and after their experience of it, the general conditions of ground combat in Europe and the Pacific, the stressful nature of combat, and the relationships among men engaged in combat duty. Also examined are the soldiers' motivations for going into combat and their attitudes toward replacement policy, rear echelons, and those on the homefront. Of special importance is a section describing the relation between masculinity and the role of the combat soldier. Other chapters are devoted to men engaged in flying combat missions and engaged in aerial combat. Psychoneurotic symptoms in the army are also described. Later chapters consider the rotation of soldiers, the end of the war, and the soldier as veteran. Volume III is concerned with the effects upon soldiers of mass communications, such as films, radio broadcasts, filmstrips, and so on. Volume IV examines theoretical and empirical analysis of problems of measurement, and problems of predicting the soldiers' postwar plans.

146. Surrey, David S. **Choice of Conscience: Vietnam Era Military and Draft Resisters in Canada.** Praeger Special Studies. New York: Praeger Publishers, J.F. Bergin Publishers, 1982. P. xi, 207. notes. index. bibliography, 189-97.

From structured interviews and the author's work with over one thousand men during and after the Vietnam era, this book surveys the history of conscription and resistance in America, the lives of the young men who left the United States for Canada during the Vietnam era, their reception in Canada, their assimilation, the effects of amnesty, and the lingering legacies of the Vietnam War.

147. Tax, Sol, ed. **The Draft: A Handbook of Facts and Alternatives.** Chicago and London: University of Chicago Press, 1967. P. ix, 497. appendix. notes. index of persons and subject index. pa.

Although dated, this collection of papers and discussions contains valuable insights on the military draft. Part I consists of twenty-five papers contributed to a conference on the draft held on December 4-7, 1966, at the University of Chicago. Authors discuss problems with the draft system, the possibilities of broadening the draft to a form of "universal" national service ("universal" usually means male-only), different perspectives on the draft (from history, other cultures, and a survey of high school students), and alternatives to the draft, especially voluntary service schemes. Part II contains discussions of the papers and pursues numerous themes introduced by them. Part III, an epilogue, consists of four postconference documents which indicate that in formulating the Selective Service Act of 1967 Congress by and large rejected innovations and reforms and stayed with the status quo. Two signs of the dated nature of the material are, first, no discussion of the place of homosexuals in the military occurs and, second, the sexist nature of a male-only draft is challenged only by Margaret Mead who, interestingly, argues that women should be conscripted but not allowed into combat because they are likely to be more savage fighters than men.

148.   Taylor, L. B., Jr. **The Draft: A Necessary Evil?** New York: Franklin Watts, 1981. P. 85. index. bibliography, 77-79.

An excellent text for high school and college students, this book reviews clearly and evenhandedly the history of conscription, the current draft situation in America, the arguments for and against drafting women, and the pros and cons of a nonvoluntary military obligation in the eighties.

149.   Uhl, Michael, and Tod Ensign. **GI Guinea Pigs: How the Pentagon Exposed Our Troops to Dangers More Deadly than War: Agent Orange and Atomic Radiation.** Chicago: Playboy Press, 1980. Distributed by Harper and Row. P. xv, 256. illustrations. appendixes. bibliography, 251-56. Reprint. New York: Wideview Books, 1980. pa.

Any man considering a military career or the possibility of being drafted would do well to contemplate this account of how the government and the military carelessly endangered the health and lives of soldiers by exposing them to radiation and Agent Orange.

150.   Williams, Roger Neville. **The New Exiles: American War Resisters in Canada.** New York: Liveright Publishers, 1971. P. xiii, 401.

During the Vietnam War, thousands of American young men were caught in the bind of having to disobey their country's conscription laws or to become part of a war they could not support in conscience. As William Sloane Coffin, Jr., says in this book's foreword, they had the choice of being either criminals or killers. Using extended interviews and other methods, Williams charts the history of about forty to one hundred thousand young men who sought refuge in Canada. The author provides an overview of the war resistance movement and the flight to Canada, as well as individual stories of draft dodgers and military deserters.

151.   Young, Peter. **The Fighting Man: From Alexander the Great's Army to the Present Day.** New York: Rutledge Press, 1981. P. 240. illustrations. index.

With the aid of over a hundred illustrations (many in color), this oversized book focuses upon the ordinary soldiers who have done the killing and the dying in major battles and campaigns. Subjects include Roman legions, Vikings, Normans of the First Crusade, the army of Frederick the Great, Napoleon's army, Billy Yank and Johnny Reb, the U.S. Marines, the Viet Minh, the French Foreign Legion, and the Israeli army.

Cross references:

3.   Anderson, Martin, and Valerie Bloom, comps. **Conscription: A Select and Annotated Bibliography.**

104. Rivkin, Robert S. **GI Rights and Army Justice: The Draftee's Guide to Military Life and Law.**

105. Rivkin, Robert S., and Barton F. Stichman. **The Rights of Military Personnel: The Basic ACLU Guide for Military Personnel.**

107. Sherrill, Robert. **Military Justice Is to Justice as Military Music Is to Music.**

292. Etheredge, Lloyd S. **A World of Men: The Private Sources of American Foreign Policy.**

295. Grinker, Roy R., and John P. Spiegel. **Men under Stress.**

502. Crane, Stephen. **The Red Badge of Courage.**

505. Homer. **The Iliad.**

507. Shaw, George Bernard. **Arms and the Man: A Pleasant Play.**

536. Remarque, Erich Maria. **All Quiet on the Western Front.**

541. Trumbo, Dalton. **Johnny Got His Gun.**

561. Barbeau, Arthur E., and Florette Henri. **The Unknown Soldiers: Black American Troops in World War I.**

MEN'S ISSUES AND TOPICS _____

HEALTH AND RELATED MATTERS

152.   Cant, Gilbert. **Male Trouble: A New Focus on the Prostate**. A Frank E.
       Taylor Book. New York: Praeger Publishers, 1976. P. xiv, 146. illustra-
       tions. index.
Cant's book has four objectives: to acquaint lay readers with basic information
about prostatic health and disease, to encourage men to seek medical attention at
the first signs of disorder, to recommend earlier routine rectal examinations, and to
indicate that despite much mystery prostatic troubles can often be treated effec-
tively. Cant describes the urogenital system, the disorders which can involve the
prostate, and different treatments of them. He describes the effects of prostatic
troubles on men and looks to future research for additional solutions.

153.   Diagram Group, The. **Man's Body: An Owner's Manual**. New York:
       Paddington Press, 1976. Unpaged (ca. P. 250). illustrations. index.
       Reprint. New York: Bantam Books, 1977. pa.
This compendium of information and statistics about men's bodies contains over
a thousand drawings, diagrams, and charts. The twelve sections of the book cover
essential information about such matters as the development of the male body from
conception to old age; life expectancy for males, including principal causes of
death; illnesses; body care, especially of skin, hair, and teeth; the mind and body
connection; physical fitness and exercise; food, including gaining and losing weight;
drugs, alcohol, and smoking; male sex organs, potency, and sterility; sexuality,
intercourse, contraception, homosexuality; and aging. The final section briefly
describes the woman's body. The attractive format makes basic information about
men's bodies readily available to a wide range of readers.

154.   Friedman, Meyer, and Ray H. Rosenman. **Type A Behavior and Your
       Heart**. New York: Alfred A. Knopf, 1974. P. x, 276, x. illustrations.
       index. Reprint. Greenwich, Conn.: Fawcett, 1978. pa.
Heart disease respects neither class nor race, but in the past it has preyed particularly on American men. Considering the sure and possible causes of this killer,
the authors of this popular study focus on "Type A behavior," a pattern marked
by stress, hurrying, and incommunicativeness. Other contributing causes are

investigated, including cholesterol, diabetes mellitus, diet, and smoking. Exercise is no cure-all and may sometimes be contributory. In the closing chapters, Friedman and Rosenman provide guidelines for modifying Type A behavior. Although the connection between the American masculine gender role and coronary disease is touched upon, some readers may wish it had been probed more thoroughly.

155. Greenberger, Monroe E., and Mary-Ellen Siegel. **What Every Man Should Know about His Prostate.** New York: Walker and Co., 1983. P. xiv, 146. illustrations. appendix. index. bibliography, 141-43.

In clear, concise language, the authors describe for the general reader the normal state and functioning of the prostate, its changes with age, the urological examination, various kinds of prostatitis (acute and chronic, congestive and irritative), enlargement of the prostate, cancer, surgery, sexual activity after surgery, and the effects of zinc and nutrition on the prostate. The appendix is a glossary of terms.

156. Julty, Sam. **Men's Bodies, Men's Selves.** New York: Dell Publishing Co., Delta, 1979. P. 453. illustrations. notes. bibliographies at the end of each chapter. pa.

Described as "the complete guide to the health and well-being of men's bodies, minds, and spirits," Julty's book is aimed at men seeking to liberate themselves from the binds inherent in traditional concepts of masculinity. The thirteen chapters include discussions of work, relationships with women, marriage and divorce, homosexuality, physical health, mental health, fathering, aging, sexuality, male genitalia, birth control and abortion, venereal disease, and rape. A storehouse of information liberally illustrated with photographs and drawings, the text of *Men's Bodies, Men's Selves* is punctuated with editorials, autobiographical accounts, documents, definitions of unfamiliar terms, and other useful materials. Each chapter closes with an annotated list of suggested readings compiled by James Creane and with a helpful listing of resources (e.g., newsletters, organizations, films, government agencies) compiled by Paul Siudzinski.

157. Pesmen, Curtis, and the Editors of *Esquire*. **How a Man Ages.** New York: Ballantine Books, Ballantine/Esquire Press Book, 1984. P. xiii, 226. illustrations. notes. index. bibliography, 215-17. pa.

In clear, concise style, Pesmen describes the aging process in males and suggests ways to minimize its deleterious effects. Chapters are devoted to skin, hair, eyes, hearing, the mouth, bones and muscles, sexuality and sex organs, the heart, lungs and kidneys, the brain and memory, stamina and fitness, and nutrition and weight control.

158. Roen, Philip R. **Male Sexual Health.** New York: William Morrow and Co., 1974. P. 190. illustrations. index.

In readable question-and-answer fashion, Roen addresses such matters as prostate troubles, impotence, sex in elderly men, venereal diseases, and vasectomy.

159. Rowan, Robert L., and Paul J. Gillette. **Your Prostate: What It Is, What It Does, and the Diseases That Affect It.** Garden City, N.Y.: Doubleday and Co., 1973. P. xv, 147. illustrations. appendix. index.

For lay readers, the authors describe the male urogenital system and the prostate's part in it. They discuss disorders of the prostate (and disorders connected with it), as well as possible treatments of them. Topics include inflammation, growths, prostatitis, benign prostatic hypertrophy, cancer, Trichomonas vaginalis, and premature ejaculation (which is sometimes related to problems in the prostate). A glossary of terms is included.

160.   Ursin, Holger, Eivind Baade, and Seymour Levine, eds. **Psychobiology of Stress: A Study of Coping Men**. New York: Academic Press, 1978. P. xv, 236. index. bibliographies after each chapter.
Investigating seventy-two young men in the Norwegian Army Parachute School in 1974, twenty-one contributors to this study assess physiological and psychological effects upon males of coping with stress.

161.   Wagenvoord, James, ed. **The Man's Book: A Complete Manual of Style**. New York: Avon Books, 1978. P. 320. illustrations. index. bibliography, 310-11. pa.
This compendium of information and advice attractively treats care of the male body and mind (including such matters as exercising, handling stress, medications, diet, skin and hair care, and aging), clothing, and social life (including jobs, money, entertaining, travel, and love and sex). The readable text is interspersed with illustrations, charts, and humorous drawings.

162.   Wallerstein, Edward. **Circumcision: An American Health Fallacy**. Focus on Men series. New York: Springer Publishing Co., 1980. P. xix, 281. illustrations. appendixes. notes. subject and author indexes. pa.
Calling circumcision "a solution in search of a problem," Wallerstein raises important questions about America's obsession with routine circumcision. About 85 percent of all American male children are circumcised. While other Western countries have abandoned routine circumcision, only the United States continues the practice. He debunks past and present rationales for the practice, arguing that circumcision does not prevent masturbation, venereal disease, premature ejaculation, or anything else. The foreskin, he argues, serves as a useful protective shield and has an erotic function. Moreover, the operation can lead to complications, and the pain and trauma of infant circumcision (usually performed without anesthetic) may have unknown harmful effects upon the male psyche. For entirely irrational reasons, the practice of routine circumcision lingers on in America, long after the medical profession should have been discouraging it. Three appendixes cover the details of the surgery, its frequency in U.S. history, and an almost unknown statement against routine circumcision issued in 1975 by the American College of Obstetricians and Gynecologists. This book is listed as the first in a Springer series called "Focus on Men"; many readers will feel that Wallerstein has gotten the series off to a good start.

163.   Young, Frank R. **Yoga for Men Only**. West Nyack, N.Y.: Parker Publishing Co., 1969. P. x, 214. illustrations. index.

Revealing "well guarded Yoga secrets" Young describes how yoga exercises can overcome the "Four Horsemen of the Mastabah" (the early grave): constant down-pull of gravity, faulty posture, weight-bearing, and ground resistance. The author makes extraordinary claims for Yoga, promising, among other things, greater sex appeal, self-mastery, personal energy, powerful muscles, and personal popularity. The book is punctuated with success stories (e.g., "How 49-Year-Old Alfred, Who Was Avoided Generally, Swept People Off Their Feet By Relieving His Subchronic Aches and Pains"). Readers will have to decide for themselves whether Young's approach represents Oriental wisdom or a snake-oil pitch.

VASECTOMY

164. Carson, Rubin. **The Coward's Guide to Vasectomy**. Marina del Rey, Calif.: Schmidt and Hill Publications, 1973. P. xiv, 174. illustrations. appendix. Reprint. New York: Pinnacle Books, 1982. pa.

Providing facts and fun for the fainthearted, Carson attempts to dispel male misgivings about vasectomy. He even devotes a chapter to female cowards considering their own sterilization. The appendix lists Planned Parenthood centers, Zero Population Growth chapters, and information concerning the Association for Voluntary Sterilization. The text is abetted by Michael Bedard's comic illustrations.

165. Fleishman, Norman, and Peter L. Dixon. **Vasectomy, Sex and Parenthood**. Garden City, N.Y.: Doubleday and Co., 1973. P. xv, 128. appendixes. bibliography, 126-28.

Stressing the need for population control, this book for lay readers includes a personal account of what it is like to undergo vasectomy, answers frequently asked questions about the operation, and raises questions which men should ask before having it. One chapter contains Diane Fleishman's account of the positive marital effects of her husband's vasectomy. The appendixes list vasectomy clinics in the United States, organizations concerned with vasectomy, and sperm banks.

166. Fried, John J. **Vasectomy: The Truth and Consequences of the Newest Form of Birth Control—Male Sterilization**. New York: Saturday Review Press, 1972. P. 148. bibliography, 144-48.

In contrast to cheerleaders for vasectomy, Fried raises questions about it. He discusses possible complications from the operation, as well as its possible effects upon the body's immune system. He stresses the irreversibility of vasectomy and its negative psychological consequences, especially when it is performed to save a rocky marriage or when the man's masculine identity is shaky. Readers will have to decide whether Fried is alarmist or soundly cautious.

167. Gillette, Paul J. **Vasectomy: The Male Sterilization Operation**. New York: Paperback Library, 1972. P. 235. illustrations. appendixes. bibliography, 229-35. pa. Reprint. **The Vasectomy Information Manual**. New York: Outerbridge and Lazard, 1972.

A popular information guide, this book examines the need for population control, what kind of men should consider vasectomy, an explanation of how conception occurs, and a description of the operation. Aside from sterilization, vasectomy usually has either positive or nonexistent effects upon male sexuality. Legally and practically, it is often difficult for a husband to obtain a vasectomy if his wife is opposed to it. Most religious denominations regard vasectomy as a morally accept-able act; the Roman Catholic hierarchy regards it as immoral, although many Catholic laymen who have had the operation apparently do not agree. Most physicians endorse vasectomy for men who do not wish to father any more children. Gillette discusses methods of reversing the operation, including the use of sperm banks for later fertilization. A chapter is devoted to salpingectomy, the female sterilization operation. The author also includes a question-and-answer section, as well as information about financial aid for obtaining a vasectomy, directories of vasectomy clinics in the United States, Planned Parenthood affiliates, family planning centers around the world, and Zero Population Growth offices. Also included are personal accounts by two men (Jim Bouton and Louis Saban) of their operations, as well as various endorsements of vasectomy as a means of population control. The book was prepared in cooperation with the Association for Voluntary Sterilization, Inc., whose executive director, John R. Rague, supplies the introduction.

168. Greenfield, Michael, and William M. Burrus. **The Complete Reference Book on Vasectomy.** New York: Avon Books, 1973. P. 253. illustrations. appendixes. bibliography, 173-253. pa.

Part I of this book answers questions raised by those considering a vasectomy. Topics include a brief history of vasectomy, men who might not be good candidates for the operation, what the operation consists of, whether it is reversible ("don't count on it"), and whether it will adversely affect masculinity ("it won't"). Part II consists of a married couple's accounts of how his vasectomy improved their lives. In part III the authors provide information for men seeking a vasectomy, including the choice of doctor, additional information about the operation, and further questions raised by candidates for it. About half of the book consists of appendixes and bibliography. The three appendixes list vasectomy clinics, genetic counseling facilities, and insurance information. An extensive annotated bibliog-raphy covers worldwide research on vasectomy.

169. Kasirsky, Gilbert. **Vasectomy, Manhood and Sex.** New York: Springer Publishing Co., 1972. P. 128. illustrations. appendixes. notes. bibliog-raphies after each chapter. pa.

This popularly written book answers principal questions about vasectomy, explains the reasons for having the operation, describes the surgical procedures, discusses its aftereffects and the possibilities of reversing the operation, and lists the ethical responses to it of major religious organizations. A chapter by Elaine Kasirsky presents her positive assessment of the operation, and the foreword by Helen Edey discusses the book's value for doctors and for men contemplating vasectomy. The appendixes show the instruments used in the operation and sample consent forms, discuss vasectomy in countries around the world, and list places where men can obtain a vasectomy in the United States.

170. Lader, Lawrence, ed. **Foolproof Birth Control: Male and Female Steriliza-tion.** Boston: Beacon Press, 1972. P. viii, 286. illustrations. appendixes. index.

This collection of forty-two brief essays on male and female sterilization considers such topics as reasons for having a vasectomy, accounts of the operation, its effects upon men's physical and mental health, the difficulty of reversing vasectomy, frozen semen banks, costs, and overcoming obstructions to voluntary sterilization. Four appendixes list vasectomy clinics in the United States, hospitals with liberal policies for female sterilization, hospitals performing female sterilization through laparoscopy and culdoscopy, and Blue Cross-Blue Shield and Medicaid insurance for voluntary sterilization.

171. Mancini, R. E., and L. Martini, eds. **Male Fertility and Sterility**. Proceedings of the Serono Symposia, vol. 5. London and New York: Academic Press, 1974. P. xvi, 588. illustrations. author index. bibliographies after each chapter.

Fifty percent of sterility in couples is due to male infertility. The thirty-two scholarly studies in this volume examine the various facets of andrology—the morphology, physiology, pathology and clinical aspects of the male genital tract—with major emphasis on understanding and treating male infertility.

172. Raspé, Gerhard, ed. **Schering Workshop on Contraception: The Masculine Gender (Berlin, November 29 to December 2, 1972)**. Advances in the Biosciences, 10. Oxford: Pergamon Press, and Braunschweig: Vieweg, 1973. P. vii, 332. illustrations. index. bibliographies after each chapter.

This collection of twenty-four papers from a workshop on male contraception consists primarily of reports and speculations on biological and biochemical research with implications for development of additional forms of male contraception. Lay readers may be most interested in Alfred Jost's paper "Becoming a Male" ("Becoming a male is a prolonged, uneasy, and risky venture; it is a kind of struggle against inherent trends toward femaleness"); Brigitta Linnér's feminist call for equality in society, in family, and in bed; and (above all) Caroline Merula Days and David Malcolm Potts's essay "Condoms and Things" dealing with male involvement in contraception. The latter authors argue that family planning programs are geared for female contraception when "male methods of contraception have been and remain numerically the most important in nearly all countries." These male methods include coitus interruptus, condoms, and vasectomy. In addition, males often take responsibility for female birth control (e.g., seeing that the woman has a supply of birth control pills and takes them regularly). The authors conclude: "Men are in the majority as family-planning users in nearly all countries." The book closes with a "manifesto" of desiderata for new forms of male contraceptives.

173. Rosenfeld, Louis J., and Marvin Grosswirth. **The Truth about Vasectomy**. Englewood Cliffs, N.J.: Prentice-Hall, 1972. P. 156. appendixes. notes. index.

In language easily comprehensible to the layperson, the authors discuss the facts of vasectomy, weighing its pros and cons. After a brief question-and-answer chapter, the book quickly surveys the history of contraception, explains the male reproductive system, and describes a vasectomy operation. The authors discuss the doctor's role in advising couples, the problems which a machismo-oriented male may encounter in considering a vasectomy, women's views of vasectomy, the usually positive aftereffects of the operation, and what can (and cannot) be done if the man changes his mind afterwards. Among the options are surgery, semen banks, and adoption. The appendixes contain a sample vasectomy release form, a list of vasectomy clinics and hospitals in which vasectomy is performed as an outpatient procedure, and a short list of semen banks.

WORK AND PLAY: CAREERS, UNEMPLOYMENT, SPORTS

174.   Glasstone, Richard. **Dancing as a Career for Men.** New York: Sterling Publishing Co., 1981. P. 114. illustrations. index. Originally published as *Male Dancing as a Career* (Tadworth, Surrey: Kaye and Ward, 1980). Although this crisply written guide to male careers in dancing is aimed at boys and their parents, others may find in it an illuminating discussion of contemporary attitudes toward male dancers. The second chapter, raising the question of whether male dancing is effeminate or homosexual, points out that males have been dancing since history began. The current association of dance with effeminacy derives from the way in which nineteenth-century classical ballet was taken over by ethereal females dancing *sur les pointes* and representing delicate or dying creatures. The male dancer was reduced to a second-class lifter and was branded with the overwhelmingly "feminine" nature of most ballet performances. Glasstone puts this aberration in the history of dance into perspective, presenting a survey of the male dancer in history. The book's opening chapter provides an overall view of dancing as a career for males, and other chapters describe the ballet scene, modern or contemporary dance, and dancing in show business. The final chapter contains a directory of practical information and useful addresses concerning professional schools, associations of dancing teachers, dance publications, bookstores, and so on. Simon Rae-Scott's photographs enhance the text.

175.   Komarovsky, Mirra. **The Unemployed Man and His Family: The Effect of Unemployment upon the Status of the Man in Fifty-nine Families.** New York: Dryden Press, 1940. P. xii, 163. appendix. index. bibliography, 163. Reprint. New York: Arno Press and New York Times, 1971.
This classic study, based upon case histories of fifty-nine families in 1935-1936, indicates that in thirteen families the husband's status declined because of his unemployment. In such cases the man was sometimes brutally blamed for being out of work and was rejected by family members. Regarded primarily as a breadwinner, these men suffered loss of authority, although the loss of self-esteem was felt by other men in the study too. Komarovsky also examines the men's tendency to blame themselves for their "failure," their altered relationships with younger and adolescent children, their social and political views, and the decline in sexual relations between husband and wife. The appendix discusses methodology.

176.   La Velle, Michael. **Red, White and Blue-Collar Views: A Steelworker Speaks His Mind about America.** New York: Saturday Review Press/E.P. Dutton and Co., 1975. P. xi, 212.
This collection of La Velle articles from the *Chicago Tribune* provides a workingman's view of big business, big unions, right to work laws (which he calls "right to

scab laws"), the ERA (which he supports, while chivalrously hoping to retain protective legislation favoring women), higher education, the news media (which, he
says, ignores blue-collar workers), worker safety, and much, much more. La Velle
writes prose in the "tough" style. His anger is real and often justified—although, as
Studs Terkel points out in his introduction, La Velle sometimes seems to take aim
at the wrong targets.

177. LeMasters, E. E. **Blue-Collar Aristocrats: Life-Styles at a Working-Class
     Tavern.** Madison: University of Wisconsin Press, 1975. P. ix, 218. notes.
     index. pa.

Between 1967 and 1972 sociologist LeMasters frequented a blue-collar tavern
which he calls the Oasis. From his interaction with approximately fifty regular
patrons, he constructs a portrait of blue-collar people and argues that the theory
of class homogenization in America has been overemphasized. The tavern men held
such jobs as carpenter, plumber, bricklayer, roofer, sheet metal worker, and so on.
Among his findings are that the men in general liked their work, that it paid well,
that blue-collar marriage had its problems but also its rewards (which included
stability and longevity), that marital failure often adversely affected blue-collar
men and women, that the battle of the sexes is alive and well at the Oasis, that
virginity was out—for girls as well as boys, that hostility toward homosexuals,
radical feminists, and radical blacks was in, that raising "unspoiled" children is the
big problem of parenting, that social life and blue-collar humor flourished at the
Oasis, that the man drank more heavily than the women, and that political views
were conservative or middle of the road. In a final chapter LeMasters assesses the
new generation of male workers and Vietnam veterans who were beginning to frequent the Oasis.

178. Mitchell, Joyce Slayton. **Choices and Changes: A Career Book for Men.**
     New York: College Entrance Examination Board, 1982. P. ix, 309. illustra-
     tions. pa.

For the male high school student, Mitchell surveys fourteen clusters of related
careers. She describes what ninety-seven individual careers are like, what education and skills are needed for them, how many people are employed in them and
where they work, typical salaries, job future, related careers, and sources of additional information. The career clusters are: art, architecture, and design; business:
administration and management; business: advertising and marketing; business:
computer operations; business: money management; business: sales; communications; education; government; health; science and technology; social service; social
science; and transportation. In the introduction Mitchell advises males to avoid the
"success object" trap by which a man is valued according to his income; she
describes a "new age" for men in which they can be more flexible about sharing
obligations and rewards—on the job and in the family—and can strive toward being
"a whole person with many choices."

179. Mitchell, Joyce Slayton. **Free to Choose: Decision Making for Young
     Men.** New York: Delacorte Press, 1976. P. xii, 263.

Written for high school males, this collection of essays is designed to raise the male
consciousness and to offer information about sexual decisions, male-female relationships, drug use, spirituality, athletics, education, and careers. Although Mitchell

has written many sections of the book, other contributors include Marc Feigen Fasteau, Richard V. Lee, Warren Farrell, Leonard Swidler, Marnin Kligfeld, Natalie M. Shepard, and Betty M. Vetter. Some readers may find Mitchell's feminist assumptions grating and the book's concept of male liberation guiltridden.

180. Mitzel, John. **Sports and the Macho Male.** 2d ed. Boston: Fag Rag Books, 1976. P. 32. illustrations. pa.

Mitzel berates organized sports in America for fostering "straight macho" values of agressiveness, militancy, and repressiveness and for downplaying the affectional, homoerotic aspects of male bonding.

181. Sabo, Donald F., and Ross Runfola, eds. **Jock: Sports and Male Identity.** Englewood Cliffs, N.J.: Prentice-Hall, 1980. P. xvii, 365. notes. index. bibliography, 339-52. pa.

"All the selections in this book," the editors note, "share the critical assumption that sports shape many undesirable elements of the male role and perpetuate sexist institutions and values." Twenty-seven essays, plus editorial introductions and conclusion, stress the negative aspects of sports in fostering such characteristics as sexism, authoritarianism, aggression (in the negative sense), paramilitary mentality, and patriotic imperialism. Among the selections are Warren Farrell's description of the Super Bowl as machismo ritual, Peter J. Stein and Steven Hoffman's analysis of sports and male role strain, Ross J. Pudaloff's discussion of sports in American literature, and Edgar Z. Friedenberg's analysis of homoerotic fantasy in spectator sports. Three essays discuss women in sports, and the concluding seven essays suggest alternatives to current attitudes and practices in sports. In the final selection, the editors trace the development of the men's liberation movement and the dissatisfaction of some men with traditional sports.

182. Swados, Harvey, ed. **The American Writer and the Great Depression.** The American Heritage Series. Indianapolis, Ind.: Bobbs-Merrill Co., 1966. P. xli, 521. illustrations. notes. index. bibliography, xxxvi-xli. pa.

The two purposes of this anthology are "to convey the impact of the depression of the 1930's on the life and thought of the American people and to present what Harvey Swados calls 'a cross section of good writing of the period.'" Many of the thirty-five short stories, essays, poems, and excerpts from longer works focus on the working man and intellectuals, providing vivid recreations of male experiences during this devastating period of American history. Stark photographs abet the literature from such writers as Sherwood Anderson, John Steinbeck, Erskine Caldwell, James T. Farrell, Nelson Algren, Richard Wright, John Dos Passos, and Thomas Wolfe.

CRIME AND VIOLENCE: RAPE, MALE RAPE, DOMESTIC VIOLENCE, BOY PROSTITUTION, INCEST

183.   Beneke, Timothy. **Men on Rape.** New York: St. Martin's Press, 1982. P. xiv, 174. appendix. notes. pa.

In the first part of this book the author attempts to sensitize male readers to what rape does to women, not just to rape victims but to women collectively. He sees a rape mentality evidenced in our society by "rape signs" in cartoons, humor, and other popular expressions. The metaphors of sex and violence in our talk constitute "rape language." Under the rubric "she asked for it" he considers the rationalizations offered for rape. Part II—the longest and most interesting section—consists of extended statements from a variety of men, including an angry rapist who was abused by his stepmother; husbands, lovers, and friends of women who have been raped; and lawyers, doctors, and policemen involved in rape cases. The range of sensitivities and viewpoints here is considerable. Some of the men are remarkably angry and callous toward women, others offer legitimate considerations which complicate the discussion of what constitutes rape, and still others demonstrate considerable compassion for victims and disgust for perpetrators. In the final section Andrea Rechtin, an advocate for rape victims, responds to assumptions underlying some of the statements from interviewees. The author concludes that rape is a men's problem which men must solve collectively. Some readers may feel that neither Rechtin nor Beneke has listened carefully to what some of the men said: Rechtin's wholesale anger at the interviewees in particular fails to discriminate among them. Any deviation from a simplistic party-line view of rape, one begins to suspect, will be condemned as insensitivity or as another form of "blaming the victim." The book considers only female victims of rape. "I wanted to interview a man who had been raped," Beneke writes, "but was unable to find a man who would consent to an interview. That fact alone may say more than the interview would have." The appendix lists men-against-rape groups in the United States and Canada.

184.   Blumenthal, Monica D., Robert L. Kahn, Frank M. Andrews, and Kendra B. Head. **Justifying Violence: Attitudes of American Men.** Ann Arbor: Institute for Social Research, The University of Michigan, 1972. P. xii, 367. illustrations. appendixes. index. bibliography, 355-58.

Based upon a survey conducted in the summer of 1969 of 1,374 men between the ages of sixteen and sixty-four, this study explores the reasons given for justifying violence in urban racial disturbances, student campus protests, and police responses. The study explores such matters as how respondents justify violence for or against social change, and how identification with the perpetrators or victims of violence can alter one's definition and perception of violence. It is perhaps a sign of the times that 58 percent of the respondents defined burning a draft card as an act of violence, while 56 percent felt that police beating of students constituted violence. In this survey taken before the turmoil at Kent State and Jackson State, almost 50 percent of the respondents felt that shooting was a good way to handle campus disturbances "almost always" or at least "sometimes."

185.   Brownmiller, Susan. **Against Our Will: Men, Women and Rape.** New York: Simon and Schuster, 1975. P. 472. notes. index. Reprint. New York: Bantam Books, 1976. pa.

An enormously influential book, *Against Our Will* examines numerous aspects of rape. Brownmiller explores the legal view of rape from biblical times to the present, and the incidence of rape during war, revolutions, riots, and pogroms. She examines the fate of white women among Indians and Indian women among whites. The racial and sexual politics of rape during slavery are seen as an institutionalized means of destroying black women's integrity. The fear of black men raping white women is traced as an element of American racial tensions, and the rape of males, especially in prison, is depicted as an exercise in male dominance. Brownmiller argues that women are trained to be victims. She questions the prevailing Freudian views of rape, even as elaborated by Helene Deutsch and Karen Horney, which posit an inherent masochism in women. Brownmiller is scornful of current attitudes toward the rape victim, particularly among police and attorneys. While Brownmiller undeniably sheds light on rape in history, law, and psychology, she is so busy scoring polemical points that she often sheds more heat than light on the subject. Influenced by radical feminists, Brownmiller uses rape as a brush to tar all men. A principal thesis in the book—"from prehistoric times to the present, I believe, rape ... is nothing more or less than a conscious process of intimidation by which *all men* keep *all women* in a state of fear"—has become notorious as a sexist absurdity. A related passage insists that rapists are the "shock troops" who do the dirty work for the entire male sex in its war against women. Consequently, Brownmiller suggests that all men secretly celebrate rapists and admire the likes of Jack the Ripper, the Boston Strangler, Richard Speck, and Charles Manson. For many readers the hatred of men in general which permeates the book will eventually undermine much of its credibility.

186.   Drew, Dennis, and Jonathan Drake. **Boys for Sale: A Sociological Study of Boy Prostitution.** New York: Brown Book Co., 1969. P. 223.

Informal rather than scholarly, this account of boy prostitution surveys historical and geographic instances. The amount of human misery hinted at in the book is appalling. The authors, however, regard man-boy sex as inevitable and suggest that society adjust to it.

187.   Groth, A. Nicholas, with H. Jean Birnbaum. **Men Who Rape: The Psychology of the Offender.** New York and London: Plenum Press, 1979. P. xviii, 227. notes. index.

Based on data from five hundred offenders, this study examines the "myths" and realities of rape and the men (and women) who commit it. The author defines rape as a "pseudo-sexual act," indicating that from a clinical viewpoint any form of sexual assault should be included. Among the "myths" surrounding rape is the idea that pornography causes it. Groth distinguishes among anger rape, power rape, and sadistic rape, discusses possible methods of resistance, and examines the multiple motives underlying rape. He notes sexual dysfunctioning of the offender, their subjective responses, and the effects of intoxication. Remarking that the majority of men are not rapists, Groth indicates that rape "appears to be the result of a core group of highly repetitive or chronic offenders." Many of these offenders had suffered sexual trauma in childhood, often some form of sexual abuse. Patterns of rape, including gang rape, are discussed. Using information from twenty offenders and seven victims, Groth explores rape of males, noting the likely under-reporting of such offenses. "Women victims do not report that they feel less of a woman for having been raped," he writes, "but men victims do often state that they feel the offender took their manhood." The under-reporting of sexual assaults upon boys is also indicated, with Groth estimating that boys and girls are probably equally the victims of such assaults. The female offender, he notes after discussing one such case, "remains an incompletely studied and insufficiently understood subject." Groth's account of rape will strike many readers as a much-needed antidote to the many political and sexist discussions of this topic.

188. Herman, Judith Lewis, with Lisa Hirschman. **Father-Daughter Incest.** Cambridge, Mass.: Harvard University Press, 1981. P. xi, 282. appendix. notes. index. pa.

Using survey data, clinical material, anthropological literature, popular literature, and pornography, Herman explores the phenomenon of father-daughter incest. She then draws upon interviews with forty victims of incest, and twenty daughters of "seductive fathers." The book's final section deals with problems of disclosing and prosecuting incest, and with remedies for healing victims and restoring families. The book's "feminist perspective" includes considerable antagonism toward males in general. Herman does not interview the fathers, nor does she try to get at the roots of their behavior. Instead, father-daughter incest is blamed on all-purpose villains (male perverseness and patriarchal society) and becomes another stick to beat males with.

189. Lloyd, Robin. **For Money or Love: Boy Prostitution in America.** New York: Vanguard Press, 1976. P. xx, 236.

After his two sons were approached by a photographer who sells his photos of nude boys, journalist Lloyd found himself increasingly interested in the topic of boy prostitution. In this account, he constructs composite pictures of typical "chickens" (boy prostitutes), and he offers a verbatim account from a "chicken hawk" (a man who patronizes boy prostitutes). Estimating the extent of such prostitution in the United States is difficult, Lloyd says, but in part I of the book he offers glimpses of the situation with accounts of mass rape and murder of boys in Houston and scandals in Boise, Idaho, and Waukesha, Wisconsin. In part II he surveys the history of boy prostitution and briefly describes the present situation in several key cities around the world. He provides an overview of the boy pornography business, and he examines the exploitation of boys in correctional facilities. Part III suggests some possible cures, including a federal department of education and youth. Lloyd raises questions about juvenile justice and the incarceration of minors, cites the potential in group homes, and stresses the need for more humane supervisors. On the question of whether boy prostitutes will develop into exclusive homosexuals, Lloyd suggests that bisexuality is a more likely outcome. The book's introduction is by Senator Birch Bayh whose senate subcommittee findings corroborate the extent of boy prostitution in America.

190. Russell, Diana E. H. **Rape in Marriage.** New York: Macmillan Co., 1982. P. xvi, 412. appendixes. notes. index. bibliography, 399-401. pa.

In this study based upon interviews with eighty-seven women, Russell examines rape in marriage, exploring its legal aspects, the difficulties of defining it, and its connection with family violence and larger social structures. Russell's approach to her subject is decidedly partisan: her anger with men stems from a contention that "the oppression of women as a class by men as a class has been ... universal" and that men regard women as property. In this study, only the wives were interviewed. The failure to interview husbands is justified on the grounds that ours is a "patriarchal culture" and that it is time for women to be heard. Men are "heard" here only through carefully selected snippets culled from such sources as *The Hite Report on Male Sexuality* and the pornographic *My Secret Life.* Using such tactics, Russell is able to minimize the number of battered men, justify wifely violence as self-defense, and create a caricature of husbands as unfeeling oppressors.

191.　Scacco, Anthony M., Jr., ed. **Male Rape: A Casebook of Sexual Aggressions.** AMS Studies in Modern Society: Political and Social Issues, no. 15. New York: AMS Press, 1982. P. xxi, 326. index. notes and bibliographies after many essays. pa.

Most of the twenty-six essays in this collection are concerned with sexual violence in which males are victims, especially in prison. As Scacco notes in the preface: "In today's world the judge who sentences a young person to reform school or prison passes male rape on him as surely as the sentence." The anthology contains both previously printed and original articles. Wilbert Rideau and Billy Sinclair's opening essay describing prison as a sexual jungle is followed by a harrowing account of the 1973 prison gang rape of peace activist Donald Tucker—which is followed by an even more harrowing essay written by Tucker nearly a decade later and revealing all too clearly the psychosexual damage which he sustained. Later essays analyze racial factors involved in such attacks (the victim is usually white, the aggressor black). Also studied is sexual violence in other institutions, e.g., juvenile correctional facilities, mental wards, military prisons, and women's prisons (Dorothy West's account of rape by female inmates is as terrifying as Tucker's story). Later sections of the volume present psychological profiles of sexual offenders, and suggest treatment and methods of reducing sexual violence in American society.

192.　Straus, Murray A., Richard J. Gelles, and Suzanne K. Steinmetz. **Behind Closed Doors: Violence in the American Family.** New York: Anchor Press/Doubleday, 1980. P. ix, 301. appendixes. notes. index. bibliography, 273-84. pa.

This important study of domestic violence based upon 2,143 interviews is relevant to men's studies for several reasons. It is one of the few studies to demonstrate the amount of violence against males in the family. Indeed, the authors note that violence against husbands is slightly more frequent than violence against wives— although they are quick to point out that these statistics do not mean that there are more battered husbands than battered wives and that numerous qualifications must temper any conclusions drawn from these figures. Furthermore, the study points out that mothers, rather than fathers, are more often child abusers and that boys, rather than girls, are more likely to be victims of parental violence. Such violence, the authors state, "may be approved of and used as a 'character builder' for boys." Moreover, they question the pure genetic theories of male predisposition toward violence: "If men have a genetic predisposition to be violent, one would expect them to be more violent at home than their wives. Yet, an examination of violence between couples and violence by parents toward children reveals that women are as violent or more violent in the home than are men." The authors argue cogently for regarding much domestic violence as cases of mutual violence among family members, in contrast to the theory that most domestic violence is perpetrated by one family member (the husband is usually suspected). *Behind Closed Doors* has demonstrated that the issue of battered husbands deserves not to be swept under the rug. It also points to the need for greater understanding of how violence inflicted upon children, especially boys, produces additional family violence when these children become parents.

193.   Straus, Murray A., and Gerald T. Hotaling, eds. **The Social Causes of Husband-Wife Violence.** Minneapolis: University of Minnesota Press, 1980. P. x, 272. notes. author and subject indexes. bibliography, 235-53. pa.

Unwilling to settle for "single cause" answers, the authors of the thirteen essays in this volume examine the interweaving of cultural norms and social organization which fosters domestic violence. Such violence grows out of the nature of social arrangements, it is argued; it is not due to mental illness but is the result of learned and socially patterned behavior. Among the findings are: men with low "resources" in a marriage find it difficult to maintain the dominance which society expects of them and may resort to violence to regain their sense of masculinity; while wife-beating is the more serious problem, evidence of considerable violence against husbands has been found; until society convinces men of the benefits to them of a more "egalitarian" marriage, many men will feel antagonistic toward such marriages; and domestic violence may be related to the general level of acceptable violence in the society. The final essay suggests ways to reduce domestic violence in America.

194.   Sussman, Les, and Sally Bordwell. **The Rapist File.** New York: Chelsea House, 1981. P. 215. appendix.

This book consists of interviews with fifteen rapists in correctional institutions in New York, Louisiana, and Illinois. The interviews are both baffling and disturbing. Often, the men's grasp of reality is strangely shaky. It is difficult to know whether they are telling the truth, putting on the interviewers, fantasizing, or simply unable to understand reality. Wild contradictions abound in their statements, as do peculiar discrepancies between thought and feeling. Some are convinced they did no wrong; others are. Some believe that their victims enjoyed being raped despite glaringly obvious evidence that they did not. A few got ideas from pornography, some did not, and one sees Dolly Parton as a pornographic turn-on. Many exhibit hostility toward women, sometimes because of their mother's abuse— or alleged abuse. One man says he was raped by a prostitute at age nine. Sal, a sadistic rapist-murderer, is chillingly psychopathic. Quentin, a Joe College type, breezily believes that most other men are rapists like him; he also believes that many women want to be raped. Nearly all agree that rapists are regarded as scum by fellow prisoners and are primary targets for rape in prison. Few of the men seem to have had psychological counseling or to have benefited from what they did have. The news that some of them would soon be released is unlikely to cheer many readers. Given the bewildering diversity of the men, the authors in their opening comments wisely counsel against pat generalizations about rapists. Unfortunately, Ellen Frankfort's introduction trots out nearly every pat generalization from the all-men-are-rapists-at-heart school of thought. The appendix consists of letters from rapists which are, if possible, less reassuring than the interviews.

PRISONS: MALE VICTIMIZATION AND SEXUAL EXPLOITATION

195. Bartollas, Clemens, Stuart J. Miller, and Simon Dinitz. **Juvenile Victimization: The Institutionalization Paradox**. New York: John Wiley and Sons, Sage Publications, 1976. P. xv, 324. illustrations. appendixes. name and subject indexes. bibliography, 275-85.

"This is not the first, nor is it likely to be the last, in a long series of books, monographs, and articles which indict the juvenile correctional system as anti-therapeutic, anti-rehabilitative, and as exploitive and demeaning to keepers and kept alike." Focusing upon a Columbus, Ohio, correctional institution for boys, the authors of this study find widespread sexual and nonsexual exploitation, with a definite and vicious pecking order among inmates. Toughness and ability to fight are essential if a boy is not to be victimized. Racial overtones of exploitation are obvious: blacks outnumber and dominate whites. The staff offers little help to victims, is sometimes victimized itself by wily inmates, and occasionally exploits some inmates. The study makes it abundantly clear why some people are urging the dissolution of such institutions.

196. Buffum, Peter C. **Homosexuality in Prisons**. Washington, D.C.: U.S. Department of Justice, Law Enforcement Assistance Administration, National Institute of Law Enforcement and Criminal Justice, 1972. P. 48. notes, bibliography, 43-48. pa.

Dispassionately, this monograph reviews the literature and assesses sexual conditions in prisons. It considers the various sex roles which prisoners assume, racial factors, the different problems involved, and the means of intervention.

197. Franklin, H. Bruce. **Prison Literature in America: The Victim as Criminal and Artist**. 2d ed. Westport, Conn.: Lawrence Hill and Co., 1982. P. xxx, 303. notes. index. pa. Originally published as *The Victim as Criminal and Artist: Literature from the American Prison* (New York: Oxford University Press, 1978).

Franklin surveys slave and prison literature in America, devoting separate chapters to slave narratives, Melville (the ship as prison), literature by convicts in America, and the contemporary scene in prison literature. He shows lively awareness of the racist implications of imprisonment in America (most prisoners are nonwhites) but seems never to have considered the sexist implications (most prisoners are males).

198. Scacco, Anthony M., Jr. **Rape in Prison**. Springfield, Ill.: Charles C. Thomas, 1975. P. xi, 127. notes. index. bibliography, 117-22.

One of the first to examine extensively sexual exploitation of males, Scacco here depicts victimization in juvenile correctional facilities and prisons. The victim is nearly always white, Scacco points out, indicating that black rapists are revenging themselves upon white society. Rape is a means of validating one's masculinity, especially to males raised in female-dominated families. Scacco connects sex and violence (relying perhaps too confidently upon Kate Millett's *Sexual Politics*) and discusses what can be done to allieviate the situation in prisons.

199.   Toch, Hans, with John J. Gibbs, Robert Johnson, and James G. Fox. **Men in Crisis: Human Breakdowns in Prison**. Chicago: Aldine Publishing Co., 1975. P. vii, 340. notes. index.

Based upon interviews with 175 prisoners and information gathered about four suicides, Toch's study analyzes the elements of breakdowns and self-injury in prisons. A chapter is devoted to women in crisis, but the bulk of the study is concerned with male prisoners.

200.   Weiss, Carl, and David James Friar. **Terror in the Prisons: Homosexual Rape and Why Society Condones It**. Indianapolis, Ind.: Bobbs-Merrill Co., 1974. P. xiv, 247.

According to the dust jacket of this book, more men than women are raped every year in America—in the prisons. Piecing together information from official reports, congressional hearings, inv0 investigative reporting, interviews, and other sources, the authors construct a mosaic of rape in the prisons. Despite numerous exposés of prison rape, this sexual violence remains one of America's best-kept secrets. The public prefers to ignore it; the system condones—and even encourages—it. The conspiracy of silence includes the victims (who are too helpless and ashamed to report it), the media, and the prison officials (who prefer silence on the subject). Nevertheless, the price of prison rape is high. The male victim's sexual identity is often shattered, and he leaves prison seeking revenge upon a society which quietly condoned the outrages done to him. One need not actually be convicted of a crime to suffer prison rape: assaults upon males waiting for trial or being held on suspicion of a misdemeanor can occur. In their radical solutions, the experts betray their desperation with the set-up: one expert suggests arguing that "the failure of the prison system to protect young men from sexual abuse rendered illegal the confinement of these young men." The authors agree that the public is amply repaid for its indifference to the prison situation by those released prisoners who are eager to avenge the abuse inflicted upon them by institutionalized sexual violence.

201.   Weiss, Karel, ed. **The Prison Experience: An Anthology**. New York: Delacorte Press, 1976. P. xxx, 366. notes. index.

This collection of over one hundred excerpts from the famous and unknown criticizes the prison system and what it does to people. Among the nineteen sections in the anthology, separate ones are devoted to such topics as slave labor, sex in prison, the keepers, and the military dissident. The editor and many of the writers note that prisons often reflect society's class and caste prejudices, but no one raises the question of whether they also reflect society's gender prejudices.

202.   Wooden, Wayne S., and Jay Parker. **Men behind Bars: Sexual Exploitation in Prison**. New York and London: Plenum Press, 1982. P. x, 264. illustrations. appendixes. notes. index.

Sexual exploitation of men in prisons is a recognized but unacknowledged and inadequately addressed problem. Based upon more than two hundred interviews and questionnaire responses from a California prison, the authors examine the prison setting, the dynamics of sexual exploitation, and the factors contributing to it. Among such factors are race or ethnic group (black, white, Chicano) and sexual orientation (heterosexual, bisexual, homosexual). The authors describe the sexual roles (jockers, punks, sissies) and the situation of homosexuals in prison. Nine percent of the heterosexual males were sexually assaulted in prison; 41 percent of the homosexuals were pressured into sex. Some solutions to alleviate the problem are offered by the authors, including policy changes in placement of prisoners, personnel requirements, and protection for inmates who complain about abuse. The appendixes provide the questionnaire and statistical tables.

Cross references:

6. Bowker, Lee H., comp. **Prison and Prisoners: A Bibliographic Guide.**

8. Franklin, H. Bruce, comp. **American Prisoners and Ex-Prisoners: Their Writings: An Annotated Bibliography of Published Works, 1798-1981.**

10. Johnson, Carolyn, John Ferry, and Marjorie Kravitz, comps. **Spouse Abuse: A Selected Bibliography.**

16. Suvak, Daniel, comp. **Memoirs of American Prisons: An Annotated Bibliography.**

71. Shostak, Arthur B., and Gary McLouth, with Lynn Seng. **Men and Abortion: Lessons, Losses, and Love.**

77. Bouton, Jim. **Ball Four, Plus Ball Five.**

86. Kopay, David, and Perry Deane Young. **The David Kopay Story: An Extraordinary Self-Revelation.**

90. Meggyesy, Dave. **Out of Their League.**

93. Richards, Renée, with John Ames. **Second Serve: The Renée Richards Story.**

106. Rudovsky, David. **The Rights of Prisoners: The Basic ACLU Guide to a Prisoner's Rights.**

132. Gaylin, Willard. **In the Service of Their Country: War Resisters in Prison.**

244. Holliday, Laurel. **The Violent Sex: Male Psychobiology and the Evolution of Consciousness.**

264. McClelland, David C., William N. Davis, Rudolf Kalin, and Eric Wanner. **The Drinking Man.**

566. Rogosin, Donn. **Invisible Men: Life in Baseball's Negro Leagues.**

WOMEN AND MEN _____

203. Bird, Caroline. **The Two-Paycheck Marriage: How Women at Work Are Changing Life in America.** New York: Rawson, Wade Publishers, 1979. P. xiv, 305. notes. index. Reprint. New York: Pocket Books, 1980. pa.

Bird presents the two-paycheck marriage as the triumph of the women's movement, but many readers will question how adequately she understands men's viewpoints on the issues she raises. Certainly, the sexist generalizations about men ("Fathers do what they like doing with children, mothers what has to be done for them") do not inspire confidence.

204. Brothers, Joyce. **What Every Woman Should Know about Men.** New York: Simon and Schuster, 1981. P. 268. Reprint. New York: Ballantine Books, 1983. pa.

For an audience of middle-class white women, Brothers summarizes in readable fashion what current studies reveal about men. Among the topics she surveys are the biological bases for maleness, the stages of the male life cycle, men and work, sexual concerns, and love and marriage. Brothers offers advice on how women can live with men as equals and lovers without being subservient or hostile. Some readers may find Brothers's discussions both lucid and helpful; others may find her views simplistic and occasionally condescending to men.

205. Ehrenreich, Barbara. **The Hearts of Men: American Dreams and the Flight from Commitment.** Garden City, N.Y.: Anchor Press/Doubleday, 1983. P. vii, 206. notes. index. pa.

Taking an original, thought-provoking look at what happened to American men between the fifties and eighties, Ehrenreich depicts the decline and fall of the "breadwinner ethic." During the fifties pressure upon men to marry and support families was intense: those who did not were "irresponsible" and "immature" losers—or, worse yet, homosexuals. But rebellion against gray-flannel conformity and "other-directed" men hinted of coming change. Rejecting "maturity" and making "irresponsibility" fashionable, *Playboy* promoted single-life sexuality; a man did not have to be a husband to be a man. The Beat Generation rejected both job and marriage. Meanwhile, experts emphasized male vulnerability, pointing to men's biological "inferiority," their greater susceptibility to heart disease, and the lethal aspects of Type A behavior. The breadwinner trap was deadly. Despite some hostility toward men, the feminist movement promised them relief once wives shared the breadwinning. The men's movement of the seventies publicized the hazards of being male and the ways in which women's liberation could mean men's liberation. But, fearful that freeing men from the breadwinner ethic would ruin the family, the New Right (the same people who defeated the ERA) created a backlash against men's liberation. Ehrenreich is admittedly uncertain whether the "male revolt" was a perfidious abandoning of responsibilities, another step toward the liberal humanistic ideal of greater freedom, or a revolt against an exploitive social system. Unsure whether it was a revolt at all or an accommodation to narcissistic consumerism, she argues that men freed themselves from economic responsibilities before women gained economic parity. In any event, family support by a single breadwinner has collapsed, aided in part by corporate failure to provide adequate wages. Drastic solutions—including the creation of a welfare state—are the only possible ones. Ehrenreich ponders whether men and women can work together as rebels to create a more humane society.

206.   Eno, Susan. **The Truth about What Women Want in Men.** New York: William Morrow and Co., 1980. P. 312. index.

After interviewing "hundreds" of women, ages 17-40, mostly single or divorced, Eno offers detailed advice to men who want to succeed with women. Appearance, assurance, assertiveness, and aliveness are the four key elements of male attractiveness. Eno advises men on such concerns as hairstyles, facial hair, clothes, body language, conversation, breaking up, and sex. Her advice is fairly traditional: women seem to prefer gentlemanly men who take the lead, who pay for dates (at least until a closer relationship develops), and who respect them—while taking the initiative in sexual matters. What Eno does not consider is why an increasing number of men find these roles contradictory and distasteful, and are reluctant to perform them.

207.   Figes, Eva. **Patriarchal Attitudes.** Women in Revolt. New York: Stein and Day, 1970. P. 191. notes. index. bibliography, 188.

Women are shaped by men, Figes argues, reciting a now-familiar litany of complaints against males as women-hating oppressors from prehistory to the present. Women "collude" in their oppression, Figes admits, but she pays little attention to mothers as the primary socializers of children. While frequently citing Margaret Mead, Figes never mentions that in *Male and Female* Mead explicitly rejects Figes's thesis that men are malicious conspirators and women are helpless dupes.

208.   Fordham, Jim, with Andrea Fordham. **The Assault on the Sexes.** New Rochelle, N.Y.: Arlington House, Publishers, 1977. P. 480. illustrations. index. bibliography, 469-74.

With wit and argument, the Fordhams take on feminist activists, experts, the media, and others who assault traditional sex roles and the family. They deplore the trendy denigration of housewives and resent the assumption of some feminists that they speak for all women. The authors question the media's love affair with fiery feminist rhetoric and their obligatory daily quota of "feminist news." They produce evidence questioning feminist scholarship, especially that in Betty Friedan's *The Feminine Mystique* and Jessie Bernard's *The Future of Marriage.*

Criticizing feminist use of language (e.g., "sexism," "male chauvinist"), they claim such language does not describe reality but is used to manipulate unthinking responses. The authors argue that the push for "equality" and "options" will actually result in enforced unisex standards and behaviors. Readers who regard the Fordhams as pro-male should consider that they support special privileges for women and are appalled at the idea of equal military obligations for women and men. Writing from a conservative viewpoint, the Fordhams say they support equal pay for equal work but argue that men are paid more because they are held legally responsible for supporting wives and families—a situation which the authors presumably do not wish to see remedied.

209. Friedman, Scarlet, and Elizabeth Sarah, eds. **On the Problems of Men: Two Feminist Conferences**. London: The Women's Press, 1982. P. ix, 262. notes. bibliographies at the end of some chapters. pa.

This collection of twenty radical feminist papers from two British conferences contains essays on such matters as family, sex, pornography, rape, fathers, male feminists, the men's movement, and raising sons. Whatever the topic, relations between the sexes are invariably reduced to male "oppression" and female "struggle."

210. Gittelson, Natalie. **Dominus: A Woman Looks at Men's Lives**. New York: Farrar, Straus and Giroux, 1978. P. ix, 291. Reprint. New York: Harcourt Brace Jovanovich, 1979. pa.

Casting a skeptical eye on the women's liberation movement of the seventies and on male reaction to it, Gittelson draws upon "hundreds" of interviews in America and Europe to argue that "the so-called feminist revolution has transformed the consciousness of American men more dramatically, more decisively—and perhaps more dangerously—than the consciousness of women." Thwarted of the opportunity to exercise *dominus* (perhaps best defined as masterly leadership), American men have settled for a variety of questionable alternatives, including "vaginal men" who disparage masculinity, nice guys who have attempted to placate militant feminists and who have become male chauvinist pigs in the process, and callous macho types who overreact to the women's challenge. Nostalgic for men who can exercise *dominus* gracefully, Gittelson paints a portrait of modern society's decadence by examining the narcissistic lives of materialistic singles, the guiltmongering of some male liberationists, and the relationships between superman and wonder woman in which caring means losing and in which freedom means loneliness. She sees black men reveling in *dominus* at the very time when white men are jettisoning it. She notes the hostility which underlies some men's support for women's rights (for these men, equality is the best revenge). After exploring the status of European gender relationships and the battle of the sexes in corporate life, Gittelson writes movingly of blue-collar workers facing angry wives and single parenthood. She is critical of the gay liberation's attempt to become gay imperialism and of the antics of sexual liberation gurus. Acidly suave and eminently quotable, Gittelson presents a stimulating case for men to rethink their rejection of *dominus*.

211. Goldberg, Herb. **The New Male-Female Relationship**. New York: William Morrow and Co., 1983. P. 274. notes. index. Reprint. New York: New American Library, Signet, 1984. pa.

This is the third in Goldberg's trilogy of books on modern gender roles. Unlike the previous two books, *The New Male-Female Relationship* focuses on both men and women (instead of primarily on men). Besides offering a critique of present gender confusions, it attempts to elaborate an ideal toward which the sexes can strive. Goldberg writes evenhandedly, refusing to blame one sex for the other's troubles, but arguing that both have been victims of restrictive gender roles. Failure is built into the traditional roles of male machine and female child, actor and reactor, success object and sex object. These roles turn romance into disillusionment, convert love into antagonism, and set sex at cross purposes. Traditional roles are not the only villains, however; liberation philosophy itself can be a form of disguised hostility toward the opposite sex. The militant feminist and the newly sensitized male can sometimes be more-liberated-than-thou hatemongers. Most women, however, need training in asserting themselves; most men need training in learning to let go, relax, and stop feeling responsible for everything. Both sexes need to rediscover playfulness, to recognize that opposition to sexism is not so much a matter of role reversals but of achieving a more open idea of the other person as a whole human being. Goldberg inveighs against the obsession with sexual techniques and standards of performance; he labels early parenthood as the source of much family discord. Looking toward a more balanced tomorrow, Goldberg believes that the battle of the sexes will become anachronistic as men and women outgrow the gender roles that have fostered so much hostility.

212. Halas, Celia. **Why Can't a Woman Be More like a Man? The 20 Questions Men Ask Most Frequently about Women.** New York: Macmillan Co., 1981. P. ix, 243.

In this book about women written for men, Halas argues that social conditioning has damaged many women. She offers insights designed to help men understand and cope with women's difficulties, especially a sense of powerlessness and inferiority. The author, a psychotherapist, draws upon case histories to answer twenty questions about women which puzzle men, e.g., why does she feel so misunderstood? why does she act so helpless? why does she cling so close and act so jealous? Perhaps inevitably, the book implies that gender problems are a one-way street: it tends to skirt the questions of whether men have been similarly damaged by their social conditioning and whether women have a corresponding obligation to understand and cope with men's difficulties.

213. Hart, Lois B., and J. David Dalke. **The Sexes at Work: Improving Work Relationships between Men and Women.** Englewood Cliffs, N.J.: Prentice-Hall, Spectrum, 1983. P. xii, 180. appendixes. index. pa.

In this popular guide, the authors isolate problem areas in the modern professional workplace and offer suggestions on such matters as sexual harassment, sexual attraction among colleagues, sex-biased language, expressing emotions, etiquette, and related matters. The discussion shows a lively sense of women's viewpoints, but some readers may question how deeply it delves into men's feelings and concerns.

214. Hoffman, Susanna M. **The Classified Man: Twenty-two Types of Men (and What to Do about Them).** New York: Coward, McCann and Geoghegan, 1980. P. 309. appendixes. Reprint. New York: G.P. Putnam's Sons, Perigee, 1980. pa.

For an audience of women the author categorizes and describes twenty-two types of men, providing each with a catchy description (e.g., The Gender Ascender, The Disaster Broker). Touching upon such characteristics as the type's identifying signs, sex signals, money matters, and family aspects, Hoffman offers advice on how to deal with each type. The author is friendly toward, but wary of, men; the book is popular rather than scholarly.

215. Kimball, Gayle. **The 50-50 Marriage.** Boston: Beacon Press, 1983. P. xiii, 312. appendixes. notes. index. bibliography, 225-26. pa.

Drawing upon extended interviews with 150 egalitarian couples, the feminist author draws a profile of the perils and payoffs of shared moneymaking, child care, housework, and decision making. The pluses outweigh the minuses in this analysis.

216. Korda, Michael. **Male Chauvinism! How It Works.** New York: Random House, 1973. P. 243. notes.

Focusing on the office, Korda analyzes the dynamics of male chauvinism as a means of obstructing women's advancement at work. Women are indoctrinated by society to be passive and submissive, thus handicapping them in competing with men who have been taught to be aggressive. Korda touches upon such matters as office politics, unequal pay, sexual harassment of women, and the stigma of success for women. Nevertheless, the modern office is a radical experiment, a fairly civilized place of work in which the possibility of equality between men and women can emerge. Women, Korda says, are coming to grips with their problems and concerns; it is time for men to do likewise. Some readers will find Korda's account of male bias in the executive suite to be enlightened; others will be put off by the book's hectoring tone which echoes angry feminist denunciations of the early seventies.

217. Kozmetsky, Ronya and George. **Making It Together: A Survival Manual for the Executive Family.** New York: Free Press, 1981. P. xii, 155.

The authors, an executive couple, offer strategies for management of dual-career families, including how to keep together, handle children, balance leadership, cope with crises, and get started and move ahead in business.

218. Malone, John. **Straight Women/Gay Men: A Special Relationship.** New York: Dial Press, 1980. P. xi, 207. notes. bibliography, 205-207.

Drawing upon interviews with 150 people, Malone depicts the special relationship which can exist between straight women and gay men. After viewing this relationship from the women's and the men's viewpoints, Malone explores its sexual complications and indecisions. He reports on marriages broken by the husband's coming out and on enduring marriages (like that of Charles Laughton and Elsa Lanchester) between gay men and straight women. After discussing the ambiguities of bisexuality, Malone concludes with a chapter assessing the current state of this special relationship.

219.   Marine, Gene. **A Male Guide to Women's Liberation**. New York: Holt, Rinehart and Winston, 1972. P. vi, 312. notes. index. bibliography, 275-303. Reprint. New York: Avon-Discus, 1974. pa.

For the confused male, Marine attempts to explain what the women's liberation movement of the late sixties and early seventies is all about. Although recognizing the excesses of some militant feminists, he regards the feminist cause as eminently just and reasonable—and he argues accordingly.

220.   Mornell, Pierre. **Passive Men, Wild Women**. New York: Simon and Schuster, 1979. P. 192. notes. bibliography, 191-92. Reprint. New York: Ballantine Books, 1980. pa.

In this informal study Mornell depicts a familiar pattern in modern man-woman relationships: *he* is emotionally withdrawn and uncommunicative, while *she* tries to be emotionally involved and communicative. For the divorced, a similar pattern emerges: the man is wary of becoming committed to a relationship, while the woman seeks to establish a close relationship with a "good" man. Mornell sees much of the male's passivity deriving from father absence in the modern family, a situation which leaves males uncertain with and chary of women. In the closing sections of the book Mornell provides suggestions for escaping the passive man-wild woman impasse.

221.   Mount, Ferdinand. **The Subversive Family: An Alternate History of Love and Marriage**. London: Jonathan Cape, 1982. P. 282. appendix. notes. index. bibliography, 272-76.

Challenging standard beliefs that history reveals a pattern of oppressed women subverting a patriarchal order, Mount argues that men and women together in the family have been the most subversive unit in human history, defying the worst that church and state, feudal lords and feminist writers, Marxists and other ideologues could do to destroy it. Those opponents of the family pass through a six-stage relationship with it. First, they attempt to devalue the family, then they reluctantly recognize its strength, and eventually they abandon efforts to replace it with alternate pseudofamilies. In the fourth stage, they reach a one-sided peace agreement with the family, and then they rewrite history to demonstrate that they were always its friend. Finally, the family imposes its own terms on its opponents. Dismissing "mass-media sociology myths" about the family, Mount argues that the nuclear family, far from being a modern invention, has been the norm throughout history; that romantic marital love existed before the troubadours sang the praises of adultery; and that divorce, no great novelty in the past, has been widely recognized as an integral part of family law and is an indication of the popularity of marriage. Mount argues that, for the most part, the church has been no friend to the family, that the state is usually jealous of the allegiance it commands and tries to weaken it, that Marxists have tried unsuccessfully to break the power of the family, and that modern feminists who began by attacking the family as a source of male oppression are now beginning to recognize its strength, and are (sometimes reluctantly) trying to come to terms with it. *The Subversive Family* makes such a heady contribution to current debate about the history of men and women in the family that one can only hope the book will become more widely known in the United States.

222. Nahas, Rebecca, and Myra Turley. **The New Couple: Women and Gay Men.** New York: Seaview Books, 1979. P. ix, 291. notes. bibliography, 285-91.

Through interviews and research, the authors informally explore three types of female-gay male relationships. In the first type, the gay man is married to the woman; such relationships usually involve serious problems. In the second, the relationship is primarily a nonsexual friendship between people with similar professional interests; these relationships usually work smoothly. In the third, sex is a part of the relationship although the male is not wholly committed to heterosexuality; these relationships can also involve tensions and misunderstandings. The authors speculate on how the conjunction of the women's liberation movement and gay liberation has fostered these new couples.

223. Nin, Anaïs. **In Favor of the Sensitive Man and Other Essays.** New York and London: Harcourt Brace Jovanovich, Harvest/HBJ Book, 1976. P. 169. pa.

In this collection of thoughtful essays and reviews, "In Favor of the Sensitive Man" contains especially pertinent reflections on "the new man." Nin fears that some women miss the old male dominance, feel bewildered by their new freedom, mistake gentleness for weakness, and construe male flexibility toward women as indifference. She exhorts liberated women not to reject the kind of man they say they have been looking for, in favor of the more success-driven male that so many women have found attractive in the past.

224. Nir, Yehuda, and Bonnie Maslin. **Loving Men for All the Right Reasons.** New York: Dial Press, 1982. P. 275. Reprint. New York: Dell Publishing Co., 1983. pa.

Writing for women, two therapists—a husband and wife team—recount a series of no-win "lovestyles" illustrating self-defeating patterns of relating to men. The authors provide four ways for women to recognize and unlearn these patterns. In a final chapter Nir and Maslin recognize that men too can be victimized by similarly defeating patterns of relating to women and that men are often less successful than women in recognizing and breaking out of them.

225. Novak, William. **The Great American Man Shortage and Other Roadblocks to Romance (and What to Do about It).** New York: Rawson Associates, 1983. P. 210. notes. index.

Puzzled by complaints from numerous attractive and intelligent women that "all the good ones are either married or gay," Novak investigates the reasons for the apparent shortage of men. He finds that, for women thirty and over, a shortage of males does exist for several reasons, including the larger number of women who survive at each age level, the shortened longevity of males, the larger number of gay men than gay women, and the tendency of some divorcés to marry much younger women. Also, the baby boom generation has created a shortage of males for females who traditionally "marry up," that is, marry slightly older men. Though real, the man shortage does not create impossible odds. In the twenty-five- to twenty-nine-year-old age bracket, a surplus of males already exists, and in the near future (as the baby boom generation ages) a surplus of slightly older men will exist for younger women to marry. Meanwhile, however, the plight of the single over-thirty woman remains, and Novak devotes the second half of this book to suggestions for coping with the man shortage. He analyzes characteristics of the times which have sabotaged romance, including hostility between the sexes fostered by "Me Decade" selfishness, the preoccupation with sexual politics, and the fact that the women's movement has not been balanced by a men's movement to articulate men's issues. Novak is usually aware of these issues and devotes an especially interesting chapter to male "talking back" to female demands and complaints. Among the men's grievances are "selective liberation" (the tendency of some women to demand equality when it benefits them and to reject equality when it does not), the general failure of women to take greater initiative in relationships and to pay their fair share, and the conflicting demands of some women ("They're looking for somebody who's John D. Rockefeller at the office and Dr. Benjamin Spock at the dinner table. ... I'm sorry, but I'm only one person, not two").

226. Rubin, Theodore Isaac, and David C. Berliner. **Understanding Your Man**: **A Woman's Guide**. New York: Ballantine Books, 1977. P. 186. pa.

In this popularly written guide for women, Rubin surveys a wide range of topics about male psychology and sexuality, including machismo, men's fears of intimacy and rejection, male dependency on women, oedipal feelings, male anxiety and guilt feelings, heterosexual relations, the importance of the penis, fantasies, masturbation, pornography, infidelity, and the male climacteric. Because some topics are controversial, readers may find themselves disagreeing occasionally with Rubin. The author heeds various messages from the women's liberation movement without being overwhelmed by them.

227. Ryglewicz, Hilary, and Pat Koch Thaler. **Working Couples: How to Cope with Two Jobs and One Home**. New York: Sovereign Books, 1980. P. 181. index.

Presented as an exploration and guide, this popularly written book offers practical advice on allocating household chores, sustaining a loving relationship between husband and wife, raising children, handling money, using leisure, creating special lifestyles (e.g., working at home), and coping with pressures and pitfalls in two-career relationships. Although more attuned to women's issues and views, the authors treat men's concerns sympathetically.

228. Seskin, Jane, and Bette Ziegler. **Older Women/Younger Men**. Garden City, N.Y.: Anchor Press/Doubleday, 1979. P. xix, 143. appendixes. notes. bibliography, 142-43.

From interviews and research, the authors examine the apparent increase in the number of older women-younger men relationships. Separate chapters are given to accounts of these relationships by the couples, by the men alone, and by the women alone. Two concluding chapters consider "expert" opinions on such romances and the authors' positive afterthoughts about them. For the younger men (who were more reluctant to speak with the authors) the advantages of such relationships include initiation into sex by an experienced partner, the unlikelihood of having children, the lowered demand for performance, and the lack of competition with the woman. The book does not pretend to be an exhaustive study, and readers should expect to find some questions unanswered.

229. Shaevitz, Marjorie Hansen, and Morton H. Shaevitz. **Making It Together as a Two-Career Couple**. Boston: Houghton Mifflin Co., 1980. P. xiii, 282. notes. index. bibliography, 269-72.

A couple working in family and career counseling, the authors have distilled their insights and experiences into practical advice on such matters as housework, parenting, child care, money decisions, finding the right employer, coping with overload, and maintaining the couple's relationship.

230. Shain, Merle. **Some Men Are More Perfect than Others: A Book about Men, and Hence about Women, and Love and Dreams**. Philadelphia and New York: J.B. Lippincott, 1973. P. ix, 117. Reprint. New York: Bantam Books, 1974. pa.

In witty informal essays on such matters as loving (as opposed to romantic ego-tripping and casual sex), marriages (both good and bad), the current battle of the sexes, affairs, rejection, divorce, and the single life (both good and bad), Shain touches upon what "the best men" are like. "Much of women's resentment toward men at the moment," she writes in a representative passage, "is related to their notion that men, since they are supposed to be superior, should meet all their needs, and that is a pretty heavy trip to lay on anyone and generally leaves men feeling they've been charged with the national debt."

231. Stapleton, Jean, and Richard Bright. **Equal Dating**. Nashville, Tenn.: Abingdon Press, 1979. P. 127.

Within a framework of traditional ideas about sexual morality, the authors argue for patterns of greater equality in dating. The accepted patterns push males and females into roles which both sexes are no longer comfortable with. Both need to take mutual responsibility in dating. Women must take the initiative more often and must pay their fair share. Men must learn that dating is not a testing ground for their masculinity; they must learn to say no to women, politely but clearly. "Chivalry is out," the authors write, "kindness is in." In calm and cogent prose Stapleton and Bright argue that casual and premarital sex are detrimental to developing a close, long-term relationship. They debunk the idea that chastity is harmful to anyone. Other chapters explore relating to each other's families, breaking up, and getting engaged. The diamond ring for women reinforces sexist roles in the relationship; it needs to be eliminated or replaced by an exchange of gifts between the couple. The penultimate chapter on getting married raises questions about who pays for what, who does the planning, and how the ceremony can be more egalitarian. A brief final chapter expresses value in the unmarried life.

232. Stapleton, Jean, and Richard Bright. **Equal Marriage**. Nashville, Tenn.: Abingdon Press, 1976. P. 144. bibliography, 141-44.

Stapleton and Bright describe a marriage of equals based upon mutual respect and commitment. They reject the betrayal of intimacy and commitment suggested in such books as *Open Marriage*, as well as the concept of a marriage between a childish wife and a fatherly husband advocated in books like *Total Woman* and *Fascinating Womanhood*. As widowed spouses now married to each other, the authors describe the gains and losses both partners can expect in an equitable union. They rule out sexual experiments with other partners as "a blow to the heart of marriage." Each partner, they argue, must learn the other's skills (he must learn housekeeping, she must learn repair and maintenance), and each must contribute to the marriage financially (or be able to do so). The authors describe the benefits of having two parents available to children, argue that sexual equality leads to sexual satisfaction, and offer suggestions on how to promote nonsexist attitudes in children. Short on polemics and long on marriage-affirming suggestions, *Equal Marriage* offers evenhanded advice to both men and women.

233. Sunila, Joyce. **The New Lovers: Younger Men/Older Women**. New York: Fawcett Gold Medal Books, 1980. P. 254. pa.

Given the raw deal older women get in our society, Sunila argues, the older woman-younger man relationship is the preferred option for truly liberated women. Contrasting the taboo against such relationships in modern America with numerous examples of them from the past, Sunila attacks the theory that these younger men are seeking mothers in older lovers. She takes a crosscultural look at such relationships, assesses current cultural depictions of them, and considers the practical issues involved. To some readers, Sunila's humane egalitarianism would be more convincing if she were less angry with and contemptuous of older men and if she were more comfortable with the idea of women financially supporting men.

234. Wagenvoord, James, Peyton Bailey, et al. **Men: A Book for Women**. New York: Avon Books, 1978. P. 383. illustrations. index. bibliography, 370-76. pa.

A popular attempt to unravel the mysteries of men for the average woman, this pleasantly designed book explores such topics as the genetic basis of maleness, men's bodies, reproducing and aging, sensuality and sexuality, men and work, marriage and separations, and fathering.

235. Wagenvoord, James, Peyton Bailey, et al. **Women: A Book for Men**. New York: Avon Books, 1979. P. 384. illustrations. index. bibliography, 370-76. pa.

A companion piece to *Men: A Book for Women*, this popularly written book explains for the average male reader such matters as the genetics of femininity, women's bodies, sexuality, working women, and motherhood.

236. Yablonsky, Lewis. **The Extra-Sex Factor: Why Over Half of America's Married Men Play Around**. New York: Times Books, 1979. P. 239. notes.

More than half of American married men engage in extramarital sex—or extra sex, in the author's terminology. Drawing upon in-depth interviews with more than fifty men and sixteen women and upon 771 responses from married men to a brief general survey questionnaire, Yablonsky argues that the motives for extrasexual activities are complex. Nevertheless, he makes the following generalizations: "total monogamy for most married people in contemporary society is a myth," about 80 percent of married men who engage in extra sex are satisfied with their wives and their marriages, about 80 percent of these men have a strong "homing drive" and have no intention of leaving their home situation, most extra sex is clandestine and is not discovered by the wife, most often it is of brief duration, and most men participate in extra sex for the companionship of other women and not simply for sex. The excerpts from the in-depth interviews which form most of the book's contents suggest that extra sex grows out of and creates considerable emotional turmoil.

237. Zola, Marion. **All the Good Ones Are Married: Married Men and the Women Who Love Them.** New York: Times Books, 1981. P. xviii, 257. Reprint. *All the Good Ones Are Married: Women Talk Frankly about Men and Love Today.* New York: Berkley Publishing Corp., 1982. pa.

Zola explores extramarital affairs from the viewpoints of "the other woman," "the man in the middle," and "the woman at home." Using interviews with two hundred women and one hundred men, she constructs scenarios of typical affairs and recounts particular intrigues, replete with soap-opera complications.

Cross references:

15. Stineman, Esther, comp., with Catherine Loeb. **Women's Studies: A Recommended Core Bibliography.**

49. Gordon, John. **The Myth of the Monstrous Male, and Other Feminist Fables.**

76. Vilar, Esther. **The Manipulated Man.**

287. Strauss, Sylvia. **"Traitors to the Masculine Cause": The Men's Campaign for Women's Rights.**

291. Dinnerstein, Dorothy. **The Mermaid and the Minotaur: Sexual Arrangements and Human Malaise.**

570. Wallace, Michele. **Black Macho and the Myth of the Superwoman.**

587. King, Florence. **He: An Irreverent Look at the American Male.**

MASCULINITY
Masculine Gender Role, Male Sex Role,
Biology, Physiology_____

GENERAL STUDIES, BIOLOGY, PHYSIOLOGY

238.   Bahr, Robert. **The Virility Factor: Masculinity through Testosterone, the
Male Sex Hormone.** New York: G.P. Putnam's Sons, 1976. P. x, 212.
appendix. index. bibliography, 197-205.

A popular scientific account of "the male hormone," this book describes how
testosterone is produced and how it functions to create maleness. After reviewing
the history of research into testosterone, Bahr describes the hormone's effects
upon the male from the embryonic stage to old age. He describes the results of
too little—and too much—testosterone, how it changes the male's appearance, how
homosexuality and prostate trouble may be connected with hormone levels, and
how testosterone can be affected by diet and drugs. Along the way, Bahr touches
on some controversial areas. He argues that male behavior is strongly affected by
the hormone: "If anything, society may actually curb a boy's natural tendency
to be his hormonal self." Macho men, however, are out of tune with their biological
selves: they attempt to counteract the effect of "female" estrogens which are a
natural part of maleness. Still, Bahr has nothing good to say about "liberated"
men who apologize for maleness. Despite attempts to broaden gender roles, Nature
has no love for unisex: conditions favor the mating of "men with very high
testosterone—i.e., aggression/sexual compulsion—levels" and "passive, submissive,
highly estrogenic" women, their offspring being "highly androgenized boys and
highly estrogenized girls." The book includes a glossary of terms.

239.   Biller, Henry B. **Father, Child, and Sex Role: Paternal Determinants of
Personality Development.** Lexington, Mass.: Heath Lexington Books,
D.C. Heath and Co., 1971. P. xi, 195. author and subject indexes. bibliog-
raphy, 137-80.

In this volume Biller surveys literature on the relationship between the father and
the child's sex role development. Distinguishing sex role orientation, preference,
and adoption, the author explores the effects of father-absence upon the boy's
masculine development, noting that such absence apparently has its most severe
effects when it occurs during the boy's first four or five years of life. Biller surveys
theories of sex role identity, stressing Freud's ideas and derivatives from them.
Examining sociocultural and constitutional variables affecting paternal influence,

Biller notes that sex role demands are heavier upon boys than upon girls, and that boys do not learn fathering as girls learn mothering. Examining paternal influence upon general personality functioning, the author touches upon such matters as cognitive, interpersonal, and conscience development. In separate chapters, Biller analyzes literature on mother-son and father-daughter relationships. A final chapter stresses the importance of effective fathering, charts directions for additional research, and makes suggestions for minimizing the impact of father-absence and maximizing the impact of father presence.

240.　Franklin, Clyde W., II. **The Changing Definition of Masculinity.** New York and London: Plenum Press, 1984. P. xi, 234. index. bibliography, 215-25.

Utilizing recent men's awareness writing (especially that of Farrell, Fasteau, Goldberg, Nichols, and Pleck), Franklin conducts a thoughtful inquiry into changing concepts of masculinity. Assessing male responses to the women's and the men's movements, he explores such topics as the socialization of males, racial differences, gender identity, marriage, work, fatherhood, male friendships, and themes in male sexuality. Sensitive to, but occasionally critical of, feminist views, Franklin's book is suitable for college courses on men. A final chapter attempts to chart future changes in the masculine gender role.

241.　Gerzon, Mark. **A Choice of Heroes: The Changing Faces of American Manhood.** Boston: Houghton Mifflin Co., 1982. P. vii, 279. notes. pa.

In an account that is personal and political, historical and contemporary, Gerzon examines American cultural images of manhood. His descriptions of The Frontiersman and of The Soldier expand into essays on virility and violence, genocide, nuclear warfare, the antiwar movement, and political machismo; the portraits of The Breadwinner and of The Expert expand into assessments of boyhood, manhood, marriage, fatherhood, and male religious images. The "emerging masculinities" or new emblems of heroism toward which some men are beginning to aspire are identified as The Healer, The Companion, The Mediator, and The Colleague. While critical of many masculine stances, Gerzon is sensitive to the psychological and social structures that create them. He argues that destructive and repressive conditions are created by men and women acting in collusion with each other and that the important task now is for the sexes to not blame each other. Rather, Gerzon concludes, "it is our shared responsibility to break the pattern."

242.　Gunther, Max. **Virility 8: A Celebration of the American Male.** Chicago: Playboy Press, 1975. P. 280.

Although, according to Gunther, it is not chic these days to be an American male, his book is nevertheless a deliberate celebration of the American man as mover, maker, and mucker-up. Arguing that for better or for worse men still dominate American society, Gunther delineates eight types of "virility" in modern times: The No-Nonsense Pragmatist who shuns "feminine" frivolity, The Recently Civilized Brute who parades his machismo, The Thinker (e.g., Dr. Samuel Johnson, Ernest Hemingway), The Rogue whose mischievous approach is irresistible to many women, The Operator-Manipulator who attracts women with money and power, The Satyr or swinger whose prototype is Lord Byron and whose present-day types include Joe Namath and Marlon Brando, The Romantic Outcasts (e.g., Thoreau,

David Carradine), and The Mild Male or self-effacing man (e.g., James Boswell and apparently Gunther himself). In the latter part of the book Gunther offers twenty-five tongue-in-cheek rules for acting male. He also discusses with good-natured humor such current issues as the "new" impotency, male leadership, the linking of manhood with career and money, and the need for male-only rituals and bonding. In contrast to recent literature deploring the state of American manhood, Gunther's book is decidedly optimistic: the final chapter is "Prognosis: OK."

243. Hapgood, Fred. **Why Males Exist: An Inquiry into the Evolution of Sex.** New York: William Morrow and Co., 1979. P. 213. index. bibliography, 189-99. Reprint. New York: New American Library, Mentor Book, 1980. pa.

A superb example of popular scientific writing, *Why Males Exist* explores the mysteries of why sexual reproduction arose in the evolutionary process and—more specifically—why males came into existence. Hapgood divides living creatures into four groups. In the first, consisting of creatures like bacteria, asexual reproduction is standard. In the second group are "bisexuals" who occasionally resort to sexual reproduction to cope with certain extreme conditions in their environment. In the third group, specialization has led to distinct sexual differences and sexual reproduction. In this stage the female generally controls the reproductive cycle, leaving the males to struggle, demonstrate their fitness, and be rewarded by being allowed to mate. These animals seldom form couples, mating is quickly achieved, and the female is left to rear the offspring. The fourth group is marked by monogamy among animal couples and by male—as well as female—parenting. Hapgood cites the gains of such an arrangement, including the opportunity to raise more highly developed young, the modification of different sexual tempi in males and females, the disappearance of sex-differentiated roles and tasks, and the mutual dependency of the two parent animals which allows for closer bonding between them and prepares for the emergence of love in the evolutionary process.

244. Holliday, Laurel. **The Violent Sex: Male Psychobiology and the Evolution of Consciousness.** Guerneville, Calif.: Bluestocking Books, 1978. P. 254. illustrations. appendixes. notes. pa.

This oddly contradictory book begins as an explanation for the layperson of how males are more psychobiologically predisposed toward violence than females are, but it ends in a man-hating diatribe that can only be described as violent. The lengthy opening chapter describing brain and hormonal differences in males and females shows the author summarizing widespread research with seemingly dispassionate lucidity. (The negative implications of these differences for males are stressed, however; any positive implications are ignored.) The second chapter on socialization argues more passionately but still convincingly that our culture too often encourages violence in males. Especially interesting are Holliday's observations that the mother's tendency to cuddle male infants less and the parents' tendency to punish boys more often and more severely are both detrimental to the male's development. Chapters 3 and 4—on the evolution of the sexes and on modern males—increasingly indulge in wild generalizations, sexist stereotypes of males as destroyers and females as nurturers, and operatic polemics. Hunting and meat eating are depicted as the "fall" of humanity, and all the world's problems are credited to men. Readers can be amused or repelled by the contradictions that follow fast and thick in the remaining sections. After pages of warning against poisoning one's body with dubious foods and chemicals, the author advises men to use marijuana to lower their testosterone levels. After pages of invective against male interference with the natural order of things, Holliday provides instructions to enable women by artificial means to bear only female children—in order not to "burden the world with any more males if you can help it." After lengthy tirades against male insensitivity to life, the author tosses off the suggestion that when a pregnant woman "learns that the fetus is not the sex of her choice" she "may decide to have an abortion."

245. Mead, Margaret. **Male and Female: A Study of the Sexes in a Changing World**. New York: William Morrow and Co., 1949. P. vi, 477. appendixes. index. bibliographies located in several places in the appendixes. pa.

One of the giants of twentieth-century anthropology, Mead in *Male and Female* crystallizes her mature thinking concerning gender roles. Recapitulating her studies among seven South Seas peoples (the Samoans, the Manus of the Admiralty Isalnds, the mountain Arapesh, the cannibal Mundugumor of the Yuat River, the lake-dwelling Tchambuli, the Iatmul headhunters of the Great Sepik River, and the Balinese), Mead discusses how sex roles are shaped by diverse societies. She explores, for example, how different cultures offer differing ways for males to respond to the oedipal conflict. Noting that girls in general are surer of their identities, Mead argues that "the recurrent problem of civilization is to define the male role satisfactorily enough ... so that the male may in the course of his life reach a solid sense of irreversible achievement." Especially significant for men's studies is Mead's ninth chapter, "Human Fatherhood Is a Social Invention," in which she concludes that societies must teach males to want to beget and cherish children. Discussing the sexes in contemporary society, Mead rejects the notion that males have conspired throughout history to oppress women: "It takes considerable effort on the part of both men and women to reorient ourselves to thinking—when we think basically—that this is a world made not by men alone, in which women are unwilling and helpless dupes and fools or else powerful schemers hiding their power under their ruffled petticoats, but a world made by mankind for human beings of both sexes." She concludes by exploring the needs for a future in which both sexes will benefit without denying the differences between them.

246. Money, John, and Patricia Tucker. **Sexual Signatures: On Being a Man or a Woman**. Boston: Little, Brown and Co., 1975. P. 250. illustrations. index. bibliography, 237-39.

Writing for the layperson in clear, readable prose, the authors explain the mysteries of gender identity and role. Gender identity is defined as the inner, private experience of one's sexuality, gender role as the public expression of that experience. The authors use the term "gender identity/role" to express the continuity and interaction of the two. They explain what creates hermaphrodites, and they define homosexuality, transvestism, and transsexualism. Describing prenatal development, the authors invoke the "Adam principle" to explain why males are at greater risk: something extra is needed to prevent the fetus from developing into a female. They explain chromosomes and hormones, as well as variations which can occur in the standard XX and XY patterning. Discussing the socialization of humans, the authors distinguish between "reannouncement" (explaining that an infant thought to be of one sex is actually of the other) and "reassignment" (a more drastic effort to clarify an uncertain identity or to rectify the condition of a person assigned to the "wrong" sex). In discussing childhood and adolescence, the authors recommend greater social flexibility toward roles. Their chapter on "The Sex Revolution" contains a section on male liberation that is "must" reading for anyone interested in what lies behind the men's movement and other indications of male discontent in America.

247.   Ong, Walter J. **Fighting for Life: Contest, Sexuality, and Consciousness.** Ithaca, N.Y.: Cornell University Press, 1981. P. 237. index. bibliography, 211-22.

Ong explores the relation between contest and sexual identity. Arguing that self-consciousness emerges from the biological but is not entirely determined by it, he focuses upon contest or adversativeness as a shaping force of male identity. In animals and humans, males live more at risk, needing to define their sexual identity in a way that females do not. Even as an embryo, the male must differentiate himself through hormonal activity or else develop into a female. Males thus have a built-in resistance to nurture; they exhibit a need to resist the prevailing female environment of existence. Boys must shift their gender identity away from the feminine by proving themselves male, and even in intercourse men must perform in order to demonstrate their masculinity. Males thus establish their identity by taking or creating risks. Ong sees irreconcilable differences between the masculine and the feminine. He speaks of the male Don Quixote tilting at windmills in pursuit of an impossible dream, and of the female Pietà lovingly relinquishing possession of her child. The male is the archetypal quester, at times ridiculous; the female is the primary parent. There can be no female Quixotes, no male Pietàs. Masculinity is external, femininity is internal. Males are dispensable, females are not. Like Adam, the male is created with a lack or need for woman; like Eve, the female is created with the lack already provided for. In surveying selected present issues, Ong discusses spectator sports (he notes the failure of women's sports to develop the life-and-death sense of contest—and hence the audience—of men's sports), politics and business (both are highly agonistic), and Christian life and worship (the essentially feminine nature of Holy Mother Church is counterbalanced by its male-only clergy). Ong notes how the agonistic nature of academic life diminished when females entered academia. Even narrative art has become interiorized with the emergence of women authors. Ong discusses both the positive and negative aspects of contest, pointing to the difficulties likely to ensue as males have fewer opportunities for creative contest and as the insecurity that comes with contest is conveyed increasingly to females.

248.   Pleck, Joseph H. **The Myth of Masculinity.** Cambridge, Mass.: MIT Press, 1981. P. ix, 229. appendixes. notes. name and subject indexes. bibliography, 189-216. pa.

By attacking the Male Sex Role Identity (MSRI) paradigm, Pleck calls into question over forty years of sex role research and some of the most widely held assumptions about masculinity. Pleck lists eleven questionable MSRI propositions, including: sex role identity derives from identification-modeling and (to a lesser extent) from reinforcement and cognitive learning of sex-typed traits, homosexuality reflects a disturbance of sex role identity, exaggerated masculine behavior indicates insecurity in some men's sex role identity, problems of sex role identity account for men's negative attitudes and behaviors toward women, and black males are particularly vulnerable to sex role identity problems. Pleck surveys past sex role research, often finding it based upon inadequately defined psychological theory, misinterpretations, contradictions, and cultural biases. He questions the validity of sex-typing scales, the idea of identification-modeling, theories of what paternal absence does to children, and arguments that schools feminize male students. In the concluding two chapters, Pleck examines an alternative explanation of male behaviors in the Sex Role Strain paradigm, which he formulates in ten propositions, including: sex roles are contradictory and inconsistent, the proportion of people who violate sex roles is high, violating sex roles has more severe consequences for males than for females, each sex experiences sex role strain in its paid work and family roles, and historical change causes sex role strain. Appendix A reviews theories that biology is the basis of male aggression; appendix B critiques the idea that biology insures weak paternal involvement. Appendix C contains a valuable list of resources for studying (or teaching) male roles. The bibliography is extensive.

249.   Rose, Frank. **Real Men.** Garden City, N.Y.: Doubleday and Co., Dolphin, 1980. P. viii, 213. illustrations. pa.

In this study of "sex and style in an uncertain age," Rose and photographer George Bennet present in-depth portraits of seven men representing highly diverse styles of masculinity. Making no claim to representativeness, Rose describes the book as "a personal and idiosyncratic survey" of different ways in which seven men have defined their masculine identity. The men are: Rick Wetherill, a cadet at the Virginia Military Institute; rock star Dee Dee Ramone; Norm Rathweg, a gay free-lancer designer of interior spaces; Pat Hickey, hockey player for the New York Rangers; Youngstown steel worker Carroll Megginson; Dallas stockbroker Billy Bob Harris; and actor Andrew Rubin.

250.   Sexton, Patricia Cayo. **The Feminized Male: Classrooms, White Collars and the Decline of Manliness.** New York: Random House, 1969. P. 214. appendix. notes. Reprint. New York: Random House, Vintage, 1970. pa.

This controversial book argues that American schools are inimical to boys and masculinity. The female presence in the classrooms (especially in the lower grades) is stifling in its pervasiveness, schools reward feminine behavior and proscribe masculine behavior, and the least masculine boys are the ones most likely to succeed in school. Sexton reaches these and similar conclusions from a survey of school children in a fictionally named town. Her survey employs the masculinity scale from the California Psychological Inventory. To correct her findings, she compares them with those from a national survey. Sexton's solution to over-feminized schools is to move more men and masculine attitudes into the schools while moving more women and feminine attitudes into the power structure of society—in effect, balancing out the presence of the sexes throughout the social system. "Paradoxically," she concludes, "it seems that the full emancipation of women must precede or accompany the emancipation of modern man. Only as the strength of women in other institutions increases, will their stranglehold on home and school weaken. Men may then be removed as targets of female resentment."

251. Tiger, Lionel. **Men in Groups.** New York: Random House, 1969. P. xx,
      255. notes. index. bibliography, 218-45. Reprint. New York: Random
      House, Vintage, 1970. pa.

Influential and controversial, Tiger's book argues that male bonding in human
societies is not only socially learned but biologically transmitted. Like the female-
offspring relationship and the male-female sexual link, the male-male bond is rooted
in an underlying biological predisposition. After discussing male bonding in animal
communities, Tiger traces the evolution of modern male associative interaction
from generations of male group hunters. A primary function of male bonding is
aggressive action to enhance the survival of the society, whether through defence
against enemies, hunting for food, or other strenuous activities. The critical nature
of such tasks leads men to "court" other men, that is, to test and select "fit" males
for inclusion in the group, often through symbolic initiation practices. The link
between aggressive action and violence, however, indicates that male aggression can
become antisocial; hence, managing such behaviors is a primary social concern.
Although Tiger favors the inclusion of more women in the public life of modern
society, he stresses the difficulty of achieving this goal: because of the predisposition to assign critical public affairs to males, in times of crisis males tend to reject
females as colleagues, and both males and females tend to reject femals as leaders.
Paradoxically, in social matters, the modern middle-class bias against widespread
adult male bonding may impoverish men's lives by failing to formulate acceptable
male-male relationships. Any hope of future progress demands that humanity recognize and deal with its biological-social heritage of male bonding.

ANTHROPOLOGICAL AND SOCIOLOGICAL STUDIES

252. Allen, M. R. **Male Cults and Secret Initiations in Melanesia.** Melbourne,
      Australia: Melbourne University Press, 1967. P. 140. illustrations. index.
      bibliography, 123-36. Reprint. London and New York: Cambridge Univer-
      sity Press, 1967.

Citing numerous studies, Allen provides an overview of male initiation rites in a
wide variety of Melanesian societies. He connects the degree of sexual polarity in
these societies to varying kin-based social structures, and he links the rites to sexual
antagonism and social arrangements. Allen also assesses several leading anthropological and psychological theories concerning the male rites, including theories of male
envy of females, oedipal rivalry between fathers and sons, and male fears of female
contamination.

253. Bettelheim, Bruno. **Symbolic Wounds: Puberty Rites and The Envious
      Male.** Rev. ed. New York: Collier Books, 1962. P. 194. appendixes. notes.
      index. pa.

Questioning prevailing psychological and anthropological explanations of puberty
rites, Bettelheim suggests that they represent an attempt by males to imitate
female powers of procreation. Both sexes envy the powers of the other sex to some
extent; some puberty rituals spring from the male's awe of the female's ability to
bear children. These rituals represent his attempt to assimilate her powers into himself: thus, the bleeding penis which results from circumcision resembles the
menstruating vagina. Although myths suggest that circumcision is imposed and

desired by women, Bettelheim warns against an oversimplified view of its origins. The author examines numerous practices and ceremonies, including circumcision, castration, self-mutilation, subincision, couvade, transvestism, and female mutilation. He argues that the secrecy surrounding many of these rites derives from the men's need to suggest that their "business" is as important as the women's. Bettelheim concludes that less pressure on males "to fight and to strut" and greater freedom to express their creative and nurturant abilities would lessen vagina envy, would help them achieve greater closeness to females and to other males, and would heighten their positive wish to create life rather than destroy it. The appendixes discuss infant circumcision in the Hebrew scriptures and puberty rites in Australia. The first edition of this book appeared in 1954.

254. Brandes, Stanley. **Metaphors of Masculinity: Sex and Status in Andalusian Folklore**. Philadelphia: University of Pennsylvania Press, 1980. P. x, 236. illustrations. index. bibliography, 215-27. pa.

Brandes describes a rapidly disappearing culture in southern Spain where the sexes are still rigidly separated and where the males adopt an aggressive-defensive stance about their masculinity. Folklore—including public celebrations, speech, customs, jokes, pranks, riddles, skits, and religious devotions—define a male's place in the social order and his relationship to females. Brandes points out both the disadvantages of these gender roles and the enriching aspects of the folklore that defines them.

255. Cohen, Albert K. **Delinquent Boys: The Culture of the Gang**. Glencoe, Ill.: The Free Press, 1955. P. 198. notes. index. Reprint. London: Routledge and Kegan Paul, 1956.

In this study Cohen explores the influence of social class and sex role strain as contributing factors to male juvenile delinquency. He also specifies what the juvenile gang offers the boy that mainstream culture does not.

256. Gold, Martin. **Status Force in Delinquent Boys**. Ann Arbor: Institute for Social Research, University of Michigan, 1963. P. xv, 229. illustrations. appendixes. index. bibliography, 221-24.

This social-psychological study examines why sons of lower-class families are more frequently delinquent than those of higher-class families. The author reviews the literature on delinquency and reports results of a study conducted in Flint, Michigan. He concludes tentatively that part of the answer involves weaker family ties and greater provocations to delinquency among lower status boys.

257. Herdt, Gilbert H. **Guardians of the Flutes: Idioms of Masculinity**. New York: McGraw-Hill Book Co., 1981. P. xviii, 382. illustrations. appendixes. notes. name and subject indexes. bibliography, 355-68.

This anthropological study examines the lives of males among the Sambia (a pseudonym) people of the East Highlands of Papua New Guinea. Because of intertribal raids, this society requires a warrior class capable of meeting surprise attacks. To turn boys into fighting men, a long-term and sometimes brutal initiation process separates young males from females. In secret, fellatio is practiced in the belief that oral insemination of boys provides them with needed manhood. Surprisingly (at least to many Westerners), such homoerotic activity does not produce homosexuals in later life. Once a male is married and has fathered a child, he is expected to become fully heterosexual. Nearly all the males do. Unsurprisingly, such a warrior culture prizes hypermasculine styles, forcibly inducts young males into its rites, despises femininity, and fosters hostility between the sexes. A myth of male parthenogenesis insists that males alone are responsible for creation, but it is also evidence of the male's fear of "femininity" within himself. In a thought-provoking final chapter, Herdt stresses the society's crucial need to convert mother-suckled infants into fierce warriors through a process of masculinization which leaves all the males literally scarred. He also indicates the significance of the study for understanding men in other societies, including our own.

258. Herdt, Gilbert H., ed. **Rituals of Manhood: Male Initiation in Papua New Guinea.** Berkeley: University of California Press, 1982. P. xxvi, 367. illustrations. notes. bibliographies after each chapter.

This collection of eight scholarly essays by ten authors (plus editor's preface) repeatedly stresses how female growth is regarded as automatic among some peoples of New Guinea but how the process of "growing" a man requires often violent social "hardening." Among the Bimin-Kuskusmin, a systematic brutalization of boys occurs. The Awa male initiation includes beatings, nose bleedings, penis cuttings, and induced vomiting. Among the Sambia, boys are coerced into fellatio as a way to make them into men. The *bau a* ceremonial hunting lodge is an alternative to initiation, but among its rituals anal insemination of boys is used to ensure male growth. The ritualized violence of the Ilahita Arapesh uses terror tactics to heighten the boys' ordeal. Although the Chambri ceremonies are decidedly more playful, even these include scarification of the male's body. Hostility toward women often is either explicit or implicit in these rituals, although the collusion of women in them is frequent. Terence E. Hays and Patricia H. Hays emphasize, in their account of men's and women's ceremonies among the Ndumba, that women's antagonism toward men equals that of men toward women. In the book's introduction Roger M. Keesing raises important questions about the difficulty of rising above partial views of these rituals to a fuller one. In the final essay Donald F. Tuzin questions what the response of anthropologists to the ceremonies should be. Significantly, he points to guilt feelings in the initiators because of their participation in ritualized violence against those whom they love. The essays provide often shocking evidence of how boys are tortured into "manhood"; inevitably, they raise questions in the reader's mind about similar practices elsewhere.

259. Hogbin, [Herbert] Ian. **The Island of Menstruating Men: Religion in Wogeo, New Guinea.** Scranton, Pa.: Chandler Publishing Co., 1970. P. xiv, 203. illustrations. index. bibliography, 197-98.

The author describes a society in which gashing the penis is used to produce "artificial menstruation," a purifying act. In this culture, the sexes exist in "balanced opposition," and elaborate secret rituals are used by adult males to separate boys from mothers and to enable them to grow into men.

260. Komarovsky, Mirra. **Dilemmas of Masculinity: A Study of College Youth.** New York: W.W. Norton and Co., 1976. P. xi, 274. index. bibliography, 259-66. pa.

"The distinguishing feature of the present study," the author writes, "is its explicit focus upon those strains that the male experiences precisely because he is a male and not a female, living in a particular social milieu." Using a case-study method which combines sociological and psychological perspectives, Komarovsky studied sixty-two seniors in an eastern Ivy League men's college. Because the interviews were held in 1969-1970, an attempt was made to update the findings with more recent literature. Also, because the book focuses on problems of role strain, the author warns against seeing the men as more conflicted than they are. Findings include such matters as the men's attitudes toward masculinity and femininity (many men accepted several traits once labeled "feminine" as masculine) and the discrepancy between some of the men's theoretical acceptance of women's equal participation in the work force and their own preference for more domestically oriented marriage partners—apparently because the men sensed the difficulties involved in a two-career family. Some of the men were uncomfortable with academically competitive or sexually aggressive women. The sexual revolution has left men more ashamed of being virgins than of being sexually experienced. Many of the men felt emotionally distant from their fathers, although conflict with their mothers was likely to produce more serious psychological effects upon them. The study found that despite the alleged advantages of being male nearly 50 percent of the men were anxious about their ability to play the masculine role. The penultimate chapter ("A Theoretical Summary") investigates six modes of sex role strain, illustrating each with reference to the study. The final chapter ("Afterword: The Author's Envoi") argues that the tendency of students to blame themselves rather than the social structure for role strain does not bode well for the needed social reforms to facilitate role changes. Despite the authoritativeness of the study, some readers may be disappointed by the smallness and unrepresentativeness of the sample, by the dated nature of the evidence, and by the feminist bias of the commentary which often seems to show greater sensitivity toward the dilemmas of femininity than of masculinity.

261. Lee, Richard B., and Irven DeVore, with Jill Nash-Mitchell, eds. **Man the Hunter**. Chicago: Aldine Publishing Co., 1968. P. xvi, 415. illustrations. notes. index. bibliography, 353-92.

Originally presented at a 1966 University of Chicago symposium, the thirty papers (plus six discussion sessions) printed here examine present and past hunting societies, with occasional focus on how hunting shapes male behavior. The scholarly anthropological essays explore such matters as ecology and economics in present-day hunting societies, social and territorial organization, marriage in Australia, demography and population, prehistoric hunter-gatherers, and the effect of hunting upon human evolution.

262. Leemon, Thomas A. **The Rites of Passage in a Student Culture: A Study of the Dynamics of Transition**. Anthropology and Education Series. New York and London: Teachers College Press, Columbia University, 1972. P. xi, 215. illustrations. appendixes. bibliography, 203.

Drawing upon Arnold van Gennep's concept of rites of passage, Leemon recounts the process by which an American college fraternity in spring 1963 initiated a group of pledges into membership. As a privileged observer of the fraternity, the author traces the three stages of passage—separation, transition, and incorporation—

in the rituals, harassments, raids, celebrations, and interactions of members and pledges.

263. Malinowski, Bronislaw. **The Father in Primitive Psychology**. New York: W.W. Norton and Co., 1927. P. vii, 95. Reprint. 1966. pa.

Studying the Trobriand Islanders of the South Pacific, Malinowski uncovers a condition which he believes is common among early societies: a belief that the mother is the sole parent of the child and that no connection exists between sexual intercourse and pregnancy. Children, it is believed, are returned spirits of the dead who are introduced into the mother's body during sleep by controlling spirits. Thus, the islanders have constructed what amounts to a "fatherless" society. Nevertheless, the father—or, to be more exact, the husband of the child's mother—has an important role in the culture as provider, protector, and caretaker of children. So important is his role that the islanders, who do not frown on extramarital sex, nevertheless consider it disgraceful for an unmarried woman to become pregnant: she has no husband to provide for her and the child. As the child grows older, the "father's" role becomes less important and is taken over to some extent usually by the mother's brother. Nevertheless, Malinowski presents classic evidence that the concept of fathering precedes even the awareness of paternity.

264. McClelland, David C., William N. Davis, Rudolf Kalin, and Eric Wanner. **The Drinking Man**. New York: Free Press, 1972. P. xiv, 402. illustrations. appendixes. index. bibliography, 379-86.

Most of this book describes experiments conducted over ten years to determine motives for men's heavy drinking. Crosscultural research is added to work done on college campuses and in working men's bars. General readers will be put off by the sociological jargon throughout most of the volume, but luckily the authors revert to plain English for the crucial sections of the book. Readers should not miss sections of chapter 13 (pp. 303-305, 309-315) and the final chapter. "Men drink primarily to feel stronger," McClelland concludes. The roots of excessive drinking are found in the role assigned to men by society. Strong demands are made for male assertiveness, but society offers low support for the male role and provides few socialized outlets for exercising power and assertiveness. Among the solutions offered are: for men and society to reduce the need for male power displays, for men to borrow strength from sources outside themselves (e.g., religious belief), for men to find ways of acting out their aggression or to satisfy the power drive vicariously, for society to socialize the male power drive, and for men to succeed at their work. Readers may suspect that the authors have discovered the dynamics underlying not only excessive drinking by males but also a good deal of other aberrant male behavior.

265. Scott, George Ryley. **Phallic Worship**. London: Luxor Press, 1966. P. xii, 234. illustrations. appendix. index. bibliography, 221-26. Reprint. London: Panther Books, 1970. pa.

Described as "a history of sex and sex rites in relation to the religions of all races from antiquity to present day," Scott's work surveys—in part I— the emergence of phallic sun gods with the awareness of the male role in reproduction. He discusses sacred harlotry and male prostitution, serpent worship, and phallicism as part of witchcraft. Part II presents a historical, geographic review of phallicism among early tribes, during biblical times, in ancient Greece and Rome, in Eastern and Western cultures, and (despite official disapproval) in Christian symbolism.

266. Strage, Mark. **The Durable Fig Leaf: A Historical, Cultural, Medical, Social, Literary, and Iconographic Account of Man's Relations with His Penis.** New York: William Morrow and Co., 1980. p. 317. illustration. notes. index. pa.

Some of the earliest known cave paintings contain representations of the phallus, an indication that humanity's fascination with the penis has a long history. Strage surveys several aspects of this fascination, beginning with the connection made by some animals and humans between the erect penis and dominance. Dysfunctioning of the penis, however, leads to male concerns about penis size, fears of insatiable women, and (according to some theorists) homosexuality. Strage describes the mechanism of erection and such matters as "premature ejaculation," "retarded ejaculation," impotence, aphrodisiacs, and the effects of drugs on the libido. Efforts to "improve" on nature include circumcision, subincision, and insertions. (Strage points to evidence that nowadays circumcision is most often encouraged by mothers, perhaps influenced by articles in women's magazines; fathers seem indifferent to the alleged benefits of circumcision.) Strage's consideration of the penis in visual arts ranges from prehistory, through the classical and medieval periods, into the Renaissance and modern ages, with special emphasis on such figures as Aubrey Beardsley and Pablo Picasso. Considering the literature of the penis, Strage begins with Boccaccio and concludes with such twentieth-century writers as D.H. Lawrence and Norman Mailer. Some readers will feel that Strage's concluding chapter, "Not Very Hopeful," is unduly pessimistic; *The Durable Fig Leaf* contains abundant evidence that man's fascination with his penis has survived the worst that puritanical and fanatical societies could do to discourage it.

267. Vanggaard, Thorkil. **Phallós: A Symbol and Its History in the Male World.** Translated by the author. New York: International Universities Press, 1974. P. 213. illustrations. notes. index. Originally published as *Phallós* (Copenhagen: Glydendal, 1969).

This anthropological and historical study explores the significance of representations of the phallus. In particular, the author focuses on two aspects of the symbolism: its use throughout history to represent homoerotic relationships between heterosexual males, and the phallus as representing male aggression. These two concerns are interwoven throughout the book. Vanggaard discusses the communal sanctioning in ancient Greece of *paiderastia*, the homoerotic relationship between heterosexual adult males and boys. In this same culture, the phallus represented and transmitted to the boy the man's *arete*, his nobility and power. After examining phallic representations in ancient Scandanavia, the author indicates that the "submissive" role has often been permissible for boys but not for adult males. Hence, an erotic relationship between two male adult peers has been difficult to sustain. Anal rape has been used as a demonstration of male dominance; Vanggaard notes that even among male baboons the erect penis is used as a sign of aggression. In the second half of the book, the author traces how homoerotic relationships were driven underground by Judaic-Christian morality, although medieval Catholicism regarded homosexuality as a serious sin only when it was linked to heresy. Such a link, however, was commonplace at times, especially in the various manifestations of Manicheanism. Likewise, the witch cults of Renaissance times were probably heretical fertility cults. Ironically, while suppressing phallic cults, society sanctioned the codpiece as a familiar representation of male aggression and nobility. In modern times, Thomas Mann's *Death in Venice* traces the tragedy of what happens when "normal" homosexual tendencies are repressed. While becoming more tolerant of homosexuals, modern society still forbids "normal" homosexual expression in heterosexual males.

268. Wilmott, Peter. **Adolescent Boys of East London.** Rev. ed. Baltimore, Md.: Penguin Books, 1969. P. 237. appendixes. notes. index. bibliography, 227-32. pa.

This readable study explores the process of growing up male in a working-class district of London. The material was gathered between 1959-1964 from conversations, formal interviews, and diaries. The study touches on boys' groups, their relationships with girls, and their family and kinship relationships. (Although frequently strained, the father-son relationship also contained much "understanding.") The book also explores schools, work, and youth clubs. Although a chapter on delinquency reveals widespread theft, as well as outbursts of antisocial aggression, it discovers little sign of a "war of generations." The appendixes describe methodology and statistical findings in detail.

269. Young, Frank W. **Initiation Ceremonies: A Cross Cultural Study of Status Dramatization.** Indianapolis, Ind.: Bobbs-Merrill Co., 1965. P. xiv, 199. appendixes. index. bibliography, 178-92.

Using data from studies of fifty-four societies, Young in this advanced anthropological treatise weighs the evidence for seeing male initiation ceremonies as a dramatization of sex-role recognition and male solidarity. Female initiation rites within the context of the family are also discussed.

HISTORICAL STUDIES

270. Brander, Michael. **The Victorian Gentleman.** London: Gordon Cremonesi Publishers, 1975. P. 215. illustrations. index. bibliography, 206-11.

In this richly illustrated book, Brander examines the life of the British Victorian gentleman from birth to adulthood. Separate chapters are devoted to birth and childhood, schooling, and university life. Adult life is covered in chapters examining taste and manners, morality and sex, sensational trials and wartime experiences, travel at home and abroad, India and empire, and sports and pastimes. Brander writes with understanding and sympathy of the masculine gender role. The text is illustrated with numerous period photographs and illustrations, some in color.

271. Cady, Edwin Harrison. **The Gentleman in America: A Literary Study in American Culture.** Syracuse, N.Y.: Syracuse University Press, 1949. P. 232. notes. index. Reprint. Westport, Conn.: Greenwood Press, 1969.

This readable, scholarly study traces the concept of the gentleman in American life and letters. Noting that gentlemanliness is as old as history, Cady explores the eighteenth-century British contrast between the rake and the Christian gentleman. In America a similar distinction contrasted the "fine" gentleman and the religious one, as well as the born gentleman of class and the natural gentleman of democracy.

Cady depicts John Adams as spectacularly a natural gentleman who had trouble reconciling his puritan pessimism about humanity with his democratic optimism. Exalting an *aristoi* of virtue and talent, Jefferson looked to universal education to bring it into existence. James Fenimore Cooper held up the idea of the agrarian gentleman, although his most memorable fictional gentleman are noble Indians and the natural gentleman, Natty Bumpo. While Oliver Wendell Holmes praised the gentlemanliness of proper Bostonians, Ralph Waldo Emerson championed the self-reliance of the natural gentleman who was also something of a social activist. Influenced by Tolstoy's writings, William Dean Howells exalted the gentleman as socialist. In a concluding chapter Cady sees the shift to feminism as making chivalry irrelevant; the new goal for the gentleman, he says, is discovering a self-validating way of life and thought.

272. Cawelti, John G. **Apostles of the Self-Made Man.** Chicago: University of Chicago Press, 1965. P. xiv, 279. illustrations. notes. index. bibliography, 259-71.

Tracing the cult of the self-made man through nineteenth- and twentieth-century America, Cawelti focuses upon three main sources of the myth: major figures like Benjamin Franklin, Thomas Jefferson, and Horatio Alger; success manuals and guides to different periods; and novels for adults and stories for children (almost always boys) in which the self-made man is a central figure. Contrasting with nineteenth-century celebrations of success and mobility in fiction and philosophy is twentieth-century ambivalence about success as a rat race rather than a dream. In addition to well-known authors like Twain, Howells, Dreiser, Fitzgerald, and Henry James, Cawelti examines the thought of John Dewey and of such popular advice givers as Norman Vincent Peale, Dale Carnegie, and Napoleon Hill. The connection between success and American masculinity, however, is not Cawelti's topic, and it must be inferred by the reader.

273. Dubbert, Joe L. **A Man's Place: Masculinity in Transition.** Englewood Cliffs, N.J.: Prentice-Hall, 1979. P. xi, 323. notes. index. essay on sources, 307-15. pa.

Dubbert traces the evolution of masculinity in the United States from the early 1800s to the present, using a rich assortment of historic and literary documents. The introduction states the case for studying men and masculinity: "Compared with what we know about the identity problems of women, we know relatively little about the American male's struggle with his identity." The American masculine gender role is traced in detail, almost decade-by-decade, as it was shaped by the frontier, capitalism, the changing nature of work, religion, family roles, wars, the women's movement, sports, and numerous other factors. In the epilogue Dubbert writes: "It has been my intention to suggest that men too have been trapped, that the identity and roles many men have assumed throughout American history have caused certain problems unique to male identity and fulfillment." The extensive notes contain a gold mine of primary materials for elucidating American masculinity.

274. Ferguson, Charles W. **The Male Attitude.** Boston: Little, Brown and Co., 1966. P. xiv, 365. notes. index.

Miffed by books like Philip Wylie's *Generation of Vipers* which blamed America's ills on Mom, Ferguson gallantly sets out to defend womanhood by denigrating manhood. The result is a debunking of American history and culture in which nearly everything that went wrong (and apparently nearly everything did) is blamed on men. Sweeping generalizations about male evil and ineptness are used to reduce history to a tale of man's inhumanity to women and to other men.

275.   Filene, Peter Gabriel. **Him/Her/Self: Sex Roles in Modern America.** New York: Harcourt Brace Jovanovich, 1974. P. xiv, 351. appendix. notes. an essay on research, 243-58. Reprint. New York: New American Library, Mentor, 1976. pa.

Filene began his study focusing on women only, but discovered that he could not understand women's roles without considering those of men: "Sex role is, by definition, a product of interaction between male and female; the history of one sex is only one half of the whole." *Him/Her/Self* begins its survey at the end of the Victorian era, 1890-1919. The first two chapters explore women and the world and women and the home. Chapter 3, "Men and Manliness," deals with such matters as the cult of success, temperance agitation, and the conflicting scripts for being a man. Chapter 4 discusses the impact of World War I on men and women. The book's second part deals with the modern era, 1920-1974, surveying the Depression, World War II, and the "domestic mystique" of the fifties. Filene concludes with an account of the turbulent sixties and the birth of the women's liberation movement and the men's movement. Filene's decision to braid the history of masculine and feminine gender roles makes sense, despite "the multitudes of books on women and the few on men." The extensive notes contain a storehouse of primary sources detailing gender roles of both sexes.

276.   Fraser, John. **America and the Patterns of Chivalry.** Cambridge, England: Cambridge University Press, 1982. P. x, 301. notes. index.

With dazzling erudition Fraser traces the influence of chivalric ideals and practices upon numerous aspects of nineteenth- and twentieth-century American life. He examines such areas as American politics, militarism, social life, literature, art, pop culture, radicalism, and education. In this study, however, the light thrown upon the American masculine gender role is usually oblique.

277.   Girouard, Mark. **The Return to Camelot: Chivalry and the English Gentleman.** New Haven, Conn. and London: Yale University Press, 1981. P. 312. illustrations. notes. index.

Although officially dead, the chivalric ideal has been an important shaper of modern masculinity, and a residue of chivalric behavior is still expected from men. Mark Girouard, an architectural historian, here traces the rise and fall of the cult of chivalry in Victorian and Edwardian England. Beginning amid the medieval yearnings of the Romantic period, the ideal of the knightly gentleman flourished during the Victorian age, influencing manners, politics, sports, love, and war. Extensively illustrated in color and black-and-white, *The Return to Camelot* demonstrates how the revival of chivalry affected the arts and literature. Girouard necessarily focuses upon the upper classes, but he also shows how chivalry affected the middle-class ideal of the gentleman, the curricula of British public (i.e., private) schools, and the manly virtues of the Boy Scout movement. In the early twentieth century, however, the concept of heroic combat trapped men in a rising tide of militarism that led them directly into the horrors of World War I trench warfare. Girouard depicts the absurdity, the nobility, and—finally—the tragedy of the neo-chivalric ideal.

278.　Haley, Bruce. **The Healthy Body and Victorian Culture**. Cambridge, Mass.: Harvard University Press, 1978. P. 296. notes. index.

Haley demonstrates how British Victorian society linked healthiness with manliness until intellectuals pressed for fuller concepts of both terms. Among the eminent Victorians discussed in depth are Carlyle, Spencer, Newman, Kingsley, the Arnolds (father and son), Thomas Hughes, George Eliot, and George Meredith.

279.　Honey, J.R. de S. **Tom Brown's Universe: The Development of the English Public School in the Nineteenth Century**. New York: Quadrangle/The New York Times Book Co., 1977. P. xv, 416. notes. index. bibliography, 408-10. Originally published in London: Millington Books, 1977.

This scholarly study of the nineteenth-century British public (i.e., private) schools indicates that even boys from the privileged classes enjoyed a decidedly mixed blessing in being sent to school, usually around eight years of age. Honey details the grinding studies, the bullying, the unsanitary conditions, the sexual immorality and exploitation, and the ruthless punishments—especially the ritual of the flogging block. Particularly interesting is the author's speculation that complacent parents knowingly sent off their sons to these torments in the belief that they would "harden" the boys and thus prepare them for assuming the male role in society.

280.　Kett, Joseph F. **Rites of Passage: Adolescence in America, 1790 to the Present**. New York: Basic Books, 1977. P. xiii, 327. illustrations. notes. index.

Kett has written a social history of adolescence in America, in particular of white male adolescents. For the purposes of this study, American history is divided into three time periods. In part I the author explores the early republic, 1790-1840. He notes the contemporary indefiniteness about age and age groups, the fact that adolescent sons were expected to work, the movement of young people from the farms to the chaotic new cities, the roles of schools and religious conversions in shaping young lives, and the mixture of oppression and freedom faced by youths. Part II, 1840-1900, describes how Americans defined adolescence first in girls, then in boys. Kett examines youthful resistance to dead-end jobs, the emergence of formal professional education, the cults of physical fitness and of muscular Christianity, and organizations like the YMCA. Part III, 1900 to the present, depicts the "invention" of adolescence and the growth of institutions geared to molding it. Kett's study is based upon a wealth of primary sources which are listed in the copious notes.

281.　Kirshner, Alan M. **Masculinity in an Historical Perspective: Readings and Discussions**. Washington, D.C.: University Press of America, 1977. P. iii, 173. illustrations. pa.

This book derives from the author's "A History of Masculinity" course at Ohlone College. Materials include lectures, edited discussions, and course reading materials on such topics as popular and scientific views of "cave man" masculinity,

masculinity in the classical world, Judaic-Christian views of masculinity, chivalry and courtly love, puritan and Victorian masculinity, Latin-American machismo, middle-class American masculinity, and new roles for men.

282.   Macleod, David I. **Building Character in the American Boy: The Boy Scouts, YMCA, and Their Forerunners, 1870-1920.** Madison: University of Wisconsin Press, 1983. P. xx, 404. notes. index.

This massive social history argues that character-building organizations for middle-class boys arose from middle-class concerns about transmitting their values. Macleod acknowledges social worries about masculinity, the feminization of schools, masturbation, and women's changing roles, but he concludes that reaction to urban life was the primary impetus behind the creation of the YMCA boys' departments, the Boy Scouts, and other groups. The copious notes reflect extensive research in primary sources. "Although the study of women's social roles has produced a large and sophisticated body of historical literature," Macleod notes, "inquiry into American men's gender roles is still highly exploratory."

283.   Pleck, Elizabeth H., and Joseph H. Pleck, eds. **The American Man.** Englewood Cliffs, N.J.: Prentice-Hall, 1980. P. xii, 433. notes. pa.

This anthology consists of sixteen previously printed essays on aspects of masculinity in American history. The introduction by the editors stresses the need to review what is known about men and to place this information in a new, gender-conscious light. Dividing American history into four periods—agrarian patriarchy (1630-1820), the commercial age (1820-1860), the strenuous life (1861-1919), and companionate providing (1920-1965)—the editors then provide an overview of each period, preparing the way for the more narrowly focused essays which follow. These studies range from Robert Oaks's account of sodomy and buggery in seventeenth-century New England to Joseph H. Pleck's analysis of the men's movement. The contributors include Eugene D. Genovese on slave husbands and fathers, Jeffrey P. Hantover on the significance of the Boy Scout movement, Joe L. Dubbert on Progressivism and the masculinity crisis, Peter Gabriel Filene on men in World War I, Mirra Komarovsky on unemployed husbands during the Depression, and Marc Fasteau on toughness in American foreign policy. Of special interest also are Blanche Glassman Hersh's account of nineteenth-century feminist marriages (which were not always made in heaven), Charles E. Rosenberg's wide-ranging assessment of sexuality, class, and role in nineteenth-century America, and Jon M. Kingsdale's view of the saloon as the "poor man's club."

284.   Pugh, David G. **Sons of Liberty: The Masculine Mind in Nineteenth-Century America.** Westport, Conn.: Greenwood Press, 1983. P. xxii, 186. notes. index. bibliography, 171-78.

Combining psychological, cultural, and historical insights, Pugh traces the American cult of masculinity from Jacksonian democracy, through the Gilded Age, and into the he-man literature of twentieth-century popular magazines. A chapter devoted to "the female foil" concludes that women were not all the passive victims depicted in current assessments.

285.   Rischin, Moses, ed. **The American Gospel of Success: Individualism and Beyond.** Chicago: Quadrangle Books, 1965. P. x, 431. bibliography, 431.

Rischin performs a valuable service by collecting forty-eight documents which define and proclaim the American gospel of success. Although rarely spelled out in the documents themselves, their relation to the American man's gender role is obvious. Selections include a sermon by Cotton Mather, an excerpt from Benjamin Franklin's *Poor Richard Improved*, P.T. Barnum on "the art of money-getting," an abridged tale by Horatio Alger, and advice from Andrew Carnegie. The editor also includes a selection of scholarly works examining the gospel's effects upon big business, as well as writings depicting the fates of outsiders (e.g., minorities, the poor, the nonbelievers in the gospel). Other writings explore the means of excluding nonconformists from becoming members of the economic elect, the fate of the gospel in recent times, and the uneasy rapprochement between Christianity and the gospel of success.

286. Stearns, Peter N. **Be a Man! Males in Modern Society**. New York: Holmes and Meier Publishers, 1979. P. 230. illustrations. notes. index. bibliography, 225-26. pa.

Starting with a discussion of manhood as a social construct, *Be a Man!* surveys changes in the masculine gender role in Western Europe and North America from the Industrial Revolution to the present. Noting the dearth of literature on men in society, Stearns conducts a quick review of history from hunting and agricultural societies to the preindustrial world of eighteenth-century Europe and America. Focusing on his principal subject, Stearns argues that industrialism fundamentally changed the traditional concepts of masculinity by changing the nature of labor and property and by moving work outside the home, thereby dividing labor more radically between the sexes. Working-class males were separated from their families, with the home becoming women's province. Middle-class males were split between the demands of work and family life, between the roles of aggressive competitor and nurturing husband-father. As the family's enforced breadwinner, the man could be overwhelmed attempting to support a growing family. Stearn's account of manhood in the twentieth century reviews the impact of World War I and the women's movement; he argues, however, that the feminist movement has not significantly affected most men, although the anti-male hostility of some feminists threatens to deflect men from making changes that were already in progress. Stearns warns against thoughtlessly abandoning familiar concepts of manhood: "It is time not so much to take a new course as to articulate the course that men have been on." The book closes with a thoughtful essay on themes in contemporary manhood.

287. Strauss, Sylvia. **"Traitors to the Masculine Cause": The Men's Campaign for Women's Rights**. Contributions in Women's Studies, no. 35. Westport, Conn.: Greenwood Press, 1982. P. xix, 292. illustrations. index. bibliography, 273-79.

Tracing the history of the Fathers of Feminism, Strauss provides a connected account of the most important men who aided the women's movement in nineteenth-century England and America. After exploring the roots of male feminism in eighteenth-century radicalism, Strauss then focuses upon such major figures as John Stuart Mill, George Bernard Shaw, and Frederick Pethick-Lawrence, whose devotion to the cause led to imprisonment, financial ruin, and eventual ostracism by Emmeline and Christabel Pankhurst. The book also devotes considerable space to a host of other males, including William Godwin, Francis Place,

William Thompson, Robert Owen, Charles Bradlaugh, John Humphrey Noyes, W.T. Stead, George Meredith, Richard Pankhurst, Henry Fawcett, Jacob Bright, Charles Dilke, Keir Hardie, and Floyd Dell. Organizations like the Men's Political Union for Women's Suffrage and the Men's League for Women's Suffrage are also studied. Strauss divides the male partisans into two camps: the domestic feminists who saw woman's lot as tied to the home and who tried to ameliorate her situation there, and the philosophical feminists who worked for women's equal participation in public life as well. The latter—and more significant—group, believing that femininity was more democratic and compassionate than masculinity, hoped that including women in the political process would help to humanize it. Strauss's narrative closes after World War I and the granting of suffrage, although she traces briefly some developments to the present and comments on the ambiguous success of the recent women's liberation movement. Despite its subject, the book accords no positive traits to masculinity: terms like "masculine" and "masculinity" carry negative connotations and are identified with exploitive capitalism, power politics, and militarism.

288. Wyllie, Irvin G. **The Self-Made Man in America: The Myth of Rags to Riches.** New Brunswick, N.J.: Rutgers University Press, 1954. P. ix, 210. illustrations. notes. index. bibliography, 197-205. Reprint. New York: The Free Press, 1966. pa.

Few American men can have escaped being influenced by the gospel of success which flourished in the nineteenth century and which, despite a lingering decline in the twentieth, still flavors American life. In this cult of the self-made man, the causes of triumph or failure were believed to lie in the man rather than in the environment. Thus, the rags-to-riches "myth" supposedly put a man's manhood to the test, a test most men were destined to fail or to pass only modestly. In this readable survey, Wyllie traces the gospel of self-reliance from early American exemplars like Benjamin Franklin through the rise of such major figures as Andrew Carnegie to the gospel's gradual dimunition in the twentieth century. The anti-idleness doctrine, which spurred on many men to hard work as a badge of manliness, was preached far and wide by Protestant clergymen, journalists, authors, lecturers, and educators. Wyllie finds that social Darwinism had less influence in America than is usually believed. He shows how the self-help gospel was attacked from the right by those who exalted aristocratic culture and from the left by those who argued that social conditions, not personal attributes, determined financial success.

Cross references:

1. Grady, Kathleen E., Robert Brannon, and Joseph H. Pleck, comps. **The Male Sex Role: A Selected and Annotated Bibliography.**

4. Astin, Helen S., Allison Parelman, and Anne Fisher, comps. **Sex Roles: A Research Bibliography.**

22. David, Deborah S., and Robert Brannon, eds. **The Forty-Nine Percent Majority: The Male Sex Role.**

25. Kriegel, Leonard, ed. **The Myth of American Manhood.**

27. Petras, John W., ed. **Sex: Male/Gender: Masculine: Readings in Male Sexuality.**

28. Pleck, Joseph H., and Jack Sawyer, eds. **Men and Masculinity.**

47. Goldberg, Steven. **The Inevitability of Patriarchy.**

205. Ehrenreich, Barbara. **The Hearts of Men: American Dreams and the Flight from Commitment.**

545. Bamber, Linda. **Comic Women, Tragic Men: A Study of Gender and Genre in Shakespeare.**

549. Kahn, Coppélia. **Man's Estate: Masculine Identity in Shakespeare.**

551. Lynn, Kenneth S. **The American Dream: A Study of the Modern American Imagination.**

565. Liebow, Elliot. **Tally's Corner: A Study of Negro Streetcorner Men.**

567. Sochen, June, ed. **The Black Man and the American Dream: Negro Aspirations in America, 1900-1930.**

568. Staples, Robert. **Black Masculinity: The Black Man's Role in American Society.**

571. Whyte, William Foote. **Street Corner Society: The Social Structure of an Italian Slum.**

PSYCHOLOGY

289. Bowskill, Derek, and Anthea Linacre. **Men: The Sensitive Sex**. London: Frederick Muller, 1977. P. vii, 150. pa.

This exercise in popular psychology offers observations on such topics as impotence, the current battle of the sexes, fantasy and masturbation, gender role traps, and therapy. Discussion is sometimes marred by trendy misandry.

290. Chesler, Phyllis. **About Men**. New York: Simon and Schuster, 1978. P. xx, 283. illustrations. bibliography, 265-81. Reprint. New York: Bantam Books, 1979. pa.

In this "multidimensional" approach to the psychosexual bases of male personality, part I is devoted to mytho-poetic interpretations of selected works of art. In stanzas of prose-poetry, Chesler touches upon infanticide and cannibalism as the masculine "original sin," uterus envy, the conflict between sons and mothers, phallic sexuality, and male-male violence. In part II the author provides vignettes from her relationships with men—with her Jewish father who drove a truck in Brooklyn; with her first husband, a Moslem, who took her home to a patriarchal family and society in central Asia where their marriage deteriorated; with an assortment of lovers who were always imperfect in some way; and with various teachers, supervisors, and colleagues who usually exhibited some masculine psychic malady. In part III, "An Essay About Men," Chesler reinterprets the oedipal drama to show the son learning how to placate a threatening and rejecting father through fear and performance. She discusses male sexuality as compulsive and egocentric, and reverts to the topic of male-male and male-female violence. An epilogue closes the book with horror stories of masculine violence from newspaper clippings. Chesler's professed compassion and concern for humanity are belied by her animosity toward the male half of humankind and by her almost entirely negative assessment of masculine psychosexuality. Reader reaction to *About Men* is likely to range from those who regard it as an imaginative descent into the lower depths of the male psyche, to those who regard it as a slick example of anti-male hate literature welling up from the lower depths of Chesler's psyche.

291. Dinnerstein, Dorothy. **The Mermaid and the Minotaur: Sexual Arrangements and Human Malaise**. New York: Harper and Row, 1976. P. xv, 288. notes. bibliography, 286-88. pa.

Deliberately quirky and convoluted, *The Mermaid and the Minotaur* argues that female domination of childrearing guarantees malaise in sexual arrangements. Because mother is the first denier of the infant's wishes, she bears the brunt of human disappointments with life. She becomes a "scapegoat goddess." The child must eventually react against her, the boy by bonding with his father and the girl by idealizing him. Male domination in society and the sexual double standard are accepted by both males and females because of a need to control female (i.e., mother's) will. But the flight from the female tyranny of childhood results in acceptance of patriarchal tyranny later in life. By blocking male access to child-rearing, mother domination deforms both sexes, shrinking the willful-executive propensities in women and the empathic-nurturant propensities in men. Only when both sexes participate in childrearing will the resulting imbalance in personality characteristics and social arrangements be remedied. Throughout the book, Dinnerstein modifies Freudian psychology with insights from such thinkers as Margaret Mead, Simone de Beauvoir, Norman O. Brown, and Herbert Marcuse. Some readers will be irritated by the book's labyrinthine prose with its interrupting notes and "boxes" of digressive observations. Others may find that, despite her frequently successful efforts to treat both sexes evenhandedly, Dinnerstein at times reproduces sexist stereotypes of males borrowed too uncritically from militant feminists. Still other readers may find that, despite its drawbacks, the book is an original, perceptive, and thought-provoking assessment of the effects of female-dominated childrearing.

292.   Etheredge, Lloyd S. **A World of Men: The Private Sources of American Foreign Policy**. Cambridge, Mass.: MIT Press, 1978. P. xv, 178. illustrations. appendixes. notes. bibliography, 157-67.

Etheredge attempts to link mistakes in American foreign policy to specific personality characteristics. Because virtually all world political figures are male, he is concerned with identifying features of male psychology which contribute to such failures. Noting the poor track record of modern political figures in planning and winning wars (the Bay of Pigs fiasco is taken as a representative case), the author examines evidence connecting officials' behavior and decisions with particular personality traits. Drawing upon a 1971-1972 State Department survey and other evidence, Etheredge finds that such charactersitics as dominance, ambition, and competitiveness—all traits which assure political ascendancy—also produce a paranoid view of political "others." "Male narcissism syndromes" are examined in which this paranoia can be linked with machismo to create in the individual a desire to see his country as a paternalistic benefactor of other nations. Etheredge presents a psychohistory of twentieth-century political decisions, linking historical particulars to individuals and personality types. He concludes that heroic ambition has its darker side and that the virtually all-male composition of world politics increases the likelihood of war.

293.   Fine, George. **Sex Jokes and Male Chauvinism**. Secaucus, N.J.: Citadel Press, 1981. P. 236.

Long on examples and short on analysis, Fine's book stresses the misogynist character of many jokes—although among the dozens of examples included many are aimed at males, many simply delight in being naughty, and many revel in women and sexuality. Fine's indignation about an ill-defined group of "male chauvinists" will strike many readers as a trendy but threadbare response to the material he presents.

294.   Freud, Sigmund. **The Standard Edition of the Complete Psychological Works of Sigmund Freud.** 24 vols. Ed. James Strachey, with Angela Richards. Translated by James Strachey, with Anna Freud, Alix Strachey, and Alan Tyson. London: Hogarth Press and The Institute of Psycho-analysis, 1966-1974. illustrations. appendixes. Notes, indexes, and bibliography in vol. 24.

Freud's understanding of male psychology permeates nearly everything he wrote and has crucially shaped modern thinking about males, if only in some cases as a point of departure for disagreement. General readers may want to start with *An Autobiographical Study* (1925, 1935), in which Freud crystallizes his career and the history of psychoanalysis, thereby providing a concise introduction to both. Fuller understanding of Freud's view of the dynamics of the mind—including such matters as the Oedipus complex, repression, fixation, and the conscious and the unconcious—can be obtained from such shorter works as *Five Lectures on Psychoanalysis* (1910), *The Ego and the Id* (1923), and *An Outline of Psychoanalysis* (1940), which shows Freud late in his career still rethinking the possibilities of his formulations. For the larger implications of Freud's ideas, *Civilization and Its Discontents* (1930, 1931) provides a succinct statement of the cost to the individual of civilized society. Those interested in the particular ramifications of Freud's views of males may want to start with the essay "The Most Prevalent Form of Degradation in Erotic Life" (1912), dealing with the boy's incestuous desires for his mother, and *Totem and Taboo* (1912, 1913) with its account of "original sin" in the primal horde consisting of the father's murder by his sons for possession of the females. Also, *Leonardo da Vinci and a Memory of His Childhood* (1910, 1919, 1923) shows Freud psychoanalyzing a famous man and "reading" several of his paintings. Individual paperbound editions of many of Freud's works are published by W.W. Norton and Co.

295.   Grinker, Roy R., and John P. Spiegel. **Men under Stress.** Rev. ed. New York: McGraw-Hill Book Co., 1963. P. xii, 484. index. bibliography, 461-63. pa.

In this classic study of the mental and emotional damage that combat can do to males, the authors present sixty-five case histories from their work with World War II Army Air Force combat fliers. The concluding chapter examines implications for civilian psychiatry. This book first appeared in 1945.

296.   Johnson, Robert A. **He! A Contribution to Understanding Masculine Psychology, Based on the Legend of Parsifal and His Search for the Grail, and Using Jungian Psychological Concepts.** King of Prussia, Pa.: Religious Publishing Co., 1974. P. 97. illustrations. bibliography, 95-96. Reprint. *He: Understanding Masculine Psychology, Based on the Legend of Parsifal and his Search for the Grail, Using Jungian Psychological Concepts.* New York: Harper and Row, Perennial Library, 1977. pa.

The subtitle epitomizes the book. Johnson traces the Parsifal story, elucidating it in Jungian terms and describing the challenges facing males throughout the life cycle. He extends his comments into practical matters, suggesting how men and women can best cope with various stages of life. He warns, for example, of the sexism which can arise if the male confuses the feminine *anima* of his own self with flesh and blood women. An appendix by Margaret Brown synopsizes the Parsifal legend according to Chrétien de Troyes. John A. Sanford's introduction summarizes the relevant elements of Jung's thought. The foreword by Ruth Tiffany Barnhouse concludes: "Men who read it will surely learn much about themselves, and women—particularly those who are unfortunately misled into thinking of men as 'the enemy'—will find it a real eye-opener."

297. Jung, C. G. **Freud and Psychoanalysis.** Translated by R.F.C. Hull. **The Collected Works of C.G. Jung**, vol. 4. Bollingen Series, XX. Princeton, N.J.: Princeton University Press, 1961, 1970. pa.

This volume contains one of Jung's few statements dealing at some length with fathers and children, "The Significance of the Father in the Destiny of the Individual," first published in 1909 and revised considerably in 1949. Jung stresses the great influence for good or evil of the father upon the child, citing four case histories illustrating the negative impact of paternal behavior. In later additions to the essay, Jung argues that the father's "magical" ability to shape children's lives derives not from the individual but from the archetype of the father carried in the collective unconscious. The danger is that an unconscious identification with the archetype by the father can result in an irresponsible and even psychotic parent-child relationship. Usually, the feelings engendered by the father archetype are referred to a positive or negative deity, a god or a devil. Jung examines the story of Sara, Raguel, and Asmodeus from the biblical "Book of Tobias" to illustrate the Janus-like character of a father's influence. Also included in this volume is Jung's *The Theory of Psychoanalysis* (1929, 1955) which contains a discussion of the Oedipus complex and the Electra complex. Sons are not the only ones to be caught in the tensions of family romance, Jung argues. In the case of both complexes, however, these tensions do not usually lead to incest but are dissipated as the libido finds other objects of desire.

298. Jung, Carl G., M. -L. von Franz, Joseph L. Henderson, Jolande Jacobi, and Aniela Jaffé. **Man and His Symbols.** London: Aldus Books Ltd., Jupiter Books, 1964. P. 320. illustrations. notes. index. pa. Reprint. New York: Dell Publishing Co., Laurel, 1968. pa.

For nonspecialists, this beautifully illustrated volume is perhaps the best introduction to Jung's psychology of men and women. It contains "Approaching the Unconscious," one of Jung's last and most clearly written summaries of his thought. Especially helpful for understanding Jung's concept of the female *anima* and the male *animus* is M. -L. von Franz's essay "The Process of Individuation." Readers should experience this exposition of Jung's vision in the Aldus edition with its larger type and clear illustrations, many in color.

299. Kiley, Dan. **The Peter Pan Syndrome: Men Who Have Never Grown Up.** New York: Dodd, Mead, and Co., 1983. P. xxvii, 281. bibliography, 275-81.

Borrowing the name of James Barrie's "boy who would not grow up," Kiley defines what he calls the Peter Pan Syndrome (PPS). Arguing that sex-role confusion, parental neglect, and social indifference have produced a large number of males who either cannot or will not assume an adult male role, Kiley plots the victim's social profile from ages twelve through fifty. Usually the oldest male child of a middle- or upper-class family, the PPS victim is often charming, exhibits a consuming interest in parties, and is often irresponsible and irresolute—except in later years when he may develop into a workaholic. He also suffers from anxiety and loneliness, which he hides beneath nice-boy or macho masks. His sex-role confusion often expresses itself in narcissism and chauvinism. Kiley provides a PPS test to aid in spotting victims, and he offers advice for parents, wives and lovers, friends and siblings, and the victims themselves in how to overcome the deleterious effects of the syndrome. "Girls have a license to actualize both the masculine and feminine sides of their personality," he writes. "Boys don't have this same license." While girls have been given new scripts for their sex roles (sometimes with contradictory directives), boys are stuck with the same old script—or left with none to follow.

300. Mitscherlich, Alexander. **Society without the Father: A Contribution to Social Psychology**. Translated by Eric Mosbacher. New York: Harcourt, Brace, and World, 1969. P. xi, 329. notes. name and subject indexes. Reprint. New York: Schocken Books, 1970. pa. Originally published as *Auf dem Weg zur vaterlosen Gesellschaft* (Munich: R. Piper and Co. Verlag, 1963).

Aimed at an audience familiar with Freudian depth psychology, *Society without the Father* explores the breakdown of "paternal" and "paternalistic" authority in modern mass society, with the accompanying difficulties of maintaining individual freedom and responsibility in the restructuring of the social order. Mitscherlich touches on a wide range of topics, including the dynamics of adaptation, the need for human "re-education," roles and masks, and the concept of taboo. General readers will probably find most accessible chapter 7, "The Invisible Father," which discusses the effects upon modern society of father absence from the home, and chapter 12, "Two Kinds of Fatherlessness," which includes discussion of the mass leader as collective father figure: "surprising as it may seem, he is much more like the imago of a primitive mother-goddess" who "demands a regressive obedience and the begging behaviour that belongs to the behaviour pattern of a child in the pre-Oedipal stage." Indeed, terms like "paternal" and "paternalistic" when applied to modern society are misleading: "The nation is still referred to out of habit as *la patrie*, the fatherland, land of the fathers, etc., but the passive, demanding attitude to it betrays a deeper tie; it is nuzzled against as if it were a mother goddess with innumerable breasts."

301. Mullahy, Patrick. **Oedipus, Myth and Complex: A Review of Psychoanalytic Theory**. New York: Hermitage Press, 1948. P. xix, 538. notes. bibliography, 532-38. Reprint. New York: Grove Press, 1955. pa.

A crucial component in twentieth-century psychology of males, the Oedipus complex is surveyed in this volume. An extended review of the theories of Sigmund Freud, Alfred Adler, C.G. Jung, Otto Rank, Karen Horney, Erich Fromm, and Harry Stack Sullivan is followed by a complete translation of the three Oedipus plays by Sophocles.

302. Rochlin, Gregory. **The Masculine Dilemma: A Psychology of Masculinity.** Boston: Little, Brown and Co., 1980. P. xii, 310. notes. index.

Rejecting the fashionable trend of treating boys and girls alike, Rochlin presents a Freudian analysis of male psychology in which the boy's need to establish his masculine identity is prelude to the man's continuing effort to do so. "There are not only special difficulties in becoming masculine," Rochlin writes, "but also in maintaining it throughout life." In childhood, when the boy must differentiate himself from the feminine, his penis is a source of pride which lowers females in his estimation. Boys engage "naturally" in aggressive play, stimulated in part by mothers who live vicariously in their achievements. Drawing upon Freud's famous studies, such as those of Little Hans, Judge Schreber, and the Wolf Man, as well as case histories from his own practice, Rochlin examines the boy's fears of loss and abandonment, which are usually more severe than those of girls. He indicates the problems that can arise when boys and girls are naively regarded as possessing the same psychological make-up. In later chapters Rochlin examines literary classics—for example, *Gilgamesh*, the Homeric epics, *Tom Sawyer*, and *Lord Jim*—and the phases of male youth and adulthood. Masculinity is depicted as "a precariously held, endlessly tested, unstable condition" which must be reaffirmed at each phase of a man's life.

303. Ruitenbeek, Henrik M., ed. **Psychoanalysis and Male Sexuality.** New Haven, Conn.: College and University Press, 1966. P. 268. notes. bibliographies after some chapters. pa.

Although dated, the fourteen articles in this collection also contain some thought-provoking observations. Contributions include Melanie Klein on early stages of the Oedipus conflict, Karen Horney on the dread of women, and Felix Boehm on the femininity complex in men, as well as discussions of such topics as initiation rites, the castration complex, phallic passivity in men, transvestism, and fetishism.

304. Skovholt, Thomas M., Paul G. Schauble, and Richard Davis, eds. **Counseling Men.** Monterey, Calif.: Brooks/Cole Publishing Co., 1980. P. x, 213. notes. index. bibliographies after each chapter.

This book collects eighteen articles about men's roles and their significance for the counselor. After an introductory overview of the men's movement and current men's issues by Thomas M. Skovholt and Art Hansen, the second section of the book assembles seven articles examining more closely several aspects of men's awareness, including Joseph H. Pleck's discussion of men's power with women and other men and Robert A. Lewis's account of the roadblocks to emotional intimacy among men. Other essays contain examinations of what constitutes a definition of a competent male, the components of male heterosexual behavior, male homosexuality, and males' reluctance to undertake psychotherapy. In the concluding section of ten essays on intervention, topics include the problems of boys' behavior in "feminized" schoolrooms, special considerations in counseling black males, characteristics and treatment of sex offenders, treatment of secondary impotence, healing the divided allegiance which men face between work and family ("The time has come to change the world outside the client," Michael Berger and Larry Wright conclude), the process of involving men in childbirth and bonding with children, a psychoeducational model for classes on fathering, fathers with child custody, helping men to cope with a child's death, and the male in marital and family therapy. Although compiled primarily for therapists and counselors, the material in this book is likely to impress other readers as both pertinent and enlightening.

305.   Solomon. Kenneth, and Norman B. Levy, eds. **Men in Transition: Theory and Therapy**. New York and London: Plenum Press, 1982. P. xiv, 503. notes. index.

An important distillation of current research and views on men's gender roles, the twenty essays in this volume provide insight and controversy. John Money's introduction makes significant distinctions among sex-irreducible roles, sex-derivative roles, sex-adjunctive roles, and sex-arbitrary roles. James M. O'Neil surveys men's changes in the seventies and the relevant literature of men's awareness, and Kenneth Solomon analyzes the current characteristics of masculinity and their effects upon men. Reviewing such people as Freud, Jung, Sullivan, Mahler, Erikson, Levinson, and Vaillant, Martin R. Wong places men's gender identity into the context of psychoanalytic-developmental theory. Solomon discusses the process of altering male roles in psychotherapy, and Marvin R. Goldfried and Jerry M. Friedman describe the gender role behavior that brings men into therapy. Androgyny is explored by Jacqueline Boles and Charlotte Tatro. Jack O. Balswick examines the causes, effects, and possible treatment for male inexpressiveness, while David A. Dosser Jr. provides a lengthy exposition of behavioral intervention for inexpressiveness. A survey of recent gay awareness is provided by Joseph L. Norton, and Robert E. Gould argues that the tidal wave of impotence caused by women's liberation is largely fictional. Theodore Nadelson and Carol Nadelson explore the pitfalls and promises of dual-career families, and Ellen Halle describes the abandoned husband. Fathers also suffer from the empty-nest syndrome, argue Robert A. Lewis and Craig L. Roberts, and Solomon describes older men. Men's groups are analyzed by Terry S. Stein. Perhaps best of all are the rebuttals: Wolfgang Lederer's and Alexandra Botwin's call for male heroism, Richard L. Grant's questioning of the new roles described for men, and (above all) Lederer's ringing riposte to current shibboleths about male inexpressiveness, androgyny, the alleged oppression of women by men, and the value of the more "feminized" man. The capstone of a distinguished volume, Lederer's "Counterepilogue" is "must" reading for anyone interested in men's awareness.

306.   von Franz, Marie-Louise. **The Problem of the Puer Aeternus**. New York: Spring Publications, 1970. P. ca. 300. illustrations. pa.

In this series of twelve lecture-discussions, von Franz examines the Jungian archetype of the *puer aeternus* or eternal boy. In antiquity he appears as a child-god (Iacchus, Dionysus, Eros) associated with vegetation and resurrection, the counterpart of such oriental deities as Tammuz, Attis, and Adonis. He appears in literature as well. Analyzing *The Little Prince* at length, von Franz links the story's symbolism with the archetype, with the author's life, and with the problem of men identified with the *puer aeternus*. Such men suffer from a "mother complex" which can result in the son's homosexuality or Don Juan-like promiscuity. *Puer aeternus* men can be charming and irresponsible, never wishing to grow up and assume an adult male role. Von Franz conducts a wide-ranging analysis which touches on such matters as the need for male initiation rites to be shielded from the mockery of the over-protective mother, as well as the frustrating relationships which can develop between *puer aeternus* men and their women. In later chapters von Franz conducts an extensive analysis of Bruno Goetz's *The Kingdom Without Space* (1919, 1925). One cure for the *puer aeternus* problem, von Franz argues, lies in work—the day-in, day-out variety that requires self-discipline and self-motivation.

307. Wellisch, E. **Isaac and Oedipus: A Study in Biblical Psychology of the Sacrifice of Isaac *The Akedah*.** London: Routledge and Kegan Paul, 1954. P. xi, 131. illustrations. author and general indexes. bibliography, 117-23.

Although many kinds of infanticide have existed, Wellisch focuses on paternal sacrifices of sons. He presents evidence of such sacrifices in early societies, explicates the Oedipus complex as a partly successful attempt to reconcile paternal-filial tensions, and views *The Akedah* (the biblical story of Abraham and Isaac) as marking the resolution of the conflict.

Cross references:

52. Hoch, Paul. **White Hero, Black Beast: Racism, Sexism and the Mask of Masculinity.**

160. Ursin, Holger, Eivind Baade, and Seymour Levine, eds. **Psychobiology of Stress: A Study of Coping Men.**

396. Colman, Arthur, and Libby Colman. **Earth Father/Sky Father: The Changing Concept of Fathering.**

SEXUALITY_____

308. Bennett, Alan H., ed. **Management of Male Impotence**. International
      Perspectives in Urology, vol. 5. Baltimore: Williams and Wilkins, 1982.
      P. xvi, 253. illustrations. index. bibliographies after each chapter.
This volume collects nineteen scholarly papers on aspects of male sexual function,
including impotence—its various causes and possible correctives.

309. Brandes, David, ed. **Male Accessory Sex Organs: Structure and Function**.
      New York: Academic Press, 1974. P. xi, 527. illustrations. author and
      subject indexes. bibliographies after each chapter.
This collection consists of nineteen scholarly articles on sex hormones, structure of
accessory sex organs, hormone action, and immunology and systematic
abnormalities.

310. Brooks, Marvin B., with Sally West Brooks. **Lifelong Sexual Vigor: How to
      Avoid and Overcome Impotence**. Garden City, N.Y.: Doubleday and Co.,
      1981. P. xii, 249. index. bibliography, 225-35.
This clear and thorough guide for general readers points out that both partners are
necessarily affected by erectile difficulties. After explaining the mechanics of
normal erections and surveying historical views of impotence, the book examines
possible causes. Physical causes include birth defects, injuries, diseases, surgery,
hormonal problems, medications, smoking, alcohol, and chemicals. Among the
psychological causes are performance anxiety, stress, parent-child problems
stemming from the male's upbringing, homosexuality, marital discord, midlife
crisis, personality characteristics, and aging. Possible treatments are surveyed,
including aphrodisiacs, sexual aids, techniques for discovering whether the problem
is physical or psychological, sex therapy, and penile prostheses. A final chapter
explores the woman's role in coping with impotence.

311. Caprio, Frank S. **The Sexually Adequate Male**. New York: Citadel Press,
      1952. P. ix, 213. illustrations. index. pa.
As a period piece showing the kind of sexual advice men were given in the fifties,
Caprio's book serves well. It is clearly written for a general audience and reflects
post-Kinsey views. Some of the advice is still valid, but readers may be intrigued
by the burdens imposed upon the honeymooning groom (he was expected to play

Prince Charming and erotic expert to a sexually ignorant virgin), as well as the views on oral sex, homosexuality, and "male menopause."

312. Carlton, Eric. **Sexual Anxiety: A Study of Male Impotence.** New York: Harper and Row, Barnes and Noble Import Division, 1980. P. viii, 197. notes. index. bibliography, 187-93. Originally published Oxford, England: Martin Robertson and Co., 1980.

Chatty, informed, and skeptical, Carlton surveys for the general reader what is known about impotence. Noting the difficulty of defining impotence, he settles upon "the conscious intention to attempt intercourse that fails for involuntary reasons," a definition he readily admits has its own problems. Equally slippery is the attempt to define "normal" sexual performance, for this can vary from one culture to another, and it can be influenced by such matters as age, illness, and drugs. Carlton provides an overview of impotence in primitive and ancient societies before sketching in the contemporary situation. Seven case histories are presented to illustrate the range of impotence. After reviewing theories of male sexual dysfunction (physiological, sensuality-deprivation, psychological, and sociological), Carlton describes and evaluates prevailing forms of sex therapy, especially those of Masters and Johnson. Among the conclusions is the link between dominant fathers and impotent sons, and that between dominant mothers and premature ejaculation in sons.

313. Castleman, Michael. **Sexual Solutions: An Informative Guide.** New York: Simon and Schuster, 1980. P. 287. illustrations. appendixes. index. bibliography, 269-72.

Aimed primarily at male readers, *Sexual Solutions* discusses an unusually wide range of sexually related topics in informal, witty, jargon-free prose. The book's basic message is that men should aspire to be neither "cavemen" nor "delivery boys," that is, neither would-be sexual superstars nor "nice guys" who let women run the entire show. Castleman advocates sensitive sensuality or mutually satisfying lovemaking, arguing that men and women are usually alike in their preferences. He rejects the term "foreplay" for "loveplay." Castleman explores male hangups (such as concern with penis size), suggests techniques for lasting longer, and describes ways of dealing with erection problems. (Castleman avoids terms like "premature ejaculation" and "impotence.") He distinguishes between orgasm and ejaculation, and describes what turns women on—and off. A chapter is devoted to how a man can cope with the situation when the woman he loves is raped. He discusses male contraception, noting that with the health hazards associated with the pill and the IUD, the condom is making a comeback. Various sexual infections are described, and the final chapter is devoted to sexual self-care for men. Appendix I describes male and female anatomies; appendix II contains a national directory (edited by Kristi Beer) of sex therapists.

314. Ellis, Albert. **Sex and the Liberated Man.** Secaucus, N.J.: Lyle Stuart, 1976. P. 347. index. bibliography, 309-36.

An extensively rewritten and updated version of Ellis's *Sex and the Single Man* (1963), this volume attempts to take into account the dramatic changes in the sexual and social landscape of America since the sixties. An enthusiastic cheerleader of the "erotic revolution," Ellis gleefully turns the tables on prudes by arguing that abstention from sex can be physically, mentally, and sexually harmful. Writing with gusto, he praises the benefits of masturbation and offers suggestions on avoiding guilt over erotic pleasure. Having listened sympathetically to feminist critics of male sexual attitudes and performance, Ellis transmits their complaints to men, repeatedly warning males not to equate sex simply with coitus. He recognizes, however, that despite women's liberation men will still have to take the initiative sexually most of the time. Discussing techniques of arousing women and of "petting" (noncoital erotic activity), he also suggests how a man can help a woman with sexual problems and how men can help themselves with such problems as fast ejaculation, lack of erection, and so on. Ellis also recognizes that sexual intercourse is still of major importance, and he devotes a chapter to techniques and positions. The concluding chapter discussing what is and is not a sexual disturbance reverts to Ellis's major themes of enjoying sex and of modifying one's behavior through the conscious method of rational-emotive therapy.

315.   Fanta, Robert D. **The Fanta Sex Report: Self-Help for Male Hang-Ups.** Los Alamitos, Calif.: Hwong Publishing Co., 1980. P. 48. appendixes. bibliography, 44-47.

Although recognizing a variety of causes, this brief report focuses on how male impotence can be created and maintained by the female partner. After reviewing research on the topic, Fanta describes ways in which the female contributes to male impotence, and he provides a chapter of self-help suggestions for alleviating the situation. One appendix lists the reasons why a person may decline sex; the other describes the Masters and Johnson technique of sex therapy.

316.   Fellman, Sheldon L., and Paul Neimark. **The Virile Man.** New York: Stein and Day, 1976. P. 228.

A urologist and surgeon, Fellman believes that most sex therapy takes too long. In this book he guides the reader through a sampling of his cases involving male sexual problems, including impotence, premature ejaculation, latent homosexuality, "castrating" women, and difficulties with attaining male ideals of performance. Fellman attepts to treat the problems in a sixty-minute session or two. Despite successes, he cannot help all patients. Discussing the cases, Fellman makes such generalizations as "men in America are now having more sexual problems than ever, and have been made to think those problems are of their own making—when much of the time the responsibility lies with their partners."

317.   Friday, Nancy. **Men in Love: Men's Sexual Fantasies: The Triumph of Love over Rage.** New York: Delacorte Press, 1980. P. xii, 528. Reprint. New York: Dell Publishing Co., 1981. pa.

From approximately three thousand responses from males describing their sexual fantasies, Friday has selected approximately two hundred for publication, making no claims concerning the representativeness of the responses. The printed fantasies are divided into twenty-one groupings (including oral sex, anal sex, bisexuals, and sadomasochism), and although sometimes abridged the responses are not expurgated. Throughout the book, Friday comments understandingly on the fantasies, relating them to psychological theory. The introductory chapter, "The Masculine Conflict," indicates that some fantasies may represent the triumph of men's love over their rage at women, especially the internalized female who proscribes sexual expression. Only a tiny minority of men, however, report rape fantasies; maso-chistic scenarios are far more common. Like the comments throughout the book, the introduction reflects sympathetic insight into men's lives and roles. "Given the way the family and society are set up," Friday asks, "is the male role so enviable?"

318.   Hass, Aaron. **Love, Sex, and the Single Man.** New York: Franklin Watts, 1983. P. 238. index.

The sexual revolution has left problems in its wake by permitting physical intimacy to outdistance emotional closeness. Distinguishing among love, sex, and intimacy, Hass points out that the new sexual freedom which promised so much to single men has actually created pitfalls for them. The divorce of sex from caring makes casual sex diasppointing; the increased pressures for performance and satisfaction leave single men with sexual problems. To truly enjoy sex, the man must like women in general and must love this woman in particular. The primacy of love is conveyed even in the title of Hass's book. The psychologist author (who is single) devotes an entire chapter to the need for recovering romance. He warns against pseudofeminists who want men to treat them as equals but cannot bring them-selves to accept men who in fact do so. Likewise, many man may be liberated in their heads but not in their hearts.

319.   Hite, Shere. **The Hite Report on Male Sexuality.** New York: Alfred A. Knopf, 1981. P. xxxiii, 1129. appendixes. index. Reprint. abridged and rev. ed. New York: Ballantine Books, 1982. pa.

Drawing upon 7,239 responses to an essay questionnaire, this much-publicized survey provides a wealth of male opinion on a wide range of sex-related topics. In the preface Hite explains and defends her methodology as scientific even if not entirely representative, and provides statistical information. The bulk of the book is devoted to excerpts from the responses, interspersed with Hite's observations—which have a way of turning into feminist sermonettes. If the commentary is some-times more political than perspicacious, the responses themselves provide an abun-dance of male experiences and viewpoints. The men talk about numerous matters, including relationships between boys and fathers (mostly aloof and unsatisfying, from the son's viewpoint); friendships between men (few have close male friends beyond the school years); relationships with women; monogamy (most of the respondents have had extramarital sex); cohabitation arrangements; men's anger at being used by women for financial security; men's tendency to identify sex with intercourse and male sexuality with orgasm during intercourse; problems with intercourse (impotence, "premature ejaculation," pressures to provide partners with orgasms); men's complaints about women's inability to stimulate them effec-tively; men's resentment at always being the initiators of sexual activity; their uncertainty about women's orgasms; and their views on aging (many say sex gets better), homosexuality, rape, pornography, and masturbation (which some say produces more intense orgasms than intercourse). The varied and unexpurgated responses in this Hite report provide a vivid montage of men and their sexuality.

320.   Janus, Sam, Barbara Bess, and Carol Saltus. **A Sexual Profile of Men in Power.** Englewood Cliffs, N.J.: Prentice-Hall, 1977. P. xxiii, 190. index. bibliography, 183-87.

The authors examine the extramarital sex lives of men in politics. Using interviews with sixty-eight elite call girls and twelve madams, as well as other material, the authors conclude that political figures are more sexually active than average men, are more likely to frequent prostitutes, often seek "kinky" or deviant sex, and spend considerable amounts of money to satisfy their sexual needs. These political figures often retain adolescent attitudes into adulthood, many were closely bound to their mothers, and a few have homosexual tendencies. The authors suggest a link between the power drive and the sex drive. Discussing deviant behaviors, the authors note that many of these men seem to be proving their manhood by enduring pain. The authors also describe political figures from other countries as well as the call girls themselves. For the typical political man pictured here, Henry Kissinger's aphorism holds true: "Power is the ultimate aphrodisiac."

321. Johnson, A.D., W.R. Gomes, and N.L. Vandemark, eds. **The Testis**. 3 vols. New York and London: Academic Press, 1970. P. xv, 684; xv, 468; xv, 596. illustrations. author and subject indexes. bibliographies after each chapter.

The twenty-eight scholarly papers in these volumes deal with development, anatomy, and physiology of the testis, biochemistry, and influencing factors.

322. Julty, Sam. **Male Sexual Performance**. New York: Grossett and Dunlap, Publishers, 1975. P. 353. illustrations. Reprint. *MSP: Male Sexual Performance*. New York: Dell Publishing Co., 1976. pa.

Impotency is the subject of this book. Informal but informed, Julty uses taped interviews to assess how men and women feel about impotency. He then analyzes for laypeople the male sexual apparatus. Using interviews with professionals (e.g., urologists, diabetes specialists, psychiatrists), he explores possible causes and solutions—both physical and mental—to impotency. Julty has negative views of the American medical system and of the cultural pressures on males to define themselves in terms of sexual performance.

323. Kelly, Gary. **Good Sex: The Healthy Man's Guide to Sexual Fulfillment**. New York: Harcourt Brace Jovanovich, 1979. P. 244. illustrations. index. bibliography, 235-38. Reprint. New York: New American Library, Signet, 1981. pa.

"This book is for males who want to work for more total sexual fulfillment through greater awareness of their bodies, emotions, and abilities to communicate." "Straight" male scripts often narrow men's sexual enjoyment, Kelly argues. Attempting to bring the whole man into sexual activity, he discusses communication with one's partner and getting beyond male myths to warmth and caring, equality, and trust and respect. Often, the penis is a barometer of a man's emotional life. Throughout the book, Kelly provides techniques of getting in touch with one's own body, slowing ejaculation timing, impotence, and other sexual problems—including women's difficulties. A final chapter discusses brotherhood (feeling between men), fatherhood, and selfhood.

324. Kinsey, Alfred C., Wardell B. Pomeroy, and Clyde E. Martin. **Sexual Behavior in the Human Male**. Philadelphia and London: W.B. Saunders Co., 1948. P. 804. illustrations. appendix. index. bibliography, 766-87.

A landmark in the study of male sexuality, this famous report continues to be a necessary reference tool for later researchers. Tracing the patterns revealed by 5,300 white males and utilizing information from a total of 12,000 persons, the study describes its methodology and findings in great detail. With the aid of numerous charts and graphs, the authors examine such matters as the kinds of sexual outlets available to males, early sexual growth and activity, adolescence, and the effects of age, marital status, social level, rural-urban background, and religious persuasion upon sexual outlets. Also studied are the various outlets, including masturbation, nocturnal emissions, heterosexual petting, premarital intercourse, marital intercourse, extramarital intercourse, intercourse with prostitutes, homosexual outlets, and animal contacts. Among the findings are: the near universality of masturbation, 37 percent of the total male population has some overt homosexual experience to orgasm, and 4 percent of white males are exclusively homosexual throughout their lives. As might be expected, some parts of the study have been criticized. In particular, recent writers have questioned the authors' belief that the rapidly ejaculating male is "superior" to the one who can prolong intercourse.

325.   Levine, Linda, and Lonnie Barbach. **The Intimate Male: Candid Discussions about Women, Sex, and Relationships**. Garden City, N.Y.: Anchor Press/Doubleday, 1983. P. xiii, 364. notes. index. bibliography, 351-52.

The authors have conducted interviews with 120 men for this frank account of sex. The men are mostly professionals, 90 percent are white, and all are college graduates. Ranging in age from less than twenty to more than seventy, the men are middle-class heterosexuals who feel positively about sex. With the authors they discuss their rejection of machismo for more intimate relationships. They indicate what makes for good sex: usually, a good relationship with the woman is primary. Other topics discussed include masturbation, first encounters, role reversals, gourmet sex, communicating with one's partner, handling sexual problems, pregnancy and the new baby, sex for parents, and sex in later years. As Bernie Zilbergeld points out in the introduction, these men are not the insensitive ignoramuses depicted in some sex surveys.

326.   Llewellyn-Jones, Derek. **EveryMan**. New York: Peter Bedrick Books, 1983. P. viii, 303. illustrations. appendix. bibliography, 292-98. Originally published London: Oxford University Press, 1981.

For the general reader, Llewellyn-Jones discusses sex differentiation, gender, sexuality, and health. He describes the development of the male fetus, socialization into the masculine role, the dynamics of male sexual response, how to be a better lover, the decision to have children, contraception, expectant fathers, sexual problems (impotency, premature ejaculation, and so on), diseases, homosexuality, middle-age sexuality, heart trouble, and aging. The appendix is a glossary of terms.

327.   McCarthy, Barry. **What You *Still* Don't Know about Male Sexuality**. New York: Thomas Y. Crowell Co., 1977. P. iv, 244. appendix. index. bibliography, 230-33.

Pleasure, not performance, is the keynote of this book. Writing primarily for the male general reader, McCarthy proclaims, "The time has come for us to escape from the rigid and oppressive male image that has so long prevented us from fully enjoying our sexuality." Instead of "foreplay," McCarthy suggests "loveplay." Surveying the "myths" of masculinity which have blocked full sensual enjoyment, he describes the body as "the world's greatest pleasure apparatus" and provides exercises for more enjoyable masturbation. He endorses sexual fantasies and contraceptives as aids to greater pleasure; premarital sex is depicted as a valid learning experience. The emphasis on mutual pleasure recurs in McCarthy's discussions of homosexual relations, oral-genital sex, marital sex, and fostering healthy attitudes in children. The benefits and costs of extramarital sex need to be weighed. McCarthy includes chapters on venereal disease, father participation in pregnancy and childbirth ("It's Your Baby, Too"), learning to increase arousal and potency and to control ejaculation (McCarthy steers away from the terms "impotency" and "premature ejaculation"), ways to perk up sex in the middle years, sex and the second-time single man, and aging and sex. The appendix discusses how to find a reliable therapist.

328. Milsten, Richard. **Male Sexual Function: Myth, Fantasy and Reality**. New York: Avon Books, 1979. P. 205. notes. index. bibliography, 197-98. pa.

Although covering a range of topics, this book for the general reader focuses on impotence. After explaining the mechanics of erection, Milsten discusses sixteen psychological and eight physical causes of impotence. A lengthy chapter is devoted to treatment. Milsten also touches upon fallacies surrounding male sexual performance (e.g., the effects of masturbation, vasectomy, and circumcision), aging in men, and the female partner. The final chapter consists of a self-evaluation questionnaire for men concerning their sexual condition and attitudes.

329. Penney, Alexandra. **How To Make Love to a Man**. New York: Clarkson N. Potter, Publishers, 1981. P. 143. Reprint. New York: Dell, 1982. pa.

For the woman mustering nerve to take the initiative, Penney provides the dos and don'ts. Similar popular advice can be found in Penney's *How to Make Love to a Woman* and *How to Make Love to Each Other*.

330. Pietropinto, Anthony, and Jacqueline Simenauer. **Beyond the Male Myth: What Women Want to Know about Men's Sexuality: A Nationwide Survey**. New York: Times Books, 1977. P. xi, 430. appendix. index. Reprint. New York: New American Library, Signet, 1978. pa.

This survey is based upon more than four thousand responses to a forty-item questionnaire. In addition, thirty-two "essay questions" were devised and divided into eight groups of four questions; each respondent was asked to answer one of these groups of four questions. The men ranged in age from eighteen to sixty-five years. The authors describe their efforts to produce a workable questionnaire, to approximate a representative sampling, and to motivate responses. The entire questionnaire is printed in the introduction; the appendix contains statistical breakdowns of the forty non-essay questions. The survey was devised to elicit information about men that would be useful to women in dealing with them. The authors debunk the "myth" of the insensitive male, and they maintain a running battle with the conclusions about men in *The Hite Report* on female sexuality. Among their survey conclusions are: half of the respondents regarded marriage with wife as only sex partner as the ideal sex life; rather than feeling threatened, most men preferred a more aggressive or active sex partner; they liked today's more liberated women; they were not threatened by women's ability to prevent pregnancy; the widespread acceptance of vasectomy indicated that they did not equate manliness with fertility; most men were interested in their partner's orgasm; they craved cuddling even when intercourse was not imminent; they enjoyed foreplay and sexual variations; and they did not fall asleep immediately after ejaculation. The authors summarize: "The notion that men want only to penetrate, thrust, and ejaculate is, as we have seen, outdated, if, indeed, it was ever true."

331.   Pomeroy, Wardell B. **Boys and Sex**. Rev. ed. New York: Delacorte Press, 1981. P. x, 189. index. Reprint. New York: Dell Publishing Co., 1981. pa.

An updated edition of Pomeroy's concise, readable guide, this book provides a boy with essential knowledge about sexual matters. A colleague of Kinsey, Pomeroy explains the book's purpose thusly: "For boys approaching or entering adolescence, I hope it will be a guide to what is happening or about to happen to them, and I hope, too, it dispels their guilt and fear about sexual behavior, leading them toward a well-adjusted sexual life as adults." After an introduction for parents and a brief statement that all boys have a sex life, subsequent chapters consider the anatomy and physiology of sex, sex play before adolescence, masturbation, homosexuality, dating, petting, intercourse, and its consequences. Following a chapter of questions and answers, a brief afterword reiterates principal themes in the book. Whether readers find Pomeroy's attitude toward sexual behavior too permissive, sufficiently cautious, or too inhibiting, most are likely to find his explanations frank and clear.

332.   Rowan, Robert L. **Men and Their Sex**. New York: Avocation Publishers, 1979. P. 159. illustrations. Reprint. New York: Irvington Publishers, 1982. pa.

In popular, light style, Rowan describes the physiology of the male reproductive system, with brief chapters on the penis, testicles, prostate gland, and the mechanics of ejaculation. The system's diseases (e.g., Peyronie's Disease, Priapism, Phimosis), congenital birth defects, and injuries are described, as well as their treatment. Rowan explains why he favors routine circumcision. Sections on venereal diseases and cancer of the penis are included. The book provides instructions for self-examination of the testicles, a procedure which Rowan urges men to follow regularly.

333.   Shanor, Karen. **The Shanor Study: The Sexual Sensitivity of the American Male**. New York: Dial Press, 1978. P. 274. appendix. bibliography, 271-74. Reprint. New York: Ballantine Books, 1978. pa.

"The American male is a more complete person than contemporary views of him allow," Shanor concludes from her study utilizing 4,062 questionnaire responses and seventy interviews. The author devotes separate chapters to orgasm (some men fake it on occasion), masturbation (it is performed more frequently since the time of Kinsey's study), and sexual fantasies. Shanor then offers profiles of men in their forties (the midlife transition is often a midlife crisis), thirties (these men are often trapped between old and new cultural values), and twenties (freer in their sexual attitudes, these males pursue traditional careers but not "seriously"). For men fifty and older, sex can be a waning activity or a continuing source of enjoyment. In their teens, males are troubled about their sexual identity and performance, but usually they are actively pursuing information and experience. Later chapters touch upon sexual activity of black men and homosexuals, impotence, sadomasochistic fantasies, and characteristic behavior during sex. The final chapter provides an overview, an attempt to fix a representative portrait of current male sexuality in transition. Numerous quotes from Shanor's respondents are incorporated in the text. The appendix provides the questionnaire and statistical information.

334.   Silber, Sherman J. **The Male: From Infancy to Old Age**. New York: Charles Scribner's Sons, 1981. P. xii, 212. illustrations. index. pa.

In readable style, Silber examines numerous facets of male sexuality. He describes how the male organs work, what can go wrong (e.g., impotence, prostate trouble, venereal diseases), the boy's problems, and gender identity and homosexuality. The discussion is aided by Scott Barrows's illustrations.

335.   Troen, Philip, and Howard R. Nankin, eds. **The Testis in Normal and Infertile Men**. New York: Raven Press, 1977. P. xiv, 578. illustrations. notes. index. bibliographies after each chapter.

This collection consists of forty-five scholarly, technical papers plus discussions from a 1976 conference in Pittsburgh.

336.   Zilbergeld, Bernie, with John Ullman. **Male Sexuality: A Guide to Sexual Fulfillment**. Boston: Little, Brown and Co., 1978. P. xii, 334. illustrations. index. notes. Reprint. New York: Bantam Books, 1978. pa.

This lively guide to male sexual fulfillment corrects popular errors about men and offers practical advice and "exercises" to change behavior and performance. Repeatedly, Zilbergeld insists that men need permission to enjoy and expand their range of sexual experiences. Believing that men as well as women have been duped by sexual misinformation, he debunks ten popular "myths" of male sexuality; he also disagrees with several sexual gurus and occasionally differs with the experts, including Masters and Johnson. While stressing men's need to rediscover and express their feelings, he explains the physical aspects of both male and female sexuality. The importance of touching and relaxation to men are emphasized; sexual encounters, he explains, need not always result in intercourse or even in orgasm. Despite intense pressure to have sex, young males should enter upon sexual experiences only when they are ready: male virginity requires no apology. Masturbation is viewed positively in this book, and periodic abstinence from sex is recommended for some men. Zilbergeld insists that men must learn to say no to sex when they do not want it, to remain passive occasionally during sexual activity, and to take active responsibility for contraception. Although skeptical of the popular notion of "premature ejaculation," he provides two chapters of advice and exercises for the man who wants to control ejaculation. Two chapters are also devoted to correcting erection problems. Attacking the "myth" of the older man's sexual incapacity, Zilbergeld also explores the effects of medical conditions (disease, injury, physical impairment) on sexuality. After examining some of the uses and misuses of sex, he devotes the final chapter to liberating men from the old restraints and grandiose expectations of sex.

Cross references:

238.   Bahr, Robert. **The Virility Factor: Masculinity through Testosterone, the Male Sex Hormone.**

HOMOSEXUALITY _____

337.   Adams, Stephen. **The Homosexual as Hero in Contemporary Fiction**. New
York: Barnes and Noble Books, 1980. P. 208. notes. index.
In contrast to the homosexual as villain or foil, the homosexual as hero appears in
many recent novels which examine changing sex roles and sexual politics. Adams
examines the work of such writers as Gore Vidal, James Baldwin, James Purdy,
John Rechy, E.M. Forster, Christopher Isherwood, Angus Wilson, and Jean Genet.

338.   Altman, Dennis. **The Homosexualization of America: The Americaniza-
tion of the Homosexual**. New York: St. Martin's Press, 1982. P. xiv, 242.
notes. index. bibliography, 227-36. Reprint. Boston: Beacon Press, 1983.
pa.
Urbane and informed, Altman traces the influence of an increasingly visible and
assertive gay culture upon American styles, fashions, cityscapes, psychological
and historical thought, consumer capitalism, politics, and sexual freedom.

339.   Bahnsen, Greg L. **Homosexuality: A Biblical View**. Grand Rapids, Mich.:
Baker Book House, 1978. P. 152. Scripture index. bibliography, 135-47.
pa.
From a study of the scriptures, Bahnsen concludes that homosexuality is sinful,
that churches should decline membership and office to unrepentant homosexuals,
and that homosexuality should be considered a civil offense. Bahnsen argues that
although scholars are uncertain about the causes of homosexuality, the Bible is
clear in condemning both homosexual orientation and acts. He warns against
"holier than thou" attitudes toward homosexuals and against indiscriminate state
persecution of them. The churches should proclaim the good news of deliverance
for homosexuals who repent.

340.   Barnhouse, Ruth Tiffany. **Homosexuality: A Symbolic Confusion**. New
York: Seabury Press, Crossroad Book, 1977. P. xiv, 190. appendixes.
notes. index.
Although she supports the decriminalization of homosexual acts and regards
persecution of homosexuals as a great evil, Barnhouse has serious reservations
about recent efforts to describe homosexuality as "normal." She questions such
recent events as the American Psychiatric Association's 1973 declaration that

homosexuality is not a mental disorder; Christian apologists for gay love are also given a skeptical review. As theologian, Barnhouse concludes that heterosexuality is "a symbol of wholeness, of the reconciliation of opposites, of the loving at-one-ment of God and creation." Its primary religious goal is not satisfaction but wholeness. In this view, homosexuality is a failure in human adaptation, a symbolic confusion.

341.   Berger, Raymond M. **Gay and Gray: The Older Homosexual Man**. Urbana: University of Illinois Press, 1982. P. 234. appendixes. index. bibliography, 223-26.

Combining an interview study and a questionnaire study, Berger discredits stereotypes of the older homosexual. The interviews present the men as individuals; the questionnaire findings indicate that they are by no means the pathetic and promiscuous creatures of popular imagination.

342.   Boswell, John. **Christianity, Social Tolerance, and Homosexuality: Gay People in Western Europe from the Beginning of the Christian Era to the Fourteenth Century**. Chicago and London: University of Chicago Press, 1980. P. xviii, 424. illustrations. appendixes. notes. index of Greek terms and general index. bibliography, 403-409. pa.

This scholarly study examines European attitudes toward gay people from the Roman empire through the High Middle Ages. Neither ancient Rome nor early Christianity appears to have stigmatized homosexual behavior. Boswell examines biblical texts and early Christian writings for allegedly antihomosexual injunctions—and finds none. During the disintegration of the Roman state, however, hostility toward gays became manifest, but from civil authorities rather than the church. During the early Middle Ages a gay subculture was tolerated, and by the eleventh century gays were prominent at many levels of society in Europe. But during the latter half of the twelfth century, hostility toward gays and homosexuality again reappeared as part of a rise of general intolerance throughout Western society. Embedded in theological, moral, and legal complications of the later Middle Ages, this hostility influenced Western thought for centuries to come. In appendix I, Boswell discusses St. Paul's epistles, and appendix II contains texts and translations of key works. Boswell's scholarship—erudite, lively, controversial—makes this a book to reckon with.

343.   Brown, Howard. **Familiar Faces, Hidden Lives: The Story of Homosexual Men in America Today**. New York and London: Harcourt Brace Jovanovich, 1976. P. 246. pa.

A well-known medical doctor who came out in the early seventies, Brown recounts with balance and sympathy the stories of numerous homosexuals, including himself, depicting what it has been like to be gay in America. Brown retells human stories rather than case histories. He examines such areas as the mistaken tendency to blame parents for their child's sexual preference, gays in small towns, married homosexuals, long-term relationships, and the ways in which religion, psychiatry, and the law have oppressed homosexuals. An epilogue looks forward to a brighter future for gays in America.

344.   Bullough, Vern L. **Homosexuality: A History**. New York: New American
        Library, Meridian, 1979. P. ix, 196. notes. index. bibliography, 163-64. pa.
In concise style, Bullough examines a number of topics—including past definitions
of homosexuality, religion, the law, schools, lesbianism, and coming out—from a
historical perspective.

345.   Burg, B.R. **Sodomy and the Perception of Evil: English Sea Rovers in the
        Seventeenth-Century Caribbean**. New York and London: New York
        University Press, 1983. P. xxiii, 215. notes. index. bibliography, 193-209.
Against the background of homosexuality in seventeenth-century England, Burg
focuses upon "sodomy" among pirates of the Caribbean.

346.   Chester, Lewis, David Leitch, and Colin Simpson. **The Cleveland Street
        Affair**. London: Weidenfeld and Nicolson, 1976. P. 236. illustrations.
        notes. bibliography, 234-36.
The most notorious of Victorian scandals, the subject of this study, involved a
brothel employing telegraph boys, high-ranking patrons (including the Heir Pre-
sumptive Albert Victor and Lord Arthur Somerset), and a massive cover-up, engin-
eered by such people as the Prince of Wales (later Edward VII) and the prime
minister, Lord Salisbury.

347.   Delph, Edward William. **The Silent Community: Public Homosexual
        Encounters**. Beverly Hills, Calif.: Sage Publications, Sage Mark Edition,
        1978. P. 187. appendix. notes. bibliography, 183-86. pa.
Delph studies the ways in which homosexuals communicate nonverbally while
making sexual contacts in public places, such as restrooms, parks, bars, and steam-
baths. Because the problems of conducting such research were (to say the least)
intriguing, readers may want to start with the appendix on methodology.

348.   D'Emilio, John. **Sexual Politics, Sexual Communities: The Making of a
        Homosexual Minority in the United States 1940-1970**. Chicago and
        London: University of Chicago Press, 1983. P. x, 257. notes. index.
This scholarly and readable study portrays the forces and events in America
between 1940-1970 that led to gay liberation. In the opening chapter, D'Emilio
surveys homosexuality in America from its founding to the 1930s; in later chapters, he provides more detailed accounts of homosexual awareness during World
War II, the formation of gay urban cultures, the crackdown on gays during the
McCarthy period, and the uneven fortunes of gay organizations like the Mattachine
Society. During the sixties, important legal decisions coincided with the rise of gay
activism on both the east and west coasts, culminating in the Stonewall riots of
1969. In a concluding chapter, the author surveys the post-Stonewall scene.

349.   Denneny, Michael, Charles Ortleb, and Thomas Steele, eds. **The Christo-
        pher Street Reader**. New York: Coward-McCann, 1983. P. 428. pa.
Forty-six contributions from the *Christopher Street* magazine are divided into
sections dealing with living the gay life, the conditions of gays in modern America,
the situation of gays abroad (e.g., Moscow, Rio, Paris, London), aspects of gay
history, and gay cultural politics in America. The contents include essays, reports,
personal reminiscences, and interviews (with, e.g., Gore Vidal and Jean Paul Sartre).

350. Ebert, Alan. **The Homosexuals**. New York: Macmillan Co., 1977. P. xii, 332.

Ebert presents inteviews with seventeen gay men, their stories providing a cross-section of modern gay experience.

351. Feinbloom, Deborah Heller. **Transvestites and Transsexuals: Mixed Views**. New York: Delacorte Press/Seymour Lawrence, A Merloyd Lawrence Book, 1976. P. ix, 303. appendixes. index. bibliography, 283-96.

The overwhelming majority of transvestites and transsexuals are males. Transvestites dress as the opposite sex. Transsexuals identify themselves as members of one sex but possess the body of the "wrong" sex. After defining terms, Feinbloom combines scholarly literature and "participant observation" to analyze the world of heterosexual transvestites, homosexual transvestites, and transsexuals. She follows the activities of a transvestite group, as well as the life of one person who undergoes a male-to-female sex change operation. Although some readers may be disappointed that the book sheds comparatively little light on the causes of male transvestism and transsexualism, Feinbloom is wisely cautious in her conclusions.

352. Galloway, David, and Christian Sabisch, eds. **Calamus: Male Homosexuality in Twentieth-Century Literature: An International Anthology**. New York: William Morrow and Co., 1982. P. 503. appendix. pa.

This anthology includes twentieth-century fiction and poetry by thirty-five international authors (not all of whom are homosexual) dealing with male homosexuality. In their foreword, the editors note the widespread violent persecution of male homosexuals (a situation not suffered by lesbians) which shapes much of the writing in this volume. They also note recurring themes and images (e.g., the handsome sailor) in literature dealing with homosexuals. Contributions include Robert Musil's "Young Törless," an account of initiation into gay sex; Constantin Cavafy's poetic hymns to male beauty; Sherwood Anderson's "Hands," a story of violent homophobia in an American small town; stories by D.H. Lawrence and Ernest Hemingway of repressed homosexuality in the military; Federico García Lorca's "Ode to Walt Whitman"; selections from Allen Ginsberg's poetry; and Yukio Mishima's "Onnagata," a tale of smoldering homosexual jealousy. Biographical information on the authors is included.

353. Goodich, Michael. **The Unmentionable Vice: Homosexuality in the Later Medieval Period**. Santa Barbara, Calif.: American Bibliographical Center— Clio Press, 1979. P. xv, 165. appendix. notes. index. bibliography, 143-55. Reprint. Santa Barbara, Calif.: Ross-Erikson, 1979. pa.

This scholarly history traces the growth of antihomosexual attitudes in medieval Europe between the eleventh and the fourteenth centuries. At first persecution of homosexuals was sporadic, although official disapproval of homosexuality was evident. Gradually, as homosexuality became linked with heresy, the Catholic hierarchy moved to impose stricter sanctions against it. Goodich traces the activities of Peter Damian and other moral reformers, the legislation concerning homosexuality issued by various councils, the development of scholastic thought on the subject, and the increasingly severe reprisals taken by secular law. The appendix provides testimony from the trial of Arnold Verniolle, a fourteenth-century French subdeacon accused of homosexual practices.

354. Goodman, Gerre, George Lakey, Judy Lashof, and Erika Thorne. **No Turning Back: Lesbian and Gay Liberation for the '80s**. Philadelphia: New Society Publishers, 1983. P. 153. notes. pa.
Despite its stridency, *No Turning Back* advocates a nonviolent undermining of American heterosexual society, which is depicted as homophobic and sexist.

355. Gottlieb, David I. **The Gay Tapes: A Candid Discussion about Male Homosexuality**. New York: Stein and Day, 1977. P. 178.
Using taped interviews with three gay men, Gottlieb explores such topics as gay experiences, fantasies, medical problems, friendships, love, jealousy, and male gays and women.

356. Harry, Joseph, and Man Singh Das, eds. **Homosexuality in International Perspective**. New Delhi, India: Vikas Publishing House, 1980. Distributed by Advent Books. P. xiii, 134. index. bibliographies after each chapter.
Nine essays explore such diverse topics as the link between homosexuality and the arts (apparently intrinsic), employment discrimination against gays, a Canadian gay community, the connection between gay culture and leisure culture, the gay ministry, why gays are disliked by heterosexuals (both effeminate behavior and sexual preference create dislike, but mainstream appearance and behavior help offset it), public attitudes toward gays in New Zealand, sexual identity problems of male prostitutes in West Germany, and homosexual practices in nineteenth-century English public schools.

357. Hart, John, and Diane Richardson, with Kenneth Plummer, Charles Dodd, Glenys Parry and Ray Lightbown, Rose Robertson, and Jeffrey Weeks. **The Theory and Practice of Homosexuality**. London, Boston, and Henley: Routledge and Kegan Paul, 1981. P. vii, 206. illustrations. index. bibliography, 190-202. pa.
This scholarly work examines homosexuality in theory and practice, raises the question of homosexual identity, and assesses the availability of professional help for those seeking it. A selected list of English and Irish groups and organizations is included.

358. Hunt, Morton: **Gay: What You Should Know about Homosexuality**. New York: Farrar, Straus and Giroux, 1977. P. 211. appendix. notes. bibliography, 207-10. Reprint. New York: Pocket Books, 1979. pa.
For the young reader, Hunt offers dispassionate information about homosexuality or—more exactly—homosexualities. Neither a homophile nor a homophobe, Hunt uses easily understood language to dispel nine common disbeliefs about homosexuals; he also surveys and assesses twelve theories of what causes homosexuality. He discusses gay rights, possible "signs" of gayness, gays in history, and (with special tact) gay sex. Without crediting militant claims of gay superiority, he surveys gay sensitivities (e.g., in the arts), gay "deviants" (e.g., transvestites, transsexuals, and leather freaks), and gay couples. A glossary of terms is included.

359.   Johnston, Gordon. **Which Way out of the Men's Room?: Options for the Male Homosexual.** South Brunswick, N.J., and New York: A.S. Barnes and Co., 1979. P. 330. notes. bibliography, 323-30.

This thoughtful, sometimes abstruse discussion explores the difficulties of establishing a satisfying homosexual identity in a predominantly heterosexual world. Some readers will feel that Johnston too neatly makes heterosexual males into scapegoats; he perceives heterosexual society as the totally evil creation of males alone.

360.   Katz, Jonathan. **Gay American History: Lesbians and Gay Men in the U.S.A.** New York: Thomas Y. Crowell Co., 1976. P. xiv, 690. illustrations. index. notes and bibliography, 567-666. pa.

This massive documentary history covers the fortunes of gay men and women in America from the sixteenth century to the present. Topics include oppression of gays, treatments to "cure" homosexuality, passing as members of the opposite sex, gays among native Americans, resistance to persecution, and love.

361.   Kleinberg, Seymour. **Alienated Affections: Being Gay in America.** New York: St. Martin's Press, 1980. P. xiii, 256. Reprint. New York: Warner Books, 1982. pa.

In a series of graceful, thoughtful essays, Kleinberg uses his own experiences as a New York Jew coping with his homosexuality, informal interviews, and research to examine a number of personal and social concerns. Among the topics touched upon are homosexual concepts of glamor in Hollywood films, gays in ballet, the relationships between gay men and straight women, transsexuals and cross dressing, the new macho style of homosexuals, sadomasochism, prison rape, the adjustments of aging gays, and psychoanalysis and homosexuality. Sometimes severely critical of gay culture, Kleinberg envies feminist solidarity and indulges in across-the-board references to heterosexual white males as "the enemy" and "the oppressor."

362.   Koranyi, Erwin K. **Transsexuality in the Male: The Spectrum of Gender Dysphoria.** American Lecture Series. Springfield, Ill.: Charles C. Thomas, 1980. P. xv, 198. illustrations. appendix. index. bibliography, 177-91.

In clear but sometimes technical language, Koranyi defines a spectrum of disorders involving a male's maladaptation to his anatomical sex. Transsexuality may be related to, but is not identical with, transvestism and homosexuality. Probing biological theories and psychological etiologies, the author presents case histories representing good and bad prospects for sex change operations. A chapter by Selwyn M. Smith and Betty J. Lynch details the medical and legal tangles surrounding sex reassignment surgery, and a chapter by Norman B. Barwin describes, with numerous drawings, the operation itself. A glossary of terms is provided.

363.   Kronemeyer, Robert. **Overcoming Homosexuality.** New York: Macmillan Co., 1980. P. viii, 220.

Arguing that homosexuality is "a pathological adaptation" to a frustrating and nonnurturing mother-child relationship, Kronemeyer advances a holistic approach (Syntonic Therapy) to get at the roots of the problem. The author believes that fathers by themselves cannot create homosexuals if the mother-child relationship is sound. He regards homosexuals as neither evil nor a social threat but as suffering from a disease that is now curable in many.

364. Levine, Martin P., ed. **Gay Men: The Sociology of Male Homosexuality.** New York: Harper and Row, 1979. P. vi, 346. index. notes and bibliographies after some chapters. pa.

This collection of twenty-one articles reflects sociology's current understanding of gay males. The essays concern oppression of gays, gay identity, various homosexual "scenes," lifestyles (including gay couples, gay fathers, women among gay men, the aging homosexual, and the black homosexual), and the gay movement from liberation to "butch."

365. Licata, Salvatore J., and Robert P. Petersen, eds. **Historical Perspectives on Homosexuality.** New York: Stein and Day, Haworth Press, 1981. P. 224. notes. index. bibliography, 191-210.

In addition to thirteen articles covering historical periods from the Middle Ages to the present, this volume also includes William Parker's annotated bibliography of homosexuality in history, as well as two reviews of current books. This is the hardbound edition of *Journal of Homosexuality,* Vol. 6, nos. 1/2 (Fall/Winter 1980/81).

366. Marotta, Toby. **The Politics of Homosexuality.** Boston: Houghton Mifflin Co., 1981. P. xiv, 369. notes. index.

Describing "how lesbians and gay men have made themselves a political and social force in modern America," this history follows the homophile movement from the fifties to the present.

367. Marotta, Toby. **Sons of Harvard: Gay Men from the Class of 1967.** New York: William Morrow and Co., 1982. P. 288. pa.

Among the best and brightest were a number of gay men, some of whom have come out of the closet. Through interviews Marotta chronicles the experiences of ten gay men from Harvard's class of 1967. The stories reflect the growing acceptance, both personal and social, of homosexuality, but the use of assumed names by nearly all of the men in this book says much about persisting intolerance.

368. Masters, William H., and Virginia E. Johnson. **Homosexuality in Perspective.** Boston: Little, Brown and Co., 1979. P. xiv, 450. index. bibliography, 413-36. Reprint. New York: Bantam Books, 1982. pa.

This study by two leading sex experts covers both the preclinical and clinical states of their twenty-year investigation into homosexuality. Topics discussed include behavior patterns, physiology, ambisexuals, male and female homosexual dysfunctioning and dissatisfactions, and therapy.

369. McNaught, Brian. **A Disturbed Peace: Selected Writings of an Irish Catholic Homosexual.** Washington, D.C.: Dignity, 1981. P. vi, 125. pa.

In a series of sensitive essays, McNaught reflects on the clash between his homosexuality and his Catholic upbringing, as well as the ways in which he has come to terms with both.

370. McNeill, John J. **The Church and the Homosexual.** Kansas City, Kans.: Sheed Andrews and McMeel, 1976. P. xiii, 211. notes.

A Jesuit priest, McNeill questions Catholicism's traditional view of homosexuality in light of scriptural, theological, moral, and scientific considerations. "In the name of a mistaken understanding of the crime of Sodom and Gomorrah," McNeill writes, "the true crime of Sodom and Gomorrah [cruel injustice] has been and continues to be repeated every day."

371. McWhirter, David P., and Andrew M. Mattison. **The Male Couple: How Relationships Develop.** Englewood Cliffs, N.J.: Prentice-Hall, 1984. P. xv, 341. appendix. index. bibliography, 303-14.

Interviewing 156 male couples, the authors trace a recurring six-stage development: blending (first year), nesting (second and third years), maintaining (fourth and fifth years), building (years six through ten), releasing (years eleven through twenty), and renewing (beyond twenty years). The authors also examine such topics as male bonding, homophobia, coming out, and sexuality. The authors describe the history of their study; the interview format is contained in the appendix.

372. Mendola, Mary. **The Mendola Report: A New Look at Gay Couples.** New York: Crown Publishers, 1980. P. xiii, 269. appendix. index.

Based upon more than four hundred responses to a questionnaire and on extended interviews with some of the couples, this report depicts life among gay couples—both lesbian and homosexual. Aside from the social pressures and legal disparities, gay couples experience many of the same joys and difficulties that heterosexual couples do. Choosing to concentrate on vignettes from the couples' experience, Mendola touches upon such matters as sexual fidelity, gays as parents, life insurance and wills for gay couples, gay divorce, gays at work, gay widowhood, and the new generation of gays. Despite some bitterness toward society for its discrimination against gays, Mendola's sympathies are extensive. Of heterosexual men she writes: "How does a man define himself if it is not in terms of his ability to 'take care of a woman.' Men are as shackled by society's role stereotyping as women are. And when can we expect a men's liberation movement? It is long overdue." The appendix contains the text of the questionnaire.

373. Mieli, Mario. **Homosexuality and Liberation: Elements of a Gay Critique.** Translated by David Fernbach. London: Gay Men's Press, 1980. P. 247. notes. pa. Originally published Turin, Italy: Giulio Einaudi editori s.p.a., 1977.

From the Italian school of gay Marxism, Mieli denounces heterosexual capitalist society. Arguing that society warps children's undifferentiating sexual impulses into heterosexuality, Mieli suggests ways to foster polymorphous sexual behavior in the early years. He attacks "psychonazis" (i.e., professional psychotherapists) for stigmatizing homosexuality as a pathology to be cured. Christianity comes under heavy fire for its repressiveness, and sports are criticized for submerging their homoerotic aspects. Mieli extols the superiority of homosexuals, arguing that only they know how to love women truly. These and other radical views make for arresting, if not always convincing, reading.

374. Newton, Esther. **Mother Camp: Female Impersonators in America.** Rev. ed. Chicago and London: University of Chicago Press, Phoenix, 1979. P. xx, 136. illustrations. appendix. notes. pa.

Distinguishing between street fairies and stage performers, Newton focuses on homosexuals who perform in drag. The author examines the conditions under which they work, describing several stage shows in detail. The appendix provides field methods, and the new preface deplores the rise of macho styles among homosexuals. This book first appeared in 1972.

375. Oraison, Marc. **The Homosexual Question.** Translated by Jane Zeni Flinn. New York: Harper and Row, 1977. P. 132. notes. pa. Originally published as *La question homosexuelle* (Paris: Éditions du Seuil, 1975).

A French priest, doctor, and psychiatrist, the author questions traditional Catholic moral teachings on homosexuality, finding them inhuman. Reviewing many aspects of homosexuality and drawing upon case histories, Oraison attempts to "open a window" to ventilate musty moral doctrines.

376. Plummer, Kenneth, ed. **The Making of the Modern Homosexual.** Totowa, N.J.: Barnes and Noble Books, 1981. P. 280. appendixes. notes. index. bibliographies, 231-39, 253-74.

Eight essays consider homosexuals in social context and explore the challenges of conducting sociological research into homosexuality.

377. Rechy, John. **The Sexual Outlaw: A Documentary.** New York: Grove Press, 1977. P. 307.

Described as a "non-fiction account, with commentaries, of three days and nights in the sexual underground," this book focuses on "Jim" as he cruises the Los Angeles world of impersonal gay sex. A series of graphic scenes form a montage which depicts, and possibly romanticizes, Jim as a sexual outlaw defying conventional morality and its police enforcers.

378. Rector, Frank. **The Nazi Extermination of Homosexuals.** New York: Stein and Day, 1981. P. 189. illustrations. notes. index. bibliography, 179-82.

Rector retells the story of Nazi persecution of gays from initial crackdowns to the death camps. Contemporary photographs help document the horrors.

379. Rofes, Eric E. **"I Thought People like That Killed Themselves": Lesbians, Gay Men and Suicide.** San Francisco: Grey Fox Press, 1983. P. x, 163. illustration. appendixes. notes. index. pa.

Because lesbians and gay men must sometimes make a choice between disgrace and self-destrucition, suicide is a serious problem among gays. Similarly, social pressure on gays can lead to despair. Scandal, blackmail, and public exposure are still threats to gay people, and "coming out" is no guarantee of immunity from them. Rofes provides numerous cases of homosexuals driven to suicide, he outlines areas of needed research, and he discusses methods of intervention, therapy, and prevention. The appendixes examine the fiction of Sappho's suicide, the dubious use of gay suicide statistics by some conservative Christian writers, common misconceptions about suicides, and techniques of counseling gays through hotlines.

380. Ross, Michael W. **The Married Homosexual Man: A Psychological Study.** London and Boston: Routledge and Kegal Paul, 1983. P. xvi, 184. appendixes. index. bibliography, 178-82. pa.

Two surveys are the basis of this study. The first, done in 1975, involved sixty-three respondents in Australia and New Zealand. The second, conducted in 1978, involved 488 respondents in Sweden, Finland, and Australia. Ross discusses such topics as the homosexuals' reasons for marrying (social hostility toward homosexuality is a major factor) and the unlikeliness that the marriage will alter the man's sexual orientation. He sketches a profile of the homosexual who is likely to marry and presents several case histories. The appendixes reprint the questionnaire and discuss methodology.

381. Rowse, A. L. **Homosexuals in History: A Study of Ambivalence in Society, Literature and the Arts.** New York: Macmillan Co., 1977. P. xiii, 346. illustrations. index.

Brilliant and bitter, Rowse provides a series of vignettes of famous homosexuals in Western history from the Renaissance to the present. The book's epigram, "Homo homini lupus," strikes the keynote of anger at the treatment of homosexuals through the ages. Among those portrayed are Leonardo da Vinci, Michelangelo, Christopher Marlowe, Henri III, Rudolf II, James I, Louis XIII, Lord Hervey, Frederick the Great, Walt Whitman, Oscar Wilde, T. E. Lawrence, Roger Casement, Ludwig Wittgenstein, and Yukio Mishima.

382. Sarotte, Georges-Michel. **Like a Brother, like a Lover: Male Homosexuality in the American Novel and Theater from Herman Melville to James Baldwin.** Translated by Richard Miller. Garden City, N.Y.: Anchor Press/Doubleday, 1978. P. xv, 339. index. bibliography, 306-27. Originally published as *Comme un frère, comme un amant* (Paris: Flammarion, 1976).

This literary and social study opens with an overview of intolerance in the United States and the emergence of the homosexual in American novels and plays. Discussing numerous authors and works, Sarotte then examines four archetypes of the homosexual in literature (adolescents, teacher and pupil, captain and soldier, and white and black), as well as the circumstances in which the homosexual is depicted in novels and plays. Individual chapters are devoted to such major figures as playwrights Tennessee Williams, William Inge, Edward Albee, and novelist Henry James. More controversial are chapters on "latent" or "sublimated" homosexuality in the works of Jack London, F. Scott Fitzgerald, Ernest Hemingway, and Norman Mailer.

383. Silverstein, Charles. **A Family Matter: A Parents' Guide to Homosexuality.** New York: McGraw-Hill Book Co., 1977. P. v, 214. bibliography, 210-14. pa.

"This book," the author states, "is for families who want to learn how to deal with a homosexual son or daughter, and come to terms with their own feelings about homosexuality." Silverstein defines and clarifies terms, dissects stereotypes of homosexuals, and presents five case histories of families coping with a homosexual member. He discusses responsible therapy for homosexuals and their families.

384. Silverstein, Charles. **Man to Man: Gay Couples in America**. New York: William Morrow and Co., 1981. P. 348. appendix. name index. pa.

Using interviews with 190 men, Silverstein addresses numerous questions concerning gay couples, including the eroticized father-son relationship, peers in school, coming out, major issues confronting male couples (e.g., the search for excitement vs. the need to build a home), and varieties of gay couples. The appendix describes the interview technique.

385. Silverstein, Charles, and Edmund White. **The Joy of Gay Sex: An Intimate Guide for Gay Men to the Pleasures of a Gay Lifestyle**. New York: Simon and Schuster, Fireside, 1977. P. 207. illustrations. index. bibliography, 201-204. pa.

In alphabetical order—from androgyny to wrestling—the authors discuss the details of gay sex and lifestyle. The numerous illustrations (some in color) are mostly by Michael Leonard, Ian Beck, and Julian Graddon.

386. Walker, Mitch. **Men Loving Men: A Gay Sex Guide and Consciousness Book**. San Francisco: Gay Sunshine Press, 1977. P. 160. illustrations. notes. pa.

This book includes a survey of homosexuality in world history, a manual of gay sex, and a discussion of gay health problems and the mystic implications of gay sexuality. Illustrations consist of a photographic essay by David Greene, drawings by Bill Warrick, and reproductions of pertinent historical art works.

387. White, Edmund. **States of Desire: Travels in Gay America**. New York: E.P. Dutton, 1980. P. xi, 336. pa. Reprint. New York: Bantam Books, 1981. pa.

In this highly acclaimed book, interviews and thoughtful assessments are woven together into a tapestry depicting the American homosexual scene in nearly two dozen major cities.

388. Ziebold, Thomas O., and John E. Mongeon, eds. **Alcoholism and Homosexuality**. New York: Haworth Press, 1982. P. 107. index. bibliographies after each chapter.

Rejecting the idea of any necessary link between alcoholism and homosexuality, the ten essays in this collection examine the causes and treatment of alcohol abuse among gays. This is the hardbound edition of the *Journal of Homosexuality*, vol. 7, no. 4.

Cross references:

7. Bullough, Vern L., W. Dorr Legg, Barrett W. Elcano, and James Kepner, comps. **An Annotated Bibliography of Homosexuality**.

9. Horner, Tom, comp. **Homosexuality and the Judeo-Christian Tradition: An Annotated Bibliography**.

11. Parker, William, comp. **Homosexuality: A Selective Bibliography of over 3,000 Items.**

12. Parker, William, comp. **Homosexuality Bibliography: Supplement, 1970-1975.**

17. Weinberg, Martin S., and Alan P. Bell, comps. **Homosexuality: An Annotated Bibliography.**

18. Young, Ian, comp. **The Male Homosexual in Literature: A Bibliography.**

31. Sutherland, Alistair, and Patrick Anderson, eds. **Eros: An Anthology of Male Friendship.**

82. Gibson, E. Lawrence. **Get Off My Ship: Ensign Berg vs. the U.S. Navy.**

85. Kantrowitz, Arnie. **Under the Rainbow: Growing Up Gay.**

86. Kopay, David, and Perry Deane Young. **The David Kopay Story: An Extraordinary Self-Revelation.**

93. Richards, Renée, with John Ames. **Second Serve: The Renée Richards Story.**

108. Stoddard, Thomas B., E. Carrington Boggan, Marilyn G. Haft, Charles Lister, and John P. Rupp. **The Rights of Gay People.**

180. Mitzel, John. **Sports and the Macho Male.**

196. Buffum, Peter C. **Homosexuality in Prisons.**

200. Weiss, Carl, and David James Friar. **Terror in the Prisons: Homosexual Rape and Why Society Condones It.**

218. Malone, John. **Straight Women/Gay Men: A Special Relationship.**

222. Nahas, Rebecca, and Myra Turley. **The New Couple: Women and Gay Men.**

540. Sherman, Martin. **Bent.**

543. White, Edmund. **A Boy's Own Story.**

MEN IN FAMILIES

FATHERS

389.   Andersen, Christopher P. **Father: The Figure and the Force**. New York: Warner Books, 1983. P. xi, 256. bibliography, 255-56.

"Nearly every adult American alive today," Andersen declares, "has been raised in his or her father's absence." Arguing that fathers have been given short shrift by American society, the author presents evidence of fathers' overwhelming importance to children. Writing in popular style, Andersen utilizes interviews with celebrities, experts, friends, and acquaintances, as well as his own experiences as son and father, to construct an informal portrait of fatherhood in modern America. He touches upon such matters as fathers as resident aliens in the family, the effects of father absence upon children, the Oedipus and Electra complexes, and father as mediator of the outside world to the child. Later chapters deal with surrogate fathers and mentors, breaking away from father, and the New Dad—whom Andersen regards as a fraud. Both Dad and Mom, he argues, are defecting from their responsibilities as parents. Despite Andersen's willingness to portray Dad with warts and all, his book is a vigorous defense of fatherhood in a society that he regards as increasingly complacent about parenting.

390.   Appleton, William S. **Fathers and Daughters: A Father's Powerful Influence on a Woman's Life**. Garden City, N.Y.: Doubleday and Co., 1981. p. xv, 198. Reprint. New York: Berkley Books, 1984. pa.

Although written for daughters, this book makes equally valid reading for fathers. The author, an M.D. with two daughters, writes lucidly of the father's profound effect upon his daughter's life. Rejecting the Freudian model which stresses childhood influences, Appleton argues that the father-daughter relationship occurs over a thirty-year period in their separate life cycles. These years he divides into three segments: oasis (when daughter is "daddy's little girl" and when father is building his career), conflict (when daughter is an adolescent and father is passing through midlife turmoil), and separation (when daughter reaches autonomy and when father is less conflicted and sees her as an adult). Although Appleton recognizes that many father-daughter relationships are warm and strengthening, he focuses upon those relationships that adversely affect women's lives in such areas as sex, careers, insecurity, and relationships. Making changes in one's life, Appleton points out, requires a process of understanding and an act of will on the woman's part.

391. Benson, Leonard. **Fatherhood: A Sociological Perspective**. New York: Random House, 1968. P. xii, 371. index. bibliography, 325-59.

Published in 1968 this book provides an early, systematic account of the literature on fatherhood. Deploring our society's comparative neglect of fathers, Benson notes: "It is apparent that the problems of women *as women* arouse our most anxious concern, while those of men rarely stir our passion for reform." Part I of the book puts fatherhood into sociological perspective, examining the linkage between masculinity and fatherhood, our society's encouragement of instrumental roles for males, the passing of patriarchal styles of fathering, and the emergence of the father-mother team. In part II Benson discusses the male as parent. He examines the father as the "weak link" in the family chain who needs more careful adjustment to marriage and family. The greater discrepancy between the husband-father roles than between the wife-mother roles also increases stress for males in families. Benson traces the various theories of sexual identification and father's roles, the urge to excel instilled by many fathers, and the pressures on male children to assume a masculine role. A discussion of father-child conflict is followed by an account of fatherlessness in families. While any individual father in a household may be expendable, Benson concludes that the institution of fatherhood is not. Part III is concerned with the conflicts between father's obligations as breadwinner and his role as parent. A final chapter of prognosis indicates that the family has become more important to fathers.

392. Biller, Henry B. **Paternal Deprivation: Family, School, Sexuality, and Society**. Lexington, Mass.: D.C. Heath and Co., Lexington Books, 1974. P. xi, 227. author and subject indexes. bibliography, 171-207.

"The thesis of this book is that paternal deprivation, including patterns of inadequate fathering as well as father absence, is a highly significant factor in the development of serious psychological and social problems." This sequel to Biller's *Father, Child, and Sex Role* examines numerous aspects of paternal deprivation, including theories of a boy's identification with his father and the resulting development of masculinity, father-infant attachments, the boy's sex role functioning, surrogate models of masculine behavior, the effects of paternal deprivation on the child's personal and social adjustment (including psychopathology), the mother-son relationship caused by paternal deprivation, effects of father-daughter relations on her emotional and interpersonal functioning, the intellectual and academic development of children (including the effects of the feminized classroom), ways of coping with paternal deprivation, and suggested solutions for alleviating the problem. Throughout the book, Biller offers impressive evidence of the need for good fathers. The bibliography is unusually full.

393. Biller, Henry, and Dennis Meredith. **Father Power**. New York: David McKay Co., 1974. P. 376. notes. index. bibliography, 361-68. Reprint. Garden City, N.Y.: Doubleday and Co., Anchor, 1975. pa.

By "father power" the authors mean the enormous influence over his child's life which a father exercises. Because Biller and Meredith are eager to harness this power for positive results, their book is both a manifesto and a guide for the man who wishes to enlarge upon older and more rigid concepts of fathering and who wishes to give his children a secure personal identity without locking them into narrow gender roles. Drawing upon research studies, their work, and their experiences as fathers, the authors offer stimulating advice on such matters as how fathers can overcome stereotyped views of fatherhood, how they can help their children to develop a fulfilling sense of masculinity or femininity, and how they can stimulate positive attitudes toward physical growth, learning, work, and morality. A separate section of the book is devoted to "special problems," e.g., divorce, stepfathering, handicapped fathers and children, black fathers, father absence, and so on. The easy-to-read style makes *Father Power* widely accessible to men who want to be more active and nurturing parents.

394. Cammarata, Jerry, with Frances Spatz Leighton. **The Fun Book of Fatherhood: Or, How the Animal Kingdom Is Helping to Raise the Wild Kids at Our House.** Los Angeles: Corwin Books, 1978. P. xiii, 303. illustrations. bibliography, 301-303. Reprint. Los Angeles: Pinnacle Books, 1979. pa.

Cammarata attracted headlines a few years ago by fighting for—and winning—a four-year paternity leave from his job. He wanted the leave not to enable his wife to go out to work (she didn't), but to enable him to be closely involved in raising their two daughters. In frenetically informal prose, Cammarata records his insights into parenting, often by way of zany analogies with animal parents. Using anecdotes from his experiences at home, the author touches upon such matters as not pressuring children to succeed, feeding, fighting, telling children about sex, discipline, education, play, and sleeping.

395. Cath, Stanley H., Alan R. Gurwitt, and John Munder Ross, eds. **Father and Child: Developmental and Clinical Perspectives.** Boston: Little, Brown and Co., 1982. P. xxv, 636. name and subject indexes. bibliography, 587-613.

Citing the father as the "forgotten parent" and deploring the "relative dearth of reflection on paternity," the editors have collected thirty-six essays (plus preface and afterword) by thirty-nine contributors with unusually impressive credentials. Although geared primarily to clinicians, *Father and Child* covers such a range of topics and is so readable that it invites a wider audience. Divided into five sections, the book begins with reviews of the psychological literature on fathers (understandably, Freud looms large in these surveys). The next two sections trace the development of the male from infancy to old age, emphasizing the father-child relationship. Among the topics discussed are engrossment (bonding between fathers and newborn infants), father hunger (the need of a father's presence, especially to modulate aggressive drive and fantasy), the father's role in establishing the child's gender identity during early childhood, fathers and adolescent sons, expectant fathers, fathers in midlife crises, grandfatherhood, and the death of the father. Section IV deals with cultural and historical variations, including the child's representation of God, the patriarchal tradition in *Genesis*, and a survey of the changing faces of fatherhood in America. Exploring clinical problems and applications, section V touches upon such matters as divorce, abusive fathers, incest, the relationship between abdicating fathers and homosexual sons, and the importance of involving fathers in clinical treatment of children. An afterword by E. James Anthony examines the internalized early-childhood father by citing the lives of Kafka, J.S. Mill, Gosse, Butler, and Freud. *Father and Child* maintains a continuity and consistency of excellence seldom found in anthologies.

396. Colman, Arthur, and Libby Colman. **Earth Father/Sky Father: The Changing Concept of Fathering.** Englewood Cliffs, N.J.: Prentice-Hall, 1981. P. xiii, 206. illustrations. notes. index. pa.

Employing Jungian concepts, the authors depict five archetypes of the father, connecting them with recent innovations in styles of fathering. The Colmans argue that men need images of the nurturing father to validate their changing roles as fathers. They need images not only of the sky father who mediates between the family and the outside world but of the earth father who functions within the family itself. Using literature, dreams, and myths, as well as interviews with fifteen men and case histories, the authors examine the archetype of Father the Creator, arguing that parenting may be a man's most significant act of creation. The archetype of the Earth Father can be found in images of male fertility and nurturance; in everyday life this kind of father is totally involved in raising children. The Sky Father is provider, judge, and protector; the man playing this role nowadays may find it frustrating and difficult. The Royal Father controls children's lives completely; at present the single parent is often forced into this role. The Dyadic Father is half of a pair of creative parents who nevertheless retain their own identities. The authors also trace varying images of the father through the life cycle— from the child's idealization of the father, through the adolescent's alienation from and ambivalence toward the father, to the adult's reconciliation with the father. In the final section the Colmans discuss non-traditional fathering, the need for males as earth-father nurturers, and the benefits for children of dyadic parents.

397. Cottle, Thomas J. **Like Fathers, like Sons: Portraits of Intimacy and Strain.** Norwood, N.J.: Ablex Publishing Corporation, 1981. P. xvii, 140. pa.

Drawing upon his work in constructing life studies, Cottle here provides ten accounts of fathers and sons. Avoiding "scientific" detachment, Cottle recreates the people and events impressionistically, thereby conveying the men's experiences of generational stress, love, and legacy. Many readers will find these accounts moving and powerful vignettes of male lives.

398. Daley, Eliot A. **Father Feelings.** New York: William Morrow and Co., 1978. P. 192. Reprint. New York: Pocket Books, 1979. pa.

Using episodes from his experiences as a father, Daley reflects upon a variety of family and men's concerns, including the emotional costs of today's frantic mobility, triumphs and pratfalls in dealing with his three children, the dubious advice of family "experts," teaching values to children, the overcomplicated mechanisms which thwart us as often as they benefit us, and the place of money in one's priorities. In the chapter with the most radical implications ("The Great Juggling Act, or Trying To Do Justice to Both a Career and a Family"), Daley writes: "Women may be tired of being regarded, culturally, as housekeepers and diaper washers; well, I'm tired of being culturally regarded as a breadwinner whose primary responsibility to the family is to be a 'good provider.' ... I'd rather be a father."

399. Dobson, James C. **Straight Talk to Men and Their Wives.** Waco, Tex.: Word Books, 1980. P. 222. illustrations.

Deploring the erosion of family leadership by men, Dobson invokes the memory of his father to redefine a Christian concept of masculinity. He discusses paternal authority and love, husband-wife relations, and men and work. Later chapters focus upon masculine identity, emotions, and religious belief.

400. Dodson, Fitzhugh. **How to Father.** Ed. Jeanne Harris. Los Angeles: Nash Publishing, 1974. P. xviii, 537. illustrations. appendixes. notes, index. bibliography, 503-20. Reprint. New York: New American Library, Signet, 1975. pa.

In this guidebook for fathers, Dodson uses the psychological stages of child development as a basis for offering practical advice on how fathers can deal effectively with children as they grow from infancy to young adulthood. Five appendixes contain guides to commercial toy and play equipment, inexpensive toys and play equipment that fathers can make, children's books, children's records, and a "survival kit" of reading materials for fathers themselves.

401. Fields, Suzanne. **Like Father, like Daughter: How Father Shapes the Woman His Daughter Becomes.** Boston: Little, Brown and Co., 1983. P. xii, 299. notes. bibliography, 291-99.

In this popular discussion of father-daughter relationships, Fields uses replies to a questionnaire, interviews, a review of psychological and sociological literature, and autobiography. Although the impact of father absence upon sons has been studied more thoroughly, Fields finds that a missing father can have devastating effects upon a daughter. The father confirms her loveableness, while she romances him and learns how to relate to other males. Although fathers tend to be more affectionate with daughters than with sons, this closeness can have its drawbacks if it creates dependence upon males in the daughter. Puberty can be troubling for both daughter and father as both become more aware of her sexuality. While not discounting the seriousness or the frequency of father-daughter incest, Fields refuses to blame it on a patriarchal plot against females. When a daughter marries, she sometimes must make a difficult adjustment to a husband who is not Big Daddy; she must make the transition from being Daddy's Little Girl to being an adult Woman-Wife. Just how trying this adjustment can be is illustrated by an account of Fields's colorful father, Samuel "Bo" Bregman, and her first years of marriage to Ted Fields. While welcoming the increased interest of many men in being better fathers, Fields is skeptical of men who worship "feminine" values while denigrating "masculine" ones: "When men pursue a feminine sensibility, women inevitably are shortchanged in their own fundamental psychic and sensual needs."

402. Gilbert, Sara D. **What's A Father For? A Father's Guide to the Pleasures and Problems of Parenthood with Advice from the Experts.** New York: Parents' Magazine Press, 1975. P. xxiii, 231. illustrations. appendix. notes. index. bibliography, 191-208, 213-18. Reprint. New York: Warner Books, 1975. pa.

With lighthearted humor and informal prose, Gilbert examines the father's roles and offers advice from the experts. She considers the reasons for wanting to be a father, coping with the demands of fatherhood, a brief history of fathering styles, avoiding sexist stereotyping of girls and boys, new forms of fathering (including dual-career fathers and househusbands), handling smaller children, coping with teens, and launching children into the world. She discusses the special problems and rewards of part-time fathers and single fathers (here dubbed felicitously double-time fathers). A final chapter deals with the difficulties of men's roles in modern society and with the father's need to develop as a fulfilled human being. "A typical married man with kids is somebody's husband, somebody's father, *and* somebody's employee," Gilbert notes for the benefit of women envying men's lot. "He can't do what he wants any more than his wife can." Comic cartoons by James Stevenson of the *New Yorker* supplement the text.

403. Grant, Wilson Wayne. **The Caring Father**. Nashville, Tenn.: Broadman Press, 1983. P. 155. appendix. notes. pa.
In the context of evangelical Christianity, Grant (an M.D.) considers the importance of fathers to children and offers advice on how fathers can maximize the beneficial aspects of their role in the family. Men need to allot time for fatherhood, stress the positive when relating to their children, and handle discipline with love and intelligence. Children need to see their fathers at work, to have fathers involved in family worship, and see that fathers love their wives. In an addendum, Grant considers the future of the family, indicating that reports of its death have been premature.

404. Green, Maureen. **Fathering**. New York: McGraw-Hill Book Co., 1976. P. ix, 230. notes. bibliography, 219-25. Reprint. *Life without Fathering*. New York: McGraw-Hill Book Co., 1977. pa. Published in Great Britain as *Goodbye Father*. London and Henley: Routledge and Kegan Paul, 1976.
In popular style, Green analyzes the crisis of modern fatherhood, arguing that either the role must be reinvented or it must be abandoned. Despite all the evils attributed to patriarchy, Green feels that feminist efforts to eliminate fathers from families are a mistake. Fathers are expendable, she warns, but their loss to the family does considerable damage to children, wives, society at large, and men themselves.

405. Hamilton, Marshall L. **Father's Influence on Children**. Chicago: Nelson-Hall, 1977. P. x, 203. index. bibliography, 173-96. pa.
Hamilton surveys research done on fathers up to 1974. Rejecting the stereotype of fathers as uninvolved incompetents, Hamilton finds indications of strong paternal involvement with children. He explores the effects of father absence on children, and of fathers' influence upon children's sex roles and development. Thumbnail sketches of people like Lee Harvey Oswald, Ralph Nader, and Indira Gandhi emphasize the father-child relationship. The concluding chapter presents characteristics of an "ideal" father.

406. Hammer, Signe. **Passionate Attachments: Fathers and Daughters in America Today**. New York: Rawson Associates, 1982. P. xi, 303. notes. index.
Drawing upon interviews, recollections, and scholarly studies, Hammer discusses uneasy father-daughter relationships in modern America. Her own father, absent during World War II, returned to dominate and discourage her search for autonomy. Similar problems afflict several accounts in the book: the fathers here seldom prepared their daughters for an independent role in the world. Hammer hypothesizes

that some fathers identify their own femininity with their daughters and want to protect and pamper them. The "successful" fathers in this book are the ones whose daughters have made it in the outside "male" world. In a concluding chapter, the author considers how dutiful daughters can undo the paralyzing effects of an overbearing father.

407. Heidebrecht, Paul, and Jerry Rohrbach. **Fathering a Son**. Chicago: Moody Press, 1979. P. 218. illustrations. appendix. bibliography, 205-14. pa.

From a biblical Christian viewpoint, the authors describe how a man can become a loving and encouraging father instead of a domineering and distant one. "We are promasculine," they state. "We believe men—and the boys growing up behind them—need to be liberated. Too many false images of masculinity have been foisted upon us." Providing a "job description" of fatherhood, the authors spell out the importance of the father's role in shaping the son's sex role, concept of God, moral values, ability to deal with society, and desire to achieve. The second part of their book recounts the boy's development from infancy to the teen years, interspersed with suggestions about how the father can foster his son's emotional and intellectual learning, spiritual development, and sexuality. Part III consists of advice on how to help sons in such matters as discipline, schoolwork, and career choices. Separate chapters briefly discuss the father-daughter relationship (the authors do not minimize its importance but indicate that it is not the subject of this book), the father who is an only parent, and what to do when the father-son relationship breaks down. In part IV interviews with four men provide personal insights into fathering. The appendix lists resources for the active father, including an annotated bibliography.

408. Johnson, Spencer. **The One Minute Father: The Quickest Way for You to Help Your Children Learn to Like Themselves and Want to Behave Themselves**. New York: William Morrow and Co., 1983. P. 112.

In this brief, easily read book, Johnson describes his "one-minute reprimand," a technique for showing disapproval of a child's behavior, showing approval for the child, and letting father's feelings get expressed. The technique leads to other practices such as positive reinforcement of desired behavior.

409. Jones, Evan, ed. **The Father: Letters to Sons and Daughters**. New York: Rinehart and Co., 1960. P. xx, 268. index.

This anthology, containing over one hundred letters to children from fathers throughout the ages, features mostly famous men (Lorenzo the Magnificent, Lord Chesterfield, Dickens, Theodore Roosevelt, Gandhi), although a few unknowns are included (an American soldier in World War II writing to his unborn child). Comments before and after the letters provide the necessary context.

410. Klein, Ted. **The Father's Book**. New York: William Morrow and Co., 1968. P. xiii, 393. illustrations. index.

This readable handbook attempts to provide a Dr. Spock-like guide for fathers. Klein's advice covers such matters as basic information for the father-to-be, understanding early childhood development, childhood diseases, father-son and father-daughter relations, absent fathers and divorced fathers, discipline, stepfathers and fosterfathers, father's role in sex education and in motivating general learning, money management, grandparents, religion, accidents and first aid, and how to get help from experts. In the eighties, some of Klein's advice seems still valid ("If you wait *too* long to become involved, you may not fit in with your child's needs and already developed behavior patterns"), while other views seem dubious and dated ("when the husband is present in the labor room—and even more often, at delivery ... he is the one who usually needs help just when the baby is born").

411.   Klinman, Debra G., Rhiana Kohl, and The Fatherhood Project at Bank Street College of Education. **Fatherhood U.S.A.: The First National Guide to Programs, Services, and Resources for and about Fathers.** New York: Garland Publishing, 1984. P. xxiv, 323. illustrations. appendixes. indexes. bibliography, 205-46. pa.

An invaluable resource book for fathers and men interested in changing male roles, *Fatherhood U.S.A.* is divided into six chapters. Chapter 1 lists programs for expectant and new fathers and for fathers of special needs children, as well as organizations concerned with male reproductive health care. Chapter 2 includes information about nurturant males in the educational setting, including child-care classes for schoolage boys, programs to encourage male involvement in schools, father-child classes, and college and university courses on fathering and on male roles. In chapter 3 are listed social and supportive services for all kinds of fathers (fathers in general, single fathers, stepfathers, teen fathers, gay fathers, and incarcerated fathers), as well as a listing of men's organizations resource centers, and support groups. Fathers and family law are covered in chapter 4, including a listing of divorce and custody mediation services and of fathers' rights organizations. Chapter 5 is devoted to fathers and work, including information about alternative work schedules, parental leave policies, and education and support programs for working fathers. A hefty chapter 6 is devoted to bibliographies and other resources for fathers and "new" men. Books and publications about numerous aspects of fathering are listed, as well as books for children featuring fathers and men in nurturing roles, films and videocassettes about fathers and nurturant males, newsletters of interest to many kinds of fathers, and information about the National Fatherhood Forum Series. The appendixes describe The Fatherhood Project and print its questionnaire. Two indexes of programs and organizations by alphabet and by geographical location are followed by a subject index. This book is testimony to the burgeoning interest in fatherhood. "Ten years ago," James A. Levine writes in the foreword, "this book could not have been written."

412.   Lamb, Michael E., ed. **The Role of the Father in Child Development.** 2d ed. A Wiley-Interscience Publication. New York: John Wiley and Sons, 1981. P. xiv, 582. illustrations. author and subject indexes. bibliographies at the end of each chapter.

In this collection of fourteen essays surveying father-child relations, literature on the following topics is surveyed: an overview of fathers and child development (by Michael E. Lamb), the development of Western fatherhood during selected historical periods (by Jonathan Bloom-Feshbach), recent developments in psychoanalytic theory of the father (by Veronica J. Mächtlinger), anthropological perspectives on the father's role (by Mary Maxwell Katz and Melvin J. Konner), the role of fathers in the Soviet Union (by Jaan Valsiner), male paternal care among monkeys and apes (by William K. Redican and David M. Taub), the father as a member of the child's social network (by Michael Lewis, Candice Feiring, and Marsha Weinraub), the influence of fathers viewed in a family context (by Frank A. Pedersen), the father's importance in the child's sex role development (by Henry B. Biller), the father's role in the child's moral internalization (by Martin L. Hoffman), the paternal role in the child's cognitive, academic, and intellectual development (by Norma Radin), the determinants of paternal involvement in caregiving and play with infants (by Ross D. Parke and Barbara R. Tinsley), the development of father-child relationships (by Michael E. Lamb), and the effects of father absence and divorce on the child's personality development (by Henry B. Biller). The bibliographies at the end of each chapter are indispensable for anyone researching father-child relationships.

413. Lamb, Michael E., and Abraham Sagi, eds. **Fatherhood and Family Policy.** Hillsdale, N.J.: Lawrence Erlbaum Associates, 1983. P. xi, 276. illustration. author and subject indexes. bibliographies at the end of each chapter.

The fourteen essays in this book examine the effects of public policy on fathers. In the introduction, Lamb stresses the importance of international and interdisciplinary perspectives on the topic. Highlights of the volume include James A. Levine and Lamb's assessment of how family policy in Sweden has not produced the effects it was supposed to; an account of the aims and undertakings of The Fatherhood Project by Lamb, Levine, and Joseph H. Pleck; Martin Wolins's delightfully irreverent discussion of the gender dilemma in social welfare; Eliezer D. Jaffe's account of fathers as the forgotten clients in welfare services; and Lois Wladis Hoffman's evaluation of the losses and gains for mothers from increased father participation. Lamb, Sagi, and Graeme Russell conclude with a chapter of recommendations for public policy in such areas as employment, law, health, and education.

414. Leenhouts, Keith J. **A Father ... A Son ... and a Three-Mile Run.** Grand Rapids, Mich.: Zondervan Publishing House, 1975. P. 140. illustrations.

In this inspirational book, a son's participation in a crucial race serves as a framework for the father's reflections upon such matters as the spiritual gifts which his own father bestowed upon him, the difficulties of raising a slow-learner son, the anguished decisions which as a judge he has had to make in the courtroom, the religious faith which has sustained him, and the fate of American fatherhood. "Where have all the fathers gone?" he wonders apprehensively. "Are we the most fatherless nation of all?"

415. Leonard, Linda Schierse. **The Wounded Woman: Healing the Father-Daughter Relationship.** Athens, Ohio: Swallow Press, Ohio University Press, 1982. P. xx, 186. notes. pa. Reprint. Boulder, Colo., and London: Shambhala, 1983. pa.

Besides the wounded daughter, the wounded father and the wounded "feminine" in men are also the subjects of this book. A Jungian analyst, Leonard discusses how both men and women are spiritually impoverished when the "feminine" is devalued, whether by narrowly masculine males or by "armored amazon" females. To illustrate her thesis, the author analyzes dreams, case histories, her own experiences with an alcoholic father, plays, films, novels, myths, and fairy tales. Leonard's approach is a healing, not a blaming, one.

416.   Levine, James A. **Who Will Raise the Children? New Options for Fathers (and Mothers).** Philadelphia and New York: J.B. Lippincott, 1976. P. 192. notes. Reprint. New York: Bantam Books, 1977. pa.

An influential book, *Who Will Raise the Children?* examines men who have chosen child care in a society that actively discourages any family role for men other than that of breadwinner. Levine examines how in the past social scientists have overlooked fathers and how courts have discriminated against them in granting custody. Drawing upon extended interviews, he describes the struggles and triumphs of fathers with sole and joint custody. Noting that full-time jobs do not accommodate the father's role as parent, Levine investigates such alternatives as part-time work, flextime, small businesses operated jointly by wife and husband, joint college teaching appointments for couples, and paternity leave policies. The single male who adopts a child faces special difficulties, including the suspicion that he is a homosexual. Because homemaking is not an esteemed career (especially for men), househusbands encounter puzzlement and hostility. Levine's concluding chapter argues that, because gender roles are interdependent, the problem of reconciling family and career is not simply a woman's problem. While much attention has been focused on women's new roles in society, little time and energy have been devoted to redirecting men's roles. Despite the discouraging evidence of widespread prejudice against men in child-caring roles, Levine's book offers heartening proof of the human rewards reaped by men who undertook them.

417.   Lockerbie, D. Bruce. **Fatherlove: Learning to Give the Best You've Got.** Garden City, N.Y.: Doubleday and Co., Doubleday-Galilee Original, 1981. P. 237.

In gracefully written essays Lockerbie uses Christian scriptures, personal anecdotes, and others' experiences to investigate such matters as the importance of the father's role, building character in children, disciplining with love and wisdom, and integrating faith into family life.

418.   Lucarini, Spartaco. **The Difficult Role of a Father.** Translated by Hugh Moran. Brooklyn, N.Y.: New City Press, 1979. P. 75. pa. Originally published as *Il Difficile Mestiere di Padre* (Roma: Città nuova, 1968).

In a series of informal essays that utilize interviews with fathers and children, Lucarini stresses children's need for a loving father's presence, examines the generation conflict between fathers and children, and advises fathers to listen carefully to their children and to talk frankly with them about sexuality "before it's too late."

419.   Lynn, David B. **The Father: His Role in Child Development.** Monterey, Calif.: Brooks/Cole Publishing Co., a division of Wadsworth Publishing Co., 1974. P. xiii, 333. illustrations. author and subject indexes. bibliography, 287-319.

Although recognizing that many fundamental questions remain unanswered, Lynn provides a clearly written synthesis of the growing body of research on fathers. In part I, Fathers and Cultures, Lynn discusses American fatherhood in transition, paternal behavior in animals and early men, the father role in different cultures, cultural experiments in restructuring the family (in the Soviet Union, Sweden, Israeli kibbutzim, and American communes), the changing nature of fatherhood in the Western world, and fathers in the United States. Part II, The Father-Child Relationship, explores theories of the father's role (with focus upon Freud and Parsons), the father-mother relationship, and the influence of fathers upon children's sex role behavior, scholastic aptitude, achievement, vocational choice, creativity, moral development, and mental health. Other chapters deal with the father's approach to childrearing (with some attention to abusive fathers) and with the effects upon children of father absence. The final chapter draws conclusions about what is known concerning fathers.

420. MacDonald, Gordon. **The Effective Father.** Wheaton, Ill.: Tyndale House Publishers, 1983. P. 256. notes. pa.

Drawing upon biblical insights and pastoral counseling experiences, MacDonald suggests how fathers can be effective parents amid the rush of secular, hedonistic life.

421. McKee, Lorna, and Margaret O'Brien, eds. **The Father Figure.** London and New York: Tavistock Publications, 1982. P. xii, 239. notes. name and subject indexes. bibliography, 208-27. pa.

This collection of thirteen readable essays by British scholars reverses the mother-focused perspective of past social science studies; in the process it challenges many cultural stereotypes about men as fathers. In the first essay the editors explore why fathering has recently become a popular topic for study, although no adequate history of fathering now exists and numerous aspects of fathering are still ignored. They offer a useful critique of the use (and misuse) of the word "patriarchy" in modern feminist writings. Other essays include a survey of the legal status of fathers in Great Britain by Nigel V. Lowe and Trevor Lummis's study of turn-of-the-century fathers which dispels the myth of the working-class brute. Martin P.M. Richards reflects on needed areas of study involving fathers, and David Owens studies the impact of infertility upon men who hoped to become fathers. Joel Richman recounts men's reactions to pregnancy and childbirth, and Angela Brown reports on the disharmony between hospital staffs and fathers participating in childbirth. Lorna McKee offers a critique of fathers' participation in infant care. Madeleine Simms and Christopher Smith examine the effects of fatherhood upon younger males, while Charlie Lewis criticizes the methodology used in recent father-infant studies. Tony Hipgrave details the trials of being a "lone" or single father ("There is, in short, no evidence that lone fathers cannot plan and organize a healthy developmental environment for themselves and their children. There is a good deal of evidence that we, the community, make it extremely hard for them to do so"). Margaret O'Brien examines the different patterns and experiences of men who became single fathers. The final essay by Jacqueline Burgoyne and David Clark explores the role of the stepfather. All of the essays exhibit scholarly acumen and a willingness to abandon stereotypes for a fresher view of the father figure.

422. Meister, Robert. **Fathers.** New York: Richard Marek Publishers, 1981. P. 227. Reprint. New York: Ballantine Books, 1983. pa.

A book about "the subjective *experience* of being a father and having one," *Fathers* consists of a series of domestic horror stories gleaned from 213 interviews with fathers and children. After revealing his own sense of failure as a son and as a father, Meister retells a number of chilling case histories, grouping them into accounts of fathers who were distant and silent, seductive, tyrannical and demanding, idealized (usually for the wrong reasons), macho and competitive, and eccentric and bizarre. Capable and loving fathers are in short supply in this volume.

423. Miller, Ted, ed. **The Christian Reader Book on Being a Caring Father.** New York: Harper and Row, 1983. P. 128. illustrations. pa.

This anthology consists of twenty-seven brief essays, written from a Christian perspective and all previously published, on a range of fathering topics. Representative titles include "The Husband Who Leads His Family" (by Robert H. Schuller), "Homes Are For Building Christians" (by Howard Hendricks), "Dad's Night at Home" (by Don Crawford), and "Fathers Can Be Beautiful!" (by Marcia Schwartz).

424. Ostrovsky, Everett S. **Children without Men.** Rev. ed. New York: Collier Books, 1962. P. 188. notes. index. pa. Originally published as *Father to the Child.*

An early and poignant account of how father absence can affect children, Ostrovsky's study uses a case history approach, drawing upon observations of children at a nursery school. Eight illustrative cases are presented in detail. One girl whose father is often away on business trips clings to the male teacher; another from a divorced home constantly needs reassurance that the male teacher is not displeased with her. A boy whose father is emotionally distant has trouble expressing his affection for others; another whose father died a year previously feels that he was deserted and responds hostilely to grown men. Perhaps most significant is Barbara, a child whose fastidious mother constantly shortcircuits her curiosity and spontaneity; closer contact with her more expansive father would help her, but he is necessarily less available to her than her mother is. The case illustrates well Ostrovsky's thesis: the absence or infrequent presence of one parent hinders the child's optimum development. Surveying the separation of fathers from families in industrial societies, Ostrovsky argues that the missing male distorts sex roles for both girls and boys, misorienting them for the future. Nor can the oedipal conflict be satisfactorily resolved when men are not around. His recommendations include fuller participation of fathers in child care and more male teachers in nursery and grade schools.

425. Parke, Ross D. **Fathers.** The Developing Child Series. Cambridge, Mass.: Harvard University Press, 1981. P. 136. notes. index. bibliography, 133. pa.

Parke describes his book as "a progress report of what we know today about how fathers act and how they influence their children." Stressing the idea that fathers influence children both directly and indirectly, this compact volume gracefully surveys such topics as the distorting "myths" about fathers (particularly from Freud and Bowlby), expectant fathers, how fathers interact with infants, and how fathers affect children's socialization, particularly their gender roles. Two final chapters explore the effects of custody decisions and of innovations in fathering—including paternity leaves, flexible working hours, work-sharing couples, dual-career couples, and role-sharing families. Parke concludes: "Fathers are no longer, if they ever were, merely a biological necessity—a social accident. ... Children need their fathers, but fathers need their children, too."

426. Pedersen, Frank A., ed. **The Father-Infant Relationship: Observational Studies in the Family Setting**. Praeger Special Studies. New York: Praeger Publishers, 1980. P. x, 185. illustrations. notes. index. bibliography, 164-79.

This collection presents five studies in infant-parent interaction, with special attention to fathers. In the introductory essay, Pedersen discusses the failure of the social sciences to examine the father-infant relationship; he points to the importance of studying that relationship in the context of the family. In the first study Michael E. Lamb, rejecting the uniqueness of the mother-child relationship, examines parent-infant attachments during the first two years of life. From the earliest ages infants are attracted to both parents, and the two relationships differ qualitatively: "Fathers are not merely occasional mother-substitutes." Ross D. Parke and Douglas B. Sawin, assessing the interaction of fathers and infants, as well as parental attitudes, find both similarities and differences in mothers' and fathers' responses; the differences are partly dependent upon the infant's sex. Frank A. Pedersen, Barbara J. Anderson, and Richard L. Cain Jr. study parent-infant and husband-wife interactions at five months. Jay Belsky examines how fathers may influence their infant's ability to explore. K. Alison Clarke-Stewart views the father's contribution to cognitive and social development in early childhood; the importance of father's play is stressed, as are his contribution to the child's social-affective development. In a concluding chapter, Pedersen evaluates the findings and reformulates questions that need to be asked about fathers, infants, and families.

427. Rapoport, Rhona, Robert N. Rapoport, and Ziona Strelitz, with Stephen Kew. **Fathers, Mothers and Society: Towards New Alliances**. New York: Basic Books, 1977. P. ix, 421. index. bibliography, 366-405. Reprint. *Fathers, Mothers and Society: Perspectives on Parenting.* New York: Random House, 1980. pa.

This rich survey of literature places men's family roles clearly in the larger context of family studies. Taking issue with the "myth" that "parenting means mothering" and with the child-focused, mother-oriented, and expert-guided view of the family prevailing throughout much of the twentieth century, the authors in chapter 1 spell out their own views of parenting in a series of twelve propositions, the first of which is the idea that parents—as well as children—are people with needs to be met. In chapter 2 the authors argue that the recognition of parents' needs by the experts has been unsatisfactory. The next six chapters consist of a packed review of and commentary upon studies of the family from several disciplines. Beginning before the birth of the first child, the survey continues through the early and middle years of active parenting and concludes with parenting of adolescent and adult children. A final chapter recapitulates the book's findings and explores new directions in parenting. The discussion has historical, academic, professional, and social implications. The bibliography is extensive.

428. Reynolds, William. **The American Father: A New Approach to Understanding Himself, His Woman, His Child**. New York and London: Paddington Press, distributed by Grosset and Dunlap, 1978. P. 227. index. pa.

Somewhat misleadingly titled, this book presents Reynolds' personal and mildly sardonic view of what is happening in the modern American upper-middle-class white family. While recounting the interactions of Father, Mother, Sonny, and Sis, Reynolds flings barbs at what he considers the trendy "experts" on mental health, marriage counseling, and child care.

429. Rue, James J., and Louise Shanahan. **Daddy's Girl, Mama's Boy**. Indianapolis, Ind., and New York: Bobbs-Merrill Co., 1978. P. xvi, 250. index. bibliography, 249-50. Reprint. New York: New American Library, Signet, 1979. pa.

Because the father-daughter and mother-son relationships can be crucial to child formation, the authors consider both their positive and negative potentials. (Homosexuality is considered one of the negative possibilities.) Throughout the book, Rue and Shanahan illustrate their theses by citing case histories and biographies of the famous—including Jacqueline Bouvier and Jack Bouvier, Elizabeth I and Henry VIII, Ella Quinland O'Neill and Eugene O'Neill, and Margaret Carnegie and Andrew Carnegie. Rejecting "avant-garde life styles" (including extramarital affairs, cohabitation, and homosexual relationships), the authors consider at some length the elements of enduring and happy marriages, and they provide a workbook by which readers may assess themselves as daddy's girls or mama's boys. In this way the book is intended to be a guide to understanding and directing the self positively.

430. Russell, Graeme. **The Changing Role of Fathers?** St. Lucia, Queensland, Australia: University of Queensland Press, 1983. P. x, 250. appendixes. index. bibliography, 238-45. pa.

Based upon investigation into 145 traditional families and seventy-one shared care-giving families, this study describes four types of fathers—uninterested and unavailable, traditional, "good," and nontraditional and highly participant. Mother's employment outside the home had a small but significant impact upon increasing father participation in child care. The fathers' competence with children is clearly established. Reviewing the literature and assessing crosscultural evidence, Russell describes the benefits and costs to parents and children in father-participant households.

431. Salk, Lee. **My Father, My Son: Intimate Relationships**. New York: G.P. Putnam's Sons, 1982. P. 255. Reprint. New York: Berkley Books, 1983. pa.

Using informal questioning techniques and making no attempt at statistical representativeness, Salk has gathered twenty-eight interviews with fathers and sons. Although some marred relationships are recounted, most of the recollections are upbeat: many men tell of strong affectional ties with their nurturing fathers, and they strive to emulate that behavior with their own sons. The importance of loving attention, physical contact, and discipline recurs in the interviews. A few of the interviewees are well known, for example, talk-show host Mike Douglas. Noting that fathers and sons either have or crave loving relationships, Salk concludes that "the acceptance of males in the nurturant role ... will contribute to the survival of the family as a social unit."

432.   Singer, Wenda Goodhart, Stephen Shechtman, and Mark Singer. **Real Men Enjoy Their Kids! How to Spend Quality Time with the Children in Your Life**. Nashville, Tenn.: Abingdon Press, 1983. P. 176. illustrations. appendix. pa.

Written as a practical guide to help men interact positively with children, this upbeat handbook contains numerous suggested activities designed to develop the child's social, emotional, cognitive, physical, and spiritual capacities. Presented in two versions (one for children six and under, the other for children ages seven to twelve), the activities include home life, the working world, leisure time, and life "crises" (new baby, separation/divorce, death). A final section of the book offers additional suggestions for encouraging a deepening relationship between men and children.

433.   Shedd, Charlie. **The Best Dad Is a Good Lover**. Kansas City, Kans.: Sheed Andrews and McMeel, 1977. P. 135. illustrations.

Father of five, author of a syndicated column "Strictly for Dads," and a Presbyterian minister, Shedd elaborates upon the thesis that "to love his children well a dad must first love their mother—and show it consistently." Brief chapters contain illustrative stories, letters from correspondents, and practical advice.

434.   Shedd, Charlie. **A Dad Is for Spending Time With**. Kansas City, Kans.: Sheed Andrews and McMeel, 1978. P. 136. illustrations. Reprint. New York: Ace Books, 1982. pa.

In brief, upbeat chapters Shedd offers suggestions for fathers who want to spend more time creatively with their children.

435.   Shedd, Charlie. **Smart Dads I Know**. New York: Sheed and Ward, 1975. P. xi, 125. illustrations. Reprint. New York: Avon Books, 1978. pa.

In this book Shedd provides examples and advice on how fathers can avoid the trap of workaholism.

436.   Stanley, Charles F. **A Man's Touch**. Wheaton, Ill.: Victor Books, 1977. P. 120. pa. Originally titled *Is There a Man in the House?*

From a conservative Christian viewpoint, Stanley describes the man's role as husband, father, and religious guide for his family.

437.   Stolz, Lois Meek, and others. **Father Relations of War-Born Children: The Effect of Postwar Adjustment of Fathers on the Behavior and Personality of First Children Born While the Fathers Were at War**. 1954. Reprint: New York: Greenwood Press, 1968. P. viii, 365. illustrations. appendixes. bibliography, 361-65. Reprint. Stanford, Calif.: Stanford University Press, 1975.

This classic study examines the effects of father absence upon children and parents alike.

438.   Sullivan, S. Adams. **The Father's Almanac**. Garden City, N.Y.: Doubleday and Co., Dolphin Book, 1980. P. xvii, 365. illustrations. index. bibliography, 339-42. pa.

In this attractive, oversized book, Sullivan offers practical information and advice on such matters as the father's role during pregnancy and childbirth, tending babies, working and fathering, everyday and special family events, child learning, and playing with children.

439. Valentine, Alan, ed. **Fathers to Sons: Advice without Consent**. Norman: University of Oklahoma Press, 1963. P. xxxii, 237. notes. index. bibliography, 219-26.

From the Middle Ages to the present, fathers have written to sons exhorting, criticizing, advising, praising, and loving them. The lettters writers in this collection, mostly well known, range from Edward II to Franklin D. Roosevelt. Valentine's introductions and notes are both witty and helpful.

440. Woolfolk, William, with Donna Woolfolk Cross. **Daddy's Little Girl: The Unspoken Bargain between Fathers and Their Daughters**. Englewood Cliffs, N.J.: Prentice-Hall, 1982. P. 220. index.

In the love of fathers and daughters, she agrees to worship him, and he agrees to serve as her protector against the world. The danger in this relationship, the authors contend, is that she may never develop her own competencies and that he may be unwilling to let her grow up. The authors, father and daughter, provide evidence from their own relationship to support this thesis, and they look for it in the lives of an unspecified number of fathers and daughters whom they interviewed. Eschewing systematic methods of observation, the book relies on "the idiosyncratic, intuitive, impressionistic method"; it is thus informal and personal rather than rigorously analytic. The authors touch upon such matters as fathers and young daughters, the conflicts created by daughters' awakening sexuality, special problems (e.g., absent fathers, single parenthood, incest, homosexuality, inadequate fathers), and separation between maturing daughters and their fathers.

441. Yablonsky, Lewis. **Fathers and Sons**. New York: Simon and Schuster, 1982. P. 218. notes.

Over a four-year period, Yablonsky interviewed in depth more than a hundred men, and processed questionnaire responses from 564 men. Drawing also upon his own, often troubled, relations with his parents, his clinical experiences with men (usually involving a technique known as psychodrama), research, novels, plays, and television, Yablonsky examines father-son relationships, warts and all. He delineates the sometimes conflicting dreams and messages from fathers to sons, and enumerates different kinds of father styles (compassionate loving-doubling, buddies, macho, psychopathic, egocentric). He also traces three phases of father-son interaction: ego-blending during the son's childhood, separation and individuation during adolescence, and man-to-man during the son's adulthood. Looking at family dynamics, the author sees the mother as a "filter" between father and son; he also discusses siblings, grandparents, divorce and separation, teachers and coaches. Among the special problems considered are deviance and emotional disorders, alcohol and drug abuse, homosexuality, and health problems. In a final chapter Yablonsky presents problems and solutions in modern fathering.

EXPECTANT FATHERS

442.   Alliance for Perinatal Research and Services, The: Rae Grad, Debora Bash, Ruth Guyer, Zoila Acevedo, Mary Anne Trause, Diane Reukauf. **The Father Book: Pregnancy and Beyond.** Washington, D.C.: Acropolis Books, 1981. P. 263. illustrations. appendixes. notes. index. bibliography, 255-59. pa.

In this informative and lucid guide, the six authors explore the choices available to fathers in such matters as preparing for childbirth, events during pregnancy, childbirth classes, father participation in child delivery, unexepcted events, (e.g., multiple births, stillborn child), the postpartum period, living with an infant, interactions and exercises (a chapter by Jan Shaffer), and recent trends in fathering. Appendix I offers information and advice about how to cope with hospital personnel and policies concerning father participation in labor and birth. Appendix II lists organizations interested in childbirth.

443.   Bittman, Sam, and Sue Rosenberg Zalk. **Expectant Fathers.** New York: Hawthorn Books, 1978. P. xxv, 291. illustrations. appendixes. notes. index. bibliography, 278-83. pa.

A full-scale look at expectant fathers, this book utilizes current literature, forty-seven interviews, and 162 questionnaire responses. Although expectant fathers often undergo difficult emotional experiences, present sex roles discourage their expression, and society tends to ignore them. The authors examine the couvade syndrome in primitive and modern societies; they trace the father's emotional and physical changes during the trimesters of pregnancy. A separate chapter is devoted to sexual relations during pregnancy. The stages of labor and birth are described with the participating father's roles during each stage. Fathers of infants are warned about men's postpartum depression and are urged to resist being pushed aside by well-meaning mothers, relatives, or friends. Despite some negative aspects, involved fatherhood has more than sufficient rewards: the new father is urged to enjoy this deepening human experience. The text is illustrated by F.X. Tobin's drawings. The appendixes list questionnaire findings, home birth agencies, contraindications for home birth, and medical emergencies during home birth. A glossary of terms is also included.

444.   Bradley, Robert A. **Husband-Coached Childbirth.** 3d ed. New York: Harper and Row, 1981. P. xiii, 238. illustrations. index.

This pioneering book, first published in 1965, recounts how Bradley (an M.D.) first became an advocate of natural childbirth and only later recognized the importance of involving the father in pregnancy, labor, and birthing. (Bradley uses "birthing" to describe natural childbirth, as opposed to "delivery" by a doctor using medication—with the father pacing in the waiting room.) Chapter 4 "Where Do Fathers Fit In?" is "must" reading for any man thinking of becoming a father. Other chapters instruct the man on the part he can play in helping his pregnant partner with physical and mental wellbeing, his role during the various stages of labor, and his function in the birthing process. Bradley also discusses postpartum family relations and the husband's role in breastfeeding. As an advocate of natural childbirth, Bradley discourages the use of chemical substances by prospective parents. Obstacles to the father's presence in the birthing room have diminished considerably since the first edition of this book, but Bradley warns against recalcitrant doctors, medical personnel, parents, and friends. The book closes with two chapters on problems during pregnancy and methods of treating them without drugs or medications. *Contra* Bradley, the foreword by Ashley Montagu advocates home birthing, while agreeing with everything else in the book. This book makes a strong case for the man's presence during birth as a part of the natural bonding of man and woman—and child.

445. Burton, Jerome, and Milt Rosen. **The Fatherhood Formula.** Chatsworth, Calif.: Major Books, 1976. P. 187. index. pa.
Dismayed by the lack of information about such matters ("men know less than women"), the authors use a question-and-answer format and a sense of humor to elucidate topics every father-to-be should know about. Contents include the male reproductive system, impregnation, the male responses to pregnancy, the development of the fetus, delivery (the authors believe the father should be present), Caesarean sections, treatment of infants (Burton recommends circumcision), and the newborn at home.

446. Gresh, Sean. **Becoming a Father: A Handbook for Expectant Fathers.** New York: Butterick Publishing, 1980. P. 144. appendixes. index. bibliography, 140-41. Reprint. New York: Bantam Books, 1982. pa.
This highly readable book provides fathers-to-be with essential information and suggestions during pregnancy, labor, childbirth, and afterward. Without pressuring men, Gresh outlines the choices available to them. He warns prospective fathers that they will be ignored by professionals and that they will experience anxieties; the rewards of active fatherhood, however, outweigh such drawbacks. Discussing men's fears (about finances, dangers of childbirth, sex, and marital relationships), Gresh stresses the importance to men of talking them out and maintaining communication with their partners. Separate chapters are devoted to men's changes during pregnancy (including the phenomenon of couvade); women's changes during each trimester of pregnancy; costs; preparations for childbirth (including choosing an obstetrician or—possibly—a midwife, childbirth education classes, and the Lamaze, the Bradley, and the Leboyer approaches to childbirth); the man's role during labor (the importance of not separating husbands and wives at this time is stressed); and adjustments to life with a newborn. The foreword by Elisabeth Bing briefly traces how separation of fathers-to-be from childbirth occurred in the nineteenth and twentieth centuries and how the situation is presently being rectified. The appendixes include a list of chapters and groups of The American Society for Psychoprophylaxis in Obstetrics, a state-by-state listing of chapters of the International Childbirth Education Association, and the Pregnant Patient's Bill of Rights and Responsibilities.

447. Heinowitz, Jack. **Pregnant Fathers: How Fathers Can Enjoy and Share the Experiences of Pregnancy and Childbirth.** Englewood Cliffs, N.J.: Prentice-Hall, 1982. P. xiii, 126. appendix. notes. index. bibliography, 117-19. pa.
Arguing that *couples* get pregnant and that the pregnant father has been almost entirely overlooked, Heinowitz offers information and suggestions to encourage males to become full partners in pregnancy. He debunks the ideas that the father is a secondary parent and that fathers' influence on infants and on growing daughters is minimal. Repeatedly, he stresses the need for men to get their feelings out in

the open, warning that some feelings (self-doubt, jealousy, insecurity, anxiety, depression, and ambivalence about becoming a parent) can be damaging to the couple's relationship if allowed to fester unexpressed. Awareness exercises are included for men, as well as advice on listening to what one's partner is saying and on communicating clearly what one wants to say. Heinowitz also discusses couvade, sympathy symptoms, and the need for "ritualizing" the pregnancy so that men can feel included in it. Advice about sex during pregnancy includes suggestions about less stressful positions and noncoital lovemaking. Childbirth classes can be helpful but may be inadequate for fathers because the teachers are unprepared to present the male's roles in pregnancy. Heinowitz reviews the options for delivery, the man's role during delivery, and his possible reactions to it. A chapter is devoted to coping with a new infant at home and to resuming sex. Despite the pitfalls of being an involved pregnant father, the rewards are great. An appendix suggests how childbirth educators and others can make their classes more helpful.

448. Kahan, Stuart. **The Expectant Father's Survival Kit.** New York: Monarch, Sovereign, 1978. P. viii, 181. index. pa.

With rare good humor, Kahan provides a guide for the expectant father. After exploring initial reactions to the news, he takes men through the nine months of pregnancy, with updates on the wife's and the child's changes. Kahan touches upon such other matters as figuring costs, finding an obstetrician, the changes men can expect to go through, sex during pregnancy, clothes for the pregnant woman, exercises, and labor and delivery—including instructions for an emergency do-it-yourself delivery. The final chapter covers coping with an infant at home.

449. Mayle, Peter. **How to Be a Pregnant Father: Including the Pregnant Father's Cookbook by Len Deighton.** Secaucus, N.J.: Lyle Stuart, 1977. P. 52. illustrations. pa.

Lighthearted advice from Mayle, a quick-meal cookbook from Deighton, and comical cartoons by Arthur Robins compose this upbeat guide for the expectant father. No advice is offered, however, about father participation in childbirth.

450. Phillips, Celeste R., and Joseph T. Anzalone. **Fathering: Participation in Labor and Birth.** 2d ed. Saint Louis, Mo.: C.V. Mosby Co., 1982. P. xv, 168. illustrations. notes. bibliographies after each chapter. pa.

Stressing the positive effects of father participation in labor and childbirth, this book argues that "since fathers tend to be undervalued in our culture ... men may have suffered as much from discrimination as have women—particularly when it comes to pregnancy and birth." Surveying the father's role in history, the authors find that his exclusion from birthing parallels his diminished role in child-rearing. The attack on nineteenth-century paternalism unfortunately also denied fatherhood. Although some hospitals still regard men as excess baggage during labor and birthing, the movement to make men active participants is growing stronger. Without insisting that every man be present at birth, the authors discuss the impact of pregnancy upon men, ways in which the physician gains from father participation, and its positive effects (e.g., father-infant bonding). Such results are movingly dramatized in a series of accounts from fathers, and sometimes mothers, of their experiences during childbirth. Photographs illustrate these accounts. An additional chapter records the memories of men who pioneered father participation. A glossary of unfamiliar medical terms is included.

451.   Sasmor, Jeannette L. **What Every Husband Should Know about Having a Baby: The Psychoprophylactic Way**. Chicago: Nelson-Hall, 1972. P. 232. illustrations. appendix. index. bibliography, 221-22.

Sasmor provides a readable guide for husbands to the psychoprophylactic method (PPM). "Prophylaxis," she explains, "is a long, unwieldy name that refers to the prevention (prophylaxis) of mental or emotional (psycho) trauma experienced by most unprepared women during the process of childbearing." In other words, the husband becomes the wife's birthing coach. Without mounting any soapboxes, Sasmor explains the value of the husband's involvement in pregnancy and child-birth. (Readers would be well advised to skip the foreword by Benjamin Segal which manages to be antagonistic toward men in a way that Sasmor never is.) She surveys the history of "natural childbirth" ideas and outlines the husband's role during pregnancy, delivery, and afterwards. As a practicing nurse, Sasmor is able to offer numerous hints for husbands about such matters as breathing and relaxation techniques, what to expect in the delivery room, episiotomy, rooming in after birth, and taking care of a new baby. Without attempting to usurp the function of husband-coached childbirth classes, Sasmor's book provides a valuable supplement.

452.   Schaefer, George. **The Expectant Father**. Rev. ed. New York: Barnes and Noble, 1972. P. xii, 167. appendixes. index. bibliography, 159-62. pa.

In concise style, Schaefer surveys the expectant father's role from premarital examination to costs of caring for an infant. He explains such matters as genes, chromosomes, and the Rh factor; he offers information and advice about living with a pregnant wife, education for parenthood, and whether to participate in childbirth.

453.   Weiss, Robert Russell, and Myron Ray Pexton. **Dr. Pexton's Guide for the Expectant Father**. North Quincy, Mass.: Christopher Publishing House, 1970. P. 208. index.

This popular guide for fathers consists of questions by Weiss and answers by Pexton, an M.D. The topics include birth control, father's presence in the delivery room, Caesarian section, vasectomy, Rh factor, postpartum blues, infant care, and so on. Some readers may find Pexton's responses refreshingly commonsensical; others may find them sometimes dubious and dated. In this book, the father's role seems largely a supportive one, in contrast to the more active role recommended by some recent fathers' advocates.

DIVORCED AND SINGLE FATHERS

454.   Atkin, Edith, and Estelle Rubin. **Part-Time Father**. New York: Vanguard Press, 1976. P. 191. Reprint. New York: New American Library, Signet, 1977. pa.

Drawing upon their experiences as therapists, the authors—both of whom possess impressive credentials—offer information and advice to divorced fathers during the breaking-up period and afterward. Topics covered include the visiting father, money problems, "bachelor" fathers, remarriage, extended families, and special problems of adolescent children. The authors' advice is calm, concise, and compassionate.

455.   Barber, Dulan. **Unmarried Fathers**. London: Hutchinson and Co., 1975.
        P. 179.

Usually ignored, dismissed, or reviled, the unmarried father deserves a closer, more humane look. Although the author of this British study concludes that most unwed fathers are unconcerned, this is not true of all. He provides extracts from interviews with eight unmarried fathers to demonstrate the range of their characteristics. Examining British law, he finds that it discourages the father's involvement with the child; by denying the unwed father nearly all rights, it also discourages his willingness to support the child. New approaches are needed to help unmarried fathers assume their responsibilities. Also, Barber calls for the same social help to single-parent fathers caring for children as is given to mothers: "A man who chooses domesticity and total daily care for his child is regarded as work-shy, perhaps a malingerer." An increasing number of men, Barber concludes, are demanding the right to be involved, caring fathers—a right often denied them now by law and society.

456.   Gatley, Richard H., and David Koulack. **Single Father's Handbook: A
        Guide for Separated and Divorced Fathers**. Garden City, N.Y.: Anchor
        Press/Doubleday, 1979. P. xvii, 196. index. pa.

For the separated or divorced father who does not have custody, the authors—both psychologists and both divorced fathers—provide helpful hints on such matters as maintaining a working relationship with the children's mother, handling grandparents and former in-laws, preparing space for the children at the father's new home, "mothering" children (the authors even provide a few favorite recipes), and bringing them together with new women friends. Above all, the authors provide support for the divorced father who must cope with society's view of him as an expendable parent, incompetent when it comes to caring for children.

457.   Kahan, Stuart. **For Divorced Fathers Only**. New York: Monarch,
        Sovereign, 1978. P. 179. bibliography, 179. pa.

Recognizing that divorce is usually a hellish experience, this supportive book offers the divorced father suggestions, information, and reassurance for coping after divorce. A divorced father himself, Kahan discusses the man's problems of establishing a new life after divorce, the dynamics of maintaining father-child relationships, and the complications of dating and remarriage. In a final chapter he provides a quick survey of the financial and legal aspects of divorce, including alimony, child support, taxes, and custody. The epilogue raises questions about the ready availability of, and the rapid resort to, divorce in America. This readable book is informed by Kahan's belief that "no matter what you may have heard, the chief victim in most divorces is the man."

458.   McCormick, Mona. **Stepfathers: What the Literature Reveals: A Literature
        Review and Annotated Bibliography**. La Jolla, Calif.: Western Behavioral
        Sciences Institute, 1974. P. iv, 76. bibliography, 42-75. pa.

Deploring the failure of researchers to attend to the father in general and to the stepfather in particular, McCormick provides a survey of such literature as there is. She notes the negative stereotypes associated with stepfathers, and she warns that the role can be difficult and perhaps never fully "successful" because the stepfather cannot—and should not try to—supplant entirely the biological father. She enumerates the factors affecting the role (including income, sexual implications, number of remarriages, the previous family situation, and the child's perception of family relationships) and the legal aspects of adoption and support. Some common problem areas are: how stepchildren and stepfathers should address each other, discipline, the child's becoming a go-between in hostile family relationships, custody, and preparation for stepfathering. McCormick reviews similar problem areas from the perspective of stepchildren, current conclusions about such familiar beliefs as "divorce is bad for children" and "children of divorce will have problems in their own marriages," and what light recent literature on the family sheds upon stepfathers. She concludes that, despite difficulties, stepfathers and stepchildren can have loving relationships. An annotated bibliography of more than 150 items illustrates the author's point that studies focusing solely on the stepfather are sparse.

459. McFadden, Michael. **Bachelor Fatherhood: How to Raise and Enjoy Your Children as a Single Parent**. New York: Walker and Co., 1974. P. 158. bibliography, 155-58.

In upbeat, "can do" style, the author—a divorced father with custody of three children—takes the reader through the basics of handling and enjoying childrearing as a single parent. In particular, McFadden is eager to show that a single father can succeed as a parent—and succeed happily. Although skeptical of the myths of happy marriage and painless divorce and aware of the difficulties in a father's gaining custody, the author argues that divorce and raising children can be a liberating, fulfilling experience for men. Using interviews with fifty divorced fathers with custody, McFadden offers advice on running a household, loving and living with small children, coping with teenagers, doing the housework, and cooking the meals (a survival handbook of basic recipes is included). In a brief afterword, McFadden suggests that the strong man of the future may be not the warrior but the peacemaker and nurturer.

460. Newman, George. **101 Ways to Be a Long-Distance Super-Dad**. Mountain View, Calif.: Blossom Valley Press, 1981. P. 108. illustrations. pa.

From creative taperecording to swapping jokes, Newman presents 101 practical suggestions for the long-distance parent who wishes to sustain an imaginative and loving relationship with his or her child.

461. Oakland, Thomas, with Nancy Vogt Wedemeyer, Edwin J. Terry, and Jane Manaster. **Divorced Fathers: Reconstructing a Quality Life**. New York: Human Sciences Press, 1984. P. 201. index.

For the man facing divorce, this book offers helpful advice—although in somewhat confusing order. Readers may want to start with chapters 7 through 9 on alternatives to divorce and legal matters, move on to discussions of child custody (chapter 6), the man's psychological and social changes during divorce (chapter 2), the effects of divorce upon children (chapters 3 through 5), life after divorce (chapter 1), and finish with information on household management and budgeting (chapters 10 and 11).

462. Pannor, Reuben, Fred Massarik, and Byron Evans. **The Unmarried Father: New Approaches for Helping Unmarried Young Parents**. New York: Springer Publishing Co., 1971. P. xii, 196. illustrations. appendix. notes. author and subject indexes.

Usually overlooked by social workers and researchers, the unmarried father is the primary focus of this study. The authors note that males are often less prepared for parenthood than females, that the unwed father is usually regarded as little more than a handy scapegoat for an unwanted pregnancy, and that society asks that he either marry the woman, or pay support, or disappear from the scene. Seldom are unmarried fathers regarded as human beings with feelings and conflicts. After describing the methodology of their study at the Vista Del Mar Child-Care Services with ninety-six fathers and 222 mothers, the authors discount stereotypes of unmarried fathers, for example, the older roué who seduces younger women or the young man who engages in casual affairs. Most of the fathers were emotionally involved with the mothers, most were reachable by the researchers, and most felt more guilt than the mothers did. In drawing a profile of the men, the authors discovered that many had masculine identity problems, often rooted in unsatisfactory relationships with their own fathers. Also, many of the men came from father-absent or conflicted families without strong religious ties. Such men may be trying to prove their masculinity by fathering a child. The authors list goals which social workers should strive for with these fathers, particularly involving them in the pregnancy and decision making. Among the options open to unmarried parents, the opportunity for the father—as opposed to the mother—to raise the child with community help is not listed, nor do the authors comment on that anomaly. They do, however, make a series of suggestions to decrease the numbers of unmarried fathers. The appendix contains the recording form used in the study.

463.   Rosenthal, Kristine M., and Harry F. Keshet. **Fathers without Partners: A Study of Fathers and the Family after Marital Separation.** Totowa, N.J.: Rowman and Littlefield, 1981. P. xxiii, 187. appendixes. index. bibliography, 167-79.

The authors, both divorced parents, explore the effects of marital breakup upon men and the father-child relationship. Drawing upon interviews with more than 129 divorced fathers, they conclude that parents need children as much as children need parents, that caring for children often stabilizes divorced fathers, and that some fathers are closer to their children after divorce. Rosenthal and Keshet also comment on numerous related matters, such as the effects of the women's liberation movement on marriages, the dynamics of father-child relationships, joint custody (though favorable toward it, they have reservations), the need for coparenting and the difficulties of achieving it, the legal system's view of the father's role, relations between men and their ex-wives, and the details of coping after divorce—housing, changed lifestyle, dating, refamilying, and cohabitation. The concluding chapter defines the family in terms of parent-child relationships rather than husband-wife relationships. "We learned," Rosenthal writes, "that fathering means many things, that divorce need not mean an inevitable distancing of a father and his children."

464.   Rowlands, Peter. **Saturday Parent: A Book for Separated Families.** New York: Continuum Publishing Corp., 1980. P. viii, 143. bibliography, 143. pa.

A divorced father, Rowlands urges similar "Saturday parents" to recognize that being involved with their children is crucially important. A psychologist by training, he offers case histories to illustrate problems and possibilities in noncustodial parenting. He also offers solid practical advice on such matters as visits, the father's "new friend," and going to court for visitation rights (this chapter is not a particularly encouraging one). Although most of Rowlands's advice is aimed at fathers, he includes a special chapter for the mother who is a Saturday parent.

465.　Shepard, Morris A., and Gerald Goldman. **Divorced Dads: Their Kids, Ex-Wives, and New Lives.** Radnor, Pa.: Chilton Book Co., 1979. P. xi, 154. notes. Reprint. New York: Berkley Publishing Corp., 1980. pa.

Joint or shared custody is the subject of this book. The authors—both divorced fathers with six preteen children between them—decided early on not to become Disneyland Dads or Sunday Heroes. Instead, each worked out a custody arrangement in which the father has the children at least 50 percent of the time. From personal experiences, they offer nuts-and-bolts suggestions about how to make joint custody work, touching on such matters as single parenting, career demands, money problems, and remarriage. Skeptical of the courts, child "experts," and public schools, the authors offer practical advice for coping with each. They report on a Brandeis University study of divorced fathers, and discuss how Sweden's family policy has affected fathers there.

466.　Silver, Gerald A., and Myrna Silver. **Weekend Fathers.** Los Angeles: Stratford Press, 1981. P. xiv, 236. appendix. bibliography, 231-36.

"If we are going to be a truly equal society," the authors write, "the next major revolution must be men's rights." Within the larger context of inequities suffered by males, this book focuses upon divorce, custody, property settlements, visitation, support, the plight of second wives and grandparents, and starting over. They find a cultural bias against males which, once divorce occurs, creates a domino effect: the man leaves the house, setting up the process by which the woman will be awarded the children and hence a good deal of the property, spouse support, and so on. Even if the man does not leave the house, judges' outmoded views of gender roles will accomplish the same effect. While support is rigidly enforced, visitation is not. No-fault divorce laws do not improve the male's disadvantage, and language changes (e.g., "alimony" becomes "spouse support") are merely cosmetic. Despite their expressed goal of sexual equality, some feminists support "selective equality" which benefits women only. The authors—both of whom have suffered painful divorces—depict the situation of Disneyland Dads, assess the impact of father absence on children, the needs of divorced men, and the various kinds of custody. They examine the economics of being male in modern America, the games children play to manipulate divorced parents, the sex bias of many judges and attorneys, and the process of picking up the pieces of one's life after divorce. A final chapter describes the men's rights movement, and the appendix lists divorce reform organizations in the U.S.

OTHER FAMILY ROLES

467.　Arcana, Judith. **Every Mother's Son.** Garden City, N.Y.: Anchor Press/ Doubleday, 1983. P. ix, 322. notes. index. bibliography, 303-9.

A divorced mother and militant feminist, Arcana confronts the problems of raising a nonsexist son. Beginning with diary episodes involving her son, Arcana uses interviews with sixty mothers and sixty sons to explore mother-son relationships. Later chapters examine myths and fairytales as accounts of patriarchal victories over matriarchy, and discuss sexual politics in modern times. Arcana's total acceptance of ideology about male power and oppression is used throughout the book to justify her extreme hostility toward males, masculinity, and fathers.

468. Beer, William R. **Househusbands: Men and Housework in American Families**. Praeger Special Studies. New York: Praeger Publishers, J.F. Bergin Publishers, 1983. P. xxi, 153. appendixes. index. bibliography, 142-48.

This vigorously written study is one of the few to deal with men and housework. Beer points out that men have traditionally done some forms of "housework"— mowing the lawn, painting the house, fixing the car, replacing a broken window, and so on. His study, however, is concerned with men who do that housework traditionally assigned to women. Dividing these men into equal-time and full-time househusbands, the author describes his own life as an equal-time house-husband and parent. Utilizing such literature as there is, as well as information from fifty-six househusbands in the New York area, Beer indicates that men are far from the stereotyped monsters who have conspired to foist housework upon women. Among men whose work schedules are flexible, he finds considerable sharing of household tasks. A man's age, a working wife, and available male role models can also influence men in taking up housework. Few of the men responding to Beer's questionnaire were consciously pioneering new sex roles; the work had to be done, and they did it. Challenging the stereotypical idea that men hate housework, Beer finds that men's attitudes toward it varied in the same way women's did. The men found it dull and repetitive but also rewarding: they could work at their own pace, they saw tangible rewards, and they took pride in their workmanship. Those least free to do housework were least enthusiastic about it. Doing housework changed few men drastically; certainly it did not feminize them. Sometimes it liberated them from overidentifying themselves with their work. If our society wishes to encourage more men to become househusbands, Beer has some forthright advice. At present, because husbands are legally required to support wives (while wives have no reciprocal obligation to support husbands), being a full-time househusband is actually illegal. Such laws will have to change. So also will social values which denigrate men who do "women's work." Finally, men's work schedules will have to be more flexible. In a summary chapter Beer argues that housework is "the last bastion of nonalienated work in modern society"; putting houseworkers on salary would reduce them to the level of other alienated wage laborers. The appendixes spell out Beer's methodology and present his questionnaire.

469. Benson, Dan. **The Total Man**. Wheaton, Ill.: Tyndale House Publishers, 1977. P. 272. notes. pa.

In a presentation designed for the conservative Christian husband-father in a middle-class marriage with a traditional housewife-mother, Benson offers advice on such matters as the pitfalls of machismo and success-obsession, fitness and diet, being a loving leader of the family, marital in-fighting, loving and disciplining the children, and putting more spark into marital sex. Readers will have to decide whether Benson is offering timely advice or describing a vanishing lifestyle.

470. Herzog, Elizabeth, and Cecelia E. Sudia. **Boys in Fatherless Families.** Washington, D.C.: U.S. Department of Health, Education and Welfare, Office of Child Development, Children's Bureau, 1971. P. iv, 120. notes. bibliography, 99-120. pa. DHEW Publication No. (OCD) 72-33.

Although dated, this review of literature on the effects of father-absence upon boys (particularly in terms of juvenile delinquency, intellectual and psychosocial functioning, and masculine identity) is still useful for pointing out the many pitfalls involved in such research. The authors' conclusions will strike some readers as no more convincing than those which they criticize.

471. Humez, Alexander, and Keith Fitzgerald Stavely. **Family Man.** Chicago: Contemporary Books, 1978. P. xiv, 262.

The authors have collected fourteen extended interviews with a variety of men who discuss their family roles—as sons, husbands, and fathers.

472. Klein, Carole. **Mothers and Sons.** Boston: Houghton Mifflin Co., 1984. P. 272. index. bibliography, 251-62.

Using responses to questionnaires and interviews, Klein surveys a number of topics from both the mother's and the son's viewpoints. Above all, she recognizes the difficulties of the son in trying to separate from identification with the mother. She examines the pressures of the masculine role and how these can lead to conflict between mothers and sons. Guilt is likely to be felt by both parties. Also examined are feminist mothers who resent motherhood, lesbian mothers and homosexual sons, the working mother, troubled sons and successful sons, sons who are pushed too early to become "the man of the house," and mothers' fears of nonaggression in sons. Divorce requires special adjustments for both mothers and sons. Many readers will find Klein's treatment both equitable and informed.

473. Newman, Joseph, ed. **Teach Your Wife How to Be a Widow.** Washington, D.C.: U.S. News and World Report Books, 1973. P. 287. illustrations. appendixes. index.

Because women outlive men so decisively, widows need to know about such matters as wills, sale of houses, Social Security, stocks and bonds, taxes, estates, and so on. While the authors of this book provide considerable information on these topics, they assume that it is the husband's responsibility to instruct his wife about them. One wishes they had addressed their advice to the wife and had thereby relieved the husband of one of those burdens which are most likely driving him to his early grave.

474. Olsen, Paul. **Sons and Mothers: Why Men Behave As They Do.** New York: M. Evans and Co., 1981. P. 192. notes. Reprint. New York: Fawcett Books, 1982. pa.

An extended essay rather than a systematic study, *Sons and Mothers* describes the ultimate power of the mother to shape a son's life. Interspersing his analysis with exceprts from case histories, Olsen sees mothers as primarily responsible for creating active sons and passive daughters. The "good enough" mother provides security, but not too much: she also stirs her son to rebel, and she permits him to be independent. In some cases, she can create a macho male to wreak vengeance upon a male world she hates. The father, in Olsen's view, is an outsider, looking in; he must be interpreted to his son by the mother. Because of the close mother-son ties, leaving home is painful to sons, and even death cannot sever their link to their mothers. Critics may feel that Olsen has overdrawn maternal bonding with sons; others may feel he has provided a needed corrective to recent studies which blame the father for perpetuating traditional sex roles in children.

475. Robertiello, Richard C. **A Man in the Making: Grandfathers, Fathers, Sons.** New York: Richard Marek Publishers, 1979. P. 185.

In this confessional search for his identity, Robertiello recalls the males who most influenced him, particularly a harsh grandfather who raised him, a second grandfather whose earthiness partly counterbalanced the acerbity of the first, his father who alternately ignored and competed with him, and his own son with whom he has been only partly successful in establishing a loving relationship. Among the patterns which emerge from these recollections is the concept that men need women so badly because men provide so little love to each other. In a final chapter Robertiello begins to formulate a psychology of the self derived from his experiences.

476. Shedd, Charlie W. **Letters to Philip: On How to Treat a Woman.** Garden City, N.Y.: Doubleday and Co., 1968. P. xii, 131. Reprint. New York: Jove Publications, 1968. pa. Reprint. Old Tappan, N.J.: Fleming H. Revell, 1969. pa.

In twenty-nine brief letters for the young husband, Shedd offers traditional Christian advice on how to treat a young wife. Suggestions include: be a leader but not a tyrant, treat her as a person, and when you disagree fight fair and constructively.

477. Vernon, Bob, and C.C. Carlson. **The Married Man.** Old Tappan, N.J.: Fleming H. Revell Co., 1980. P. 160.

An assistant chief of police of Los Angeles, Vernon presents a conservative Christian view of the married man's role. Quoting scripture and recounting events from his police work, Vernon offers advice on such matters as male leadership in family and society, disciplining children, and the importance of moral conviction. Each chapter is introduced with a few paragraphs by Carole C. Carlson. Some readers will find the book a refreshing endorsement of fundamentalist concepts of masculinity; others will find it simplistic and authoritarian.

478. Voth, Harold M. **The Castrated Family.** Kansas City, Kans.: Sheed Andrews and McMeel, 1977. P. xvii, 241. appendix. bibliography, 223-34.

The author, a psychiatrist and psychoanalyst, argues for a return to traditional family roles for men and women. He details the psychological damage which can be sustained by children in nontraditional or "castrated" households. Skeptical of current trends in sexual and personal liberation, Voth regards homosexuals as "very sick people" and encourages parents to foster strongly differentiated sex roles in their children.

Cross references:

13. Schlesinger, Benjamin. **The One-Parent Family: Perspectives and Annotated Bibliography.**

14. Sell, Kenneth D., comp. **Divorce in the 70s: A Subject Bibliography.**

51. Herzig, Alison Cragin, and Jane Lawrence Mali. **Oh Boy! Babies!**

79. Clary, Mike. **Daddy's Home.**

80. Covington, Jim. **Confessions of a Single Father.**

88. McGrady, Mike. **The Kitchen Sink Papers: My Life as a Househusband.**

91. Nichols, Beverley. **Father Figure.**

94. Seabrook, Jeremy. **Mother and Son.**

95. Sifford, Darrell. **Father and Son.**

96. Stafford, Linley M. **One Man's Family: A Single Father and His Children.**

97. Steinberg, David. **fatherjournal: Five Years of Awakening to Fatherhood.**

221. Mount, Ferdinand. **The Subversive Family: An Alternate History of Love and Marriage.**

239. Biller, Henry B. **Father, Child, and Sex Role: Paternal Determinants of Personality Development.**

263. Malinowski, Bronislaw. **The Father in Primitive Psychology.**

300. Mitscherlich, Alexander. **Society without the Father: A Contribution to Social Psychology.**

482. Gordon, William J., and Steven D. Price. **The Second-Time Single Man's Survival Handbook.**

546. Davis, Robert Con, ed. **The Fictional Father: Lacanian Readings of the Text.**

550. Lee, M. Owen. **Fathers and Sons in Virgil's** *Aeneid:* **Tum Genitor Natum.**

554. Reich, Hanns, comp. **Children and Their Fathers.**

555. Sadoff, Dianne F. **Monsters of Affection: Dickens, Eliot, and Brontë on Fatherhood.**

589. Myer, Andy. **The Liberated Father's Handbook.**

590. Schoenstein, Ralph. **Yes, My Darling Daughters: Adventures in Fathering.**

591. Stewart, D. L. **Fathers Are People Too.**

See section on Literature for literary works about men in families.

SINGLE MEN

479.   Anderson, Nels. **The Hobo: The Sociology of the Homeless Man**. Rev. ed.
        Chicago and London: University of Chicago Press, 1961. P. xxix, 296.
        illustrations. appendixes. notes. index. bibliography, 287-93. pa.
First published in 1923, this study has become a classic describing the lives of
homeless men in "Hobohemia"; its influence upon sociology has been considerable.
In the new introduction, the author notes that the hobo has vanished with the
world described in these pages.

480.   Gilder, George. **Naked Nomads: Unmarried Men in America**. New York:
        Quadrangle/The New York Times Book Co., 1974. P. ix, 180. notes.
        index.
In this controversial study, Gilder attempts to debunk the single life, especially
for men. Rejecting the stereotype of the swinging playboy, he depicts single men
as unhappier, poorer, more criminal, more disturbed, and more suicidal than
married men. Arguing that men need the stability of marriage and children more
than women do, Gilder excoriates the sexual revolution for attempting to short-
circuit marriage. He deplores competition between men and women fostered by
the entrance of large numbers of women into corporate life. Males, Gilder concludes, are at their best when they are able to adjust to women's sexual and pro-
creative rhythms in monogamous family life.

481.   Gillette, Paul. **The Single Man's Indispensable Guide and Handbook**.
        Chicago: Playboy Press, 1973. P. x, 333. illustrations. bibliographies
        after many chapters.
For the would-be swinging bachelor, Gillette provides detailed information on
where the swinging women are ("Ohio doesn't make it"), how to set up one's
apartment, how to play the successful host for a tête-à-tête, party, or orgy (recipes
and drink mixes are included), dating, sex terminology, where the swinging women
are abroad ("Moscow doesn't make it in any department"), international travel,
finding and holding a job, income and investments, and clothes. The illustrations,
by the way, are strictly of apartment floor plans.

482.   Gordon, William J., and Steven D. Price. **The Second-Time Single Man's
        Survival Handbook**. New York: Praeger Publishers, 1975. P. 175.
        illustrations.

Maintaining a light touch, the authors consider the lot of the divorced male, offering suggestions about sharing living quarters with another male, checking out apartments, furnishings, housecleaning, operating in the kitchen, keeping oneself in clothes, dating again, and coping with kids. The humorous cartoons are by Roy Doty. (William J. Gordan is sometimes listed under the name William J. Goode.)

483. Greenblatt, Edwin. **Suddenly Single: A Survival Kit for the Single Man.** New York: Quadrangle/New York Times Book Co., 1973. P. 156.

In humorous, upbeat style, Greenblatt advises the suddenly single male how to make the best of the situation. Advice covers such areas as finding and checking out an apartment, furnishing it, maintaining the kitchen, cooking (thirty recipes are given), housecleaning, keeping up a wardrobe, entertaining children, and women in one's life.

484. Kohn, Jane Burgess, and Willard K. Kohn. **The Widower.** Boston: Beacon Press, 1978. P. xvi, 169. index. bibliography, 157-66.

Concerned by the few studies of widowers and the casual assumption that widowers face few problems, the authors—both of whom had been widowed before their marriage to each other—combine their efforts to present a personal and professional view of widowers. Each of the eight chapters follows the same pattern: Bill, a plant superintendent, recounts his experiences during and after the terminal illness of his first wife, Beth; Jane, a professor of sociology, draws upon interviews with thirty-five widowed persons and fifteen young persons who had lost parents to comment more broadly on the experiences of widowers. Topics covered include the immediate reactions to a loved one's death, the acceptance of death and recovery from grief, helping one's children to cope with death and grief (when Beth Kohn died, Bill had six daughters to raise; Jane points out that 550,000 widowers, half of whom have children to care for, are accounted for yearly), the man's ability to function as a single parent (this chapter is titled: "It's a Fact—Men Are Capable of Parenthood"), the widower's reentry into paired society, dating again, the decision to remain single or remarry, and the problems and possibilities of remarriage. Although extensive on related matters, the bibliography demonstrates how few works have been written about widowers. Both authors write with exceptional sensitivity and humaneness.

Cross references:

318. Hass, Aaron. **Love, Sex, and the Single Man.**

530. Lopate, Phillip. **Bachelorhood: Tales of the Metropolis.**

584. Friedman, Bruce Jay. **The Lonely Guy's Book of Life.**

MALE MIDLIFE TRANSITION _____

485.   Bergler, Edmund. **The Revolt of the Middle-Aged Man.** 2d ed. New York:
        Hill and Wang, 1957. P. xiii, 312.
One of the earliest assessments of male midlife crisis, Bergler's 1957 study depicts
the middle-aged man as rebelling and yet wanting his rebellion to fail. Through
extensive accounts of interviews with patients, the psychiatrist author argues that
midlife rebellion is doomed to failure; at best, it can be survived and converted into
an instrument of personal growth. The younger women with whom such men sometimes become involved are depicted as neurotic; wives are advised to hang on to
their marriages, for the husband's midlife storm will pass. Biological changes are not
the source of male midlife changes, and divorce is not the solution because it does
not provide the needed therapy. Bergler's view of middle-aged men as suffering
from psychic masochism and his judgmental view of patients, wives, and "other
women" may strike some readers nowadays as simplistic.

486.   Bowskill, Derek, and Anthea Linacre. **The Male Menopause.** Los Angeles:
        Brooke House Publishers, 1977. P. 195. appendix. bibliography, 195.
Despite the unfelicitous title (and the authors had ample warning about it from
those they interviewed), *The Male Menopause* offers vivid firsthand accounts of
male midlife crises from Great Britain. The authors present extended extracts
concerning midlife problems from medical practitioners, wives, and men themselves. If the organic evidence of midlife changes is debatable, the psychological
and emotional evidence seldom is. Midlife symptoms include disillusionment with
success or disappointment at not having achieved it, awareness of physical decline,
the desire to be attractive to women, impotence, extramarital affairs, dissatisfaction
with work, personality changes, and a feeling that no one cares. "As there is minimal or no sanction for a man to grieve in our society," remarks one man, "there is
also neither one for him to grow old." The authors review some of the remedies
for midlife anxiety, suggesting that the solution lies in two achievements (neither
of which is easy)—fixing a new midlife identity and facing squarely the certainty
of death. An extensive appendix contains extracts reviewing organic evidence for
midlife changes, their emotional implications, and female menopause; much of
the material is, as the authors note, contradictory.

487. Chew, Peter. **The Inner World of the Middle-Aged Man.** New York: Macmillan Co., 1976. P. xix, 278. notes. index. Reprint. Boston: Houghton Mifflin, 1977. pa.

This popular account of midlife crisis draws upon the work of Daniel J. Levinson, Elliott Jaques, and others. A journalist, Chew uses interviews and wide reading to explore such midlife concerns as stocktaking, extramarital affairs, impotence, work, leisure, and age discrimination.

488. Farrell, Michael P., and Stanley D. Rosenberg. **Men at Midlife.** Boston: Auburn House Publishing Co., 1981. P. xix, 242. illustrations. appendixes. notes. index. bibliography, 227-35. pa.

Begun in 1971, this study combines a wide sample of 450 men with more detailed study of twenty selected subjects. Instead of a single pattern of predictable male midlife crisis, the authors discovered four distinct paths through midlife: that of the antihero or dissenter who exhibits alienation, identity struggle, and orientation toward his own ego; that of the transcendent-generative male who thrives during this period and is marked by openness to feelings; that of the pseudo-developed man who cultivates a facade of satisfaction but is actually undergoing a midlife crisis; and that of the punitive-disenchanted or authoritarian man who is highly dissatisfied and often in conflict with his children. Farrell and Rosenberg stress that the man's experience of midlife must be seen in the larger context of family relationships. They also point to the importance of class in influencing the man's midlife experience, with upper-class or educated middle-class males more likely to weather the period positively. The authors explore husband-wife relationships ("middle age represents the doldrums of marriage in our culture"), parent-child relationships, extended family relationships, and male friendship groups during midlife. Of the four paths through midlife, only one is described positively. The authors conclude that because "most men strive to conform to a limited range of cultural stereotypes of masculinity," their lives "become increasingly burdensome, particularly in relation to work and family."

489. Hallberg, Edmond C. **The Grey Itch.** N.p.: Ombudsman Press, 1977. Reprint. Rev. ed. *The Gray Itch: The Male Metapause Syndrome.* New York: Stein and Day, 1978. P. ix, 228. notes. index. bibliography, 209-22. Reprint. New York: Warner Books, 1980. pa.

Writing for corporate and professional white men, Hallberg spells out the ingredients of male metapause, a word signifying a midlife pause in the man's life changes. In part I ("Is That All There Is?") Hallberg explores the concept of life stages and the symptoms of male metapause, including dissatisfaction with work, fear of aging and death, marital boredom, memory slips, distaste for the role of "family money machine," and (above all) an identity crisis. Part II ("Let Me Out of Here!") examines in greater detail the problem areas of men at midlife, including work identity confusion, problems of declining physique, sexual dilemmas, marital problems, disengaging from marriage, sex role strain, and parent-child tensions. Each chapter concludes with a quiz (called the Hallberg Index of Male Metapause) that allows the reader to gauge his own situation in each of these matters. Part III ("You Only Go Around Once") offers suggestions for coping and changing in the various areas covered in part II: the reader can focus on advice in those areas where he has found himself to have the most serious problems. The final chapter deals with "emansumation," a term and a concept combining "man," "sum," and "emancipation."

490. Levinson, Daniel J., and Charlotte N. Darrow, Edward B. Klein, Maria H. Levinson, and Braxton McKee. **The Seasons of a Man's Life**. New York: Alfred A. Knopf, 1978. P. xiv, 367. illustrations. notes. index. Reprint. New York: Ballantine Books, 1979. pa.

An extremely influential book, this study has affected both scholarly and popular conceptions of the male life cycle. Building upon the work of Jung and Erikson, Levinson presents a developmental perspective on men in adulthood, based upon in-depth biographical interviews of forty men, ages thirty-five to forty-five, in four occupations: hourly workers in industry, business executives, university biologists, and novelists. In addition, Levinson refers to a secondary sampling of famous men and fictional characters. The study concludes that male adult development proceeds through a series of eras, each of which occurs at an average or most frequent age: 17-22 (Early Adult Development), 22-28 (Entering the Adult World), 28-33 (Age 30 Transition), 33-40 (Settling Down), 40-45 (Midlife Transition), 45-50 (Entering Middle Adulthood), 50-55 (Age 50 Transition), 55-60 (Culmination of Middle Adulthood), 60-65 (Late Adult Transition), 65 and beyond (Late Adulthood). At each era, the man must perform certain developmental tasks or risk impeding his individuation process. Usually at age forty, the man enters midlife transition in which he must reappraise the past, modify his life structure, continue individuation, and reconcile four polarities: young/old, destruction/creation, masculine/feminine, and attachment/separation. Levinson describes five different pathways through midlife tranisition: advancement within a stable life structure, serious failure or decline within a stable life structure, breaking out or trying for a new life structure, advancement which itself produces a change in life structure, and unstable life structure. A humane and literate book, *The Seasons of a Man's Life* is both moving and thought provoking.

491. Mayer, Nancy. **The Male Mid-Life Crisis: Fresh Starts after Forty**. Garden City, N.Y.: Doubleday and Co., 1978. P. xv, 295. notes. index. bibliography, 275-83. Reprint. New York: New American Library, Signet, 1979. pa.

In readable style, Mayer examines sympathetically what is known about the male midlife crisis and offers advice about how it can be directed positively. Supplementing her researches with interviews, Mayer surveys the thought of Freud, Jung, and Erikson, as well as the more recent findings of Daniel J. Levinson and others. She explores the traditional masculine gender role and its liabilities (e.g., workaholism, disillusionment with "success," exploitation in the marketplace, impacted emotions, early death), as well as the symptoms of midlife transition (e.g., penis angst, the quaking marriage, the pressure of unwanted responsibilities). Nevertheless, Mayer's outlook is essentially optimistic as she details the possibilities for growth and renewal that midlife transition can offer.

492. McGill, Michael E. **The 40- to 60-Year-Old Male: A Guide for Men—And the Women in Their Lives—To See Them through the Crises of the Male Middle Years**. New York: Simon and Schuster, Fireside, 1980. P. 299. appendix. pa.

Based upon a four-year research effort involving five hundred questionnaires completed by men and women, as well as two hundred interviews, this book examines the male midlife crisis. McGill argues that insufficient research has been done on it, that the focus of too many studies has been on its negative aspects, and that a lack of good advice for dealing with it has emerged. Keeping an eye on the women, children, friends, employers, and other involved with the midlife male, the author reviews seven possible causes of the crisis: the "goal gap" in which the man experiences a discrepancy between what he hoped to achieve and what he actually has achieved, "the dream" that has come true but proved empty, the "step aside" pattern in which the man finds himself surpassed by younger men, "vanity and virility" in which aging takes its toll on mind and body, "the empty nest" syndrome in which a man loses his role as father-provider, "meeting mortality" or the awareness of one's own approaching death, and "the search for adventure" in which the man seeks to renew his interest in living by experimenting with a new way of life. To cope with the midlife crisis, McGill suggests five steps for the man: recognition that there is a problem, acknowledgement that the crisis is indeed a crisis, a consideration of the consequences of any actions he takes upon himself and others, a deliberate decision to change in a specific way, and integration of the change into his personality. For women wishing to help a man through midlife crisis, the author suggests ways to help him see, understand, and change himself. After answering ten frequently asked questions about male midlife crisis, McGill concludes that two current causes are increasing role demands on men in our society and the self-absorption of "Me Generation" thinking. The common denominator of midlife crisis lies in a threat to the man's identity; thus, men who define themselves narrowly will be more prone to the crisis. "Men and women, all of us, need to encourage men as individuals to explore who they are as whole men."

493. McMorrow, Fred. **Midolescence: The Dangerous Years.** A Strawberry Hill Book. New York: Quadrangle/New York Times Book Co., 1974. P. xiv, 366.

"This book is not a sociological or psychoanalytical study," the publishers note. "It makes no pretensions. There is nothing scientific about it in conception or execution." The author presents, usually verbatim, question-and-answer dialogue from interviews concerning midlife crisis. Those interviewed are seven experts (e.g., a psychiatrist, a psychoanalyst and sociologist, and a labor-relations lawyer), seven midlife men, and seven women involved with midlife men. Three concluding chapters are devoted to the midlife crisis in history, in literature, and in recent headline stories; midolescence and awakening homosexuality; and what lies in the years beyond midolescence.

494. Osherson, Samuel D. **Holding On or Letting Go: Men and Career Change at Midlife.** New York: Free Press, 1980. P. xii, 258. appendix. notes. index. bibliography, 250-54.

For this study Osherson reviews the literature on male midlife crisis and interviewed twenty men who made radical career changes at midlife. The author places the midlife years between thirty-five and fifty; he uses a free-associative interview procedure described in the appendix. For each man, five sessions over a two-week period were held. The twenty men were white research scientists, engineers, business managers or executives, lawyers, and university faculty who exchanged their careers at midlife for work in arts or crafts, e.g., acting, visual arts, and pottery. In particular, Osherson draws extensively from interviews with six men. He finds that a pre-change period or stage often precedes the actual crisis, which is characterized by a sense of loss. The self is called into question, and the man seeks to reconstitute a new self. Career change, for many men, is part of this transformation. In young adulthood men may rigidly define part of the self in career and marriage. At midlife the inadequacy of this definition becomes painfully obvious, and the man faces ambivalent feelings about holding on to, or letting go of, the old self. Osherson contrasts premature "foreclosed" resolutions with fuller "sculpted" ones: the first may be somewhat defensive, the second more fully integrative. The midlife crisis, the author argues, is rooted in adolescent conflicts with an "ideal" self transmitted from parents. He discusses the impact upon sons of the "strong mother-unavailable father" family pattern. In his conclusion, Osherson points to the wisdom of adaptively holding on as well as letting go, that is, of integrating wisely both the old and the new.

495. Ruebsaat, Helmut J., and Raymond Hull. **The Male Climacteric**. New York: Hawthorn Books, 1975. P. xviii, 190. illustration. appendix. index.

Ruebsaat (an M.D.) and Hull (a writer) explain to lay readers the nature of the male climacteric which usually occurs between the ages of forty-one and fifty. The introduction consists of Hull's diary-like account of his own climacteric, which included trancelike interludes, memory lapses, bouts of depression, and loss of libido. Part I enumerates systematically the symptoms of climacteric. Physical symptoms can include urinary irregularities, fluid retention, hot flashes, heart problems, peptic ulcers, air hunger, and osteoporosis; mental and emotional symptoms can include irritability, fatigue, insomnia, moodiness and depression, weakened mental ability, loss of self-confidence, and severe behavior fluctuations. Marital relationships may be upset by the man's interest in younger women and by his unwillingness to discuss his problems with anyone. Alluding to famous men of the past—Dickens, Tolstoy, Shakespeare, Napoleon, Mussolini—the authors explore the social dimensions of the climacteric. Contrasting male climacteric with female menopause, the authors reject the term male menopause. Part II traces the causes of the climacteric, indicating an interrelationship of physical, psychological, and social contributing factors. In Part III the authors offer advice to men (they include self-analysis charts to help pinpoint areas of difficulty) and to others dealing with midlife men in personal relationships or in public life. A glossary of terms is included.

496. Still, Henry. **Surviving the Male Mid-Life Crisis**. New York: Thomas Y. Crowell Co., 1977. P. xi, 240. notes. index. bibliography, 227-28.

In the first section of this popular account of male midlife crisis, Still characterizes the physical and emotional changes in men between the ages of forty and forty-five. The lost dreams, awareness of mortality, the death of one's parents, and the empty nest—all can combine with the rigid gender role of American masculinity to precipitate crisis in many men's lives. In section II Still explores "the personal equation" of midlife crisis—physical decline, tired marriage, sagging sexuality, and the inability to express feelings or to explore different modes of loving. The book's final section deals with "professional reckonings"—work dissatisfaction and burnout, the discovery by some men that they have sacrificed their lives in careers they never really wanted, and the problems of retirement. Especially interesting are Still's idea of granting sabbaticals to midlife men to allow them breathing space to recover and his chapter on the need for lifetime learning. Despite the book's grim picture of middle age, Still believes that "the mid-life crisis of the American male ... is an opportunity for new growth and directions."

497. Tamir, Lois M. **Men in Their Forties: The Transition to Middle Age.** Focus on Men series. New York: Springer Publishing Co., 1982. P. x, 150. appendixes. index. bibliography, 144-48. pa.

A sociologist and lifespan developmental psychologist, Tamir has tapped a national survey conducted in 1976 by the University of Michigan in order to draw a picture of men in midlife transition. "Ages 40 to 49 years in the life of the adult male," she finds, "comprise a major transitional period that is reflected in the quality of life experience, with repercussions in the worlds of work, family, and social relationships." Tamir includes in her study only men in their forties who are married parents; she uses an educational control, distinguishing college-educated men from non-college-educated men. As for quality of life, middle-aged college-educated men displayed a lack of zest, indicating possible psychological distress, while the other group suffered low self-esteem. For both groups, satisfaction with marriage and parenthood dropped, although toward the end of the decade marriage satisfaction began to rise again. Self-respect became a dominant value for both groups. Although job satisfaction increased (particularly among college-educated men), this satisfaction was no longer linked with personal wellbeing: apparently midlife men disengage from work as a source of personal fulfillment. For college-educated men, marriage became a more important source of personal satisfaction, although heightened awareness of marital problems also surfaced at this time. Increasingly, the men sought social relationships, perhaps to share midlife troubles with others. Despite the evident difficulties of midlife transition, Tamir cautions against seeing it too bleakly and points to its rewards and opportunities. She concludes with suggestions for future research.

498. Vaillant, George E. **Adaptation to Life.** Boston: Little, Brown and Co., 1977. P. xvii, 396. appendixes. notes.

Ninety-five men from an elite private college are followed through thirty-five years of development in this study. Most of the men were predictably "successful," but success did not mean trouble-free lives. Vaillant studies in detail the men's methods of adapting to reality. Their midlife years were troubled by what Erik Erikson designates as a search for "generativity," a desire for socially creative achievement. Midlife crises, however, were neither universal nor chronologically regular among the men. One appendix contains a glossary of defenses; the other two concern methodology.

Cross references:

23. Filene, Peter, ed. **Men in the Middle: Coping with the Problems of Work and Family in the Lives of Middle-Aged Men.**

506. Homer. **The Odyssey**.

517. Fitzgerald, F. Scott. **Tender Is the Night**.

523. Heller, Joseph. **Something Happened**.

532. Maugham, W. Somerset. **The Moon and Sixpence**.

553. Merriam, Sharan B. **Coping With Male Midlife: A Systematic Analysis Using Literature as a Data Source**.

LITERATURE

CLASSIC LITERATURE (pre-1900)

499.   Anonymous. **Pearl: A New Verse Translation**. Translated by Marie Borroff.
New York: W.W. Norton and Co., 1977. P. xxii, 40. pa.
This beautiful poem from late fourteenth-century England is many things—a
father's lament for his dead daughter, a religious allegory, and a poem of consola-
tion. It also gives the lie to those who assert that before modern times parents—
especially fathers—were emotionally detached from their young chidren, regarding
them as hardly human. Whether the poem is autobiographical, it clearly assumes
an audience which understands that fathers—no less than mothers—can be deeply
grieved by the death of a young child. Readers who prefer to tackle the poem in
the original Middle English should see *Pearl*, ed. E.V. Gordon (New York: Oxford
University Press, 1953).

500.   Besant, Walter. **The Revolt of Man**. Edinburgh and London: William Black-
wood and Sons, 1882. P. 358.
Though hardly a classic, Besant's half-comic, half-serious novel deserves to be better
known, especially for its depiction of England in the future after the Great Transition. Women exercise political and social power, the monarchy has been abolished,
the state is a matriarchal theocracy worshiping The Perfect Woman, and the men
are kept in guilty subjection by such devices as public hysteria over wife-beating.
At last a young nobleman, coached by his female professor of ancient and modern
history, leads a revolt of the men. Despite its outlandishness, the novel occasionally
manages to be both pertinent and perceptive.

501.   Clemens, Samuel Langhorne [Mark Twain]. **The Adventures of Huckle-
berry Finn**. 1884. Reprint. Eds. Sculley Bradley, Richmond Croom
Beatty, E. Hudson Long, and Thomas Cooley. 2d. ed. New York: W.W.
Norton, Norton Critical Edition, 1977. P. xi, 452. appendixes. notes.
bibliography, 451-52. pa.
One of the great reads of American literature, *The Adventures of Huckleberry
Finn* is also a hymn to male bonding, to the friendship between man and boy in a
hostile world, and to the good will that can exist between black and white males.
Persecuted by his brutal "pap," Huck Finn takes off downriver on a raft with an
escaped slave, Jim. As their adventures multiply, Huck becomes increasingly aware

of Jim's compassionate humanity, and in one of the book's most memorable scenes he decides to violate his "conscience" and to help Jim become a free man. Although many readers are disappointed with the last quarter of the novel when Tom Sawyer appears in the story, few readers have been unmoved by the eloquence and humor of the novel's great middle section, with Huck and Jim drifting down the Mississippi, discovering their brotherhood. Like other Norton Critical Editions, this one contains useful background materials and critical essays.

502. Crane, Stephen. **The Red Badge of Courage**. 1895. Reprint. Eds. Sculley Bradley, Richmond Croom Beatty, E. Hudson Long, and Donald Pizer. 2d ed. New York: W.W. Norton and Co., 1976. P. viii, 364. appendixes. notes. bibliography, 361-64. pa.

Vividly recreating a young soldier's first taste of battle during the Civil War, *The Red Badge of Courage* shows how Henry Fleming's growing sense of valor is linked with his growing sense of manhood. Setting out with dreams of glory, Henry is at first demoralized by the reality of war. Having fled in combat and abandoned another soldier in distress, Henry returns to the war, fiercely engages in battle, and even becomes a "heroic" standard bearer. At the end, he is able to beat down his shameful memories and quietly bask in his newfound heroism: "He felt a quiet manhood, nonassertive but of sturdy and strong blood. ... He was a man." But Crane's pervasive irony has left many readers wondering whether Henry has achieved a genuine manhood or has tragically internalized a destructive social definition of masculinity. The Norton Critical Edition includes textual notes, background materials, and critical essays.

503. Dickens, Charles. **Dombey and Son**. 1848. Reprint. Ed. Peter Fairclough. New York: Penguin Books, 1970. P. 992. illustrations. appendix. notes. bibliography, 37. pa.

Perhaps the most profound of Dickens's portraits of fatherhood corrupted by monetary concerns, *Dombey and Son* is—ironically—the name of a business "house" rather than a description of a parent-child relationship. A wealthy businessman, Mr. Dombey regards his daughter Florence as insignificant (she cannot succeed to the firm); his fragile son Paul is regarded less as a son than as a business successor and Mr. Dombey's bid for immortality. When Paul dies midway through the novel, the suggestion is that lack of love is partly responsible: Paul's mother had died at his birth, and his father has remained sternly aloof from him. After Paul's death, Mr. Dombey "buys" a new wife, Edith, from the marriage market. Repelled by what she is doing, Edith nevertheless consents to marry Mr. Dombey, only to make life miserable for him, herself, and Florence. When his financial structure collapses, partly as a result of Edith's desperate attempts to escape from her marriage, Mr. Dombey at last awakens to the "feminine" qualities of love and caring embodied in his daughter. In this novel, the most attractive father-figure is the warm-hearted Captain Cuttle, and he—significantly—has no business acumen. Another kindly father, Mr. Toodles, is a poor workingman. In dramatic terms *Dombey and Son* depicts the incompatibility of laissez-faire capitalist ideals and loving fatherhood. The Penguin edition contains the original illustrations of the novel by Hablot K. Browne (known as "Phiz") and an introduction by Raymond Williams.

504.   Dostoevsky, Fyodor. **The Brothers Karamazov**. 1879-80. Reprint. Translated by Constance Garnett, revised by Ralph E. Matlaw. Ed. Ralph E. Matlaw. New York: W.W. Norton and Co., 1976. P. xiii, 887. appendixes. notes. bibliography, 887. pa.

Dostoevsky's crowning achievement as a novelist is, among other things, a psychological thriller that exposes the heart of darkness—and light—in fathers and sons. When the depraved Fyodor Karamazov is murdered, the killer could be any of his four sons—the passionate Dmitri, who has been locked in an oedipal struggle with his father for the attentions of the earth-mother Grushenka; the intellectual Ivan, who has come to the belief that because God has disappeared "all is permitted"; the Christlike Alyosha whose steps are nevertheless haunted by a dark "double" named Rakitin; and the diabolical Smerdyakov, who is apparently the illegitimate son of Fyodor and an idiot girl whom he wronged. While the sensual Fyodor and the saintly Father Zosima represent opposite extremes of father figures, the four brothers are volatile compounds of passion, intellect, demonic hate, and mystical love. (The women in the novel are equally temptestuous, especially the hot-blooded Grushenka and the brittle Katerina.) Perhaps no other novel has portrayed so vividly the range of men's spiritual possibilities and the fury of their hidden torments. The Norton edition includes backgrounds and sources of the novel, as well as essays by such authors as Harry Slochower on the book's incest theme, D.H. Lawrence and Albert Camus on the Grand Inquisitor section, and Ralph E. Matlaw on the novel's religious myth and symbol.

505.   Homer. **The Iliad**. Translated by Robert Fitzgerald. Garden City, N.Y.: Anchor Press/Doubleday, 1974. P. 595. illustrations. note. Reprint. Garden City, N.Y.: Anchor Press/Doubleday, Anchor Books, 1975. pa.

This grim and glorious epic represents perhaps the earliest and most electrifying account of combat warfare and its effect upon men. Retelling an episode from the legendary Trojan war, the poem focuses on the Akhaian warrior Akhilleus whose quarrel with King Agamemnon leads to Akhilleus' angry withdrawal from battle. During his absence, his friend Patroklos is killed by the Trojan hero, Hektor, an act which unites the Akhaian forces and sends Akhilleus furiously back into battle. His mania for revenge knows no bounds, even after he has killed Hektor. Only when Hektor's father, the pathetic King Priam, quietly asks Akhilleus for the return of his son's body does the hero's fury subside into a tragic sense of the human situation. Although *The Iliad* is crowded with a multitude of vivid characters both human and divine, Akhilleus is at its center. Is he a cold-blooded soldier-killer, obsessed with military slaughter and triumph? Is he a deluded young man who has taken the only path to glory that his culture exalts? Is he a tragic figure who comes to realize the futility of his way of life? After nearly three thousand years, *The Iliad* still raises these and other disturbing questions about the nature of war and civilization, about freedom and necessity in the human lot, and about the relationship between combat warfare and men's behavior. The Robert Fitzgerald translation has received numerous accolades for its vigor, clarity, and ingenuity.

506.   Homer. **The Odyssey**. Translated by Robert Fitzgerald. Garden City, N.Y.: Doubleday and Co., 1961. P. 474. illustrations. appendix. Reprint. Garden City, N.Y.: Doubleday and Co., Anchor Books, 1963. pa.

This magnificent epic, which has haunted the Western mind for nearly three thousand years, celebrates a family-oriented hero. Having spent ten years fighting the Trojan war, Odysseus incurs the wrath of the god Poseidon who delays his return to Ithaka for another ten years. Wandering about the Mediterranean Sea, Odysseus encounters numerous adventures before facing a final challenge—a group of lawless suitors who have invaded his household, who are pressuring his wife Penelope to marry one of them, and who have murderous designs upon his son Telemakhos. With the aid of the goddess Athene, Odysseus slays the suitors and reestablishes himself within his family and his kingdom. Modern audiences can see the epic as the interrelated stories of a man's midlife search for identity and of a son's search for his father. Odysseus rejects the youthful heroic ideal of early death in battle and instead finds his identity in his roles as husband to Penelope, father to Telemakhos, son to Laertes, and leader of his island community. Although frequently tempted to abandon the struggle of masculine life, Odysseus rejects such entrapment—violently when he drags himself away from the Lotus Eaters, cleverly when he listens to the song of the sirens without heeding their destructive call, and graciously when he turns down a subtle marriage proposal from the nubile princess Nausikaa. A far different kind of hero than Akhilleus, Odysseus speaks from the heart when he says that "the best thing in the world" is "a strong house held in serenity / where man and wife agree." Robert Fitzgerald's lively verse translation has been widely acclaimed by scholars and general readers alike.

507.   Shaw, George Bernard. **Arms and the Man: A Pleasant Play**. 1884. New York: Penguin Books, 1955. P. 78. pa.

The sparkling wit of Shaw's dialogue is deadly serious about several matters, including how men are socialized to become soldiers, how men and women manipulate each other into playing frustrating gender roles, how masculinity is associated with combat aggressiveness, and how war is glamorized. This improbable antiromantic comedy concerns a young Bulgarian woman who rescues a fleeing Swiss mercenary by hiding him in her bedroom, but that is just the start of the zany plot twists which Shaw uses to puncture cultural balloons about sex roles, war, and honor.

508.   Strindberg, August. **The Father**. 1887. Reprint. August Strindberg. *Pre-Inferno Plays: The Father, Lady Julie, Creditors, The Stronger, The Bond*. Translated by Walter Johnson. Seattle: University of Washington Press, 1970. P. x, 243. illustrations. notes. bibliography, 237-43. Reprint. New York: W.W. Norton and Co., 1976. pa.

Anyone interested in men's awareness needs to know Strindberg, especially his 1887 drama *The Father*. The play depicts the struggle between the Captain and his wife Laura over the future of their daughter. The father wishes her to be a teacher in the event that she does not marry; the mother has grandiose schemes of her becoming a great artist who will prove that women can be as good as men. The Captain loses decisively, as Laura drives him to violence and insanity, but the play contains numerous insights to prevent other men from being victimized by the manipulative woman. The Captain's dependency upon women, his little-boy need for mothering, his chivalrous attitude that prevents his fighting Laura as an equal, his overdependence upon "rational" thought, and his foolish susceptibility to suggestions that he is not the father of his child—all are exposed in the play as typical male weaknesses. Repeatedly, the play offers astonishing and radical depictions of the present-day male condition. It shows that anti-male hatred flourishes as much as racism, it protests against the "enslavement" of men to supporting women and children, and it urges the discarding of stereotypes of males. In anguish the Captain asks, "Why shouldn't a man complain, a soldier weep? Because it's unmanly! What is unmanly?" In a stunning echo of Shylock's famous speech from *The Merchant of Venice* the Captain protests that men as well as women must be considered as human beings not just as hated stereotypes. Walter Johnson's translations are both readable and actable, and his collection contains four other plays depicting the battle of the sexes written before Strindberg's "Inferno" period. Among them, *The Bond* (1892) dramatizes a furious custody trial that makes *Kramer Versus Kramer* look like child's play.

509. Strindberg, August. **Getting Married**. 1884, 1886. Translated by Mary Sandbach. New York: Viking Press, 1972. P. 384. notes.

The publication of part I of *Getting Married* in 1884 gave such offense to Swedish feminists and right-wing pietists that Strindberg found himself facing prosecution for blasphemy. The whole improbable story of Strindberg's ordeal is recounted in Sandbach's introduction to this translation of thirty short stories embellished with polemical prefaces. A favorite target in part I of the collection is Ibsen's play *A Doll's House,* which Strindberg dissects as a sham in his preface and assaults further in a short story titled "A Doll's House." Other stories in part I deal with the hazards faced by men in marriage. Typical of Strindberg's views is "Love and the Price of Grain" in which the hapless young hero finds he must pay and pay and pay again for the privilege of being married. Part II, published in 1886 after Strindberg had been acquitted of blasphemy, shows him defiantly unrepentant. After declaring in the preface that women ruthlessly manipulate men, he dramatizes the point unflinchingly in such stories as "The Bread-Winner." Whether one regards Strindberg as an outrageous misogynist or as the father of men's liberation, it is difficult to disagree with Sandbach's conclusion that "he alone among contemporary Swedish writers refused to be castrated or muzzled."

510. Whitman, Walt. **Leaves of Grass**. 1855-1891. Reprint. Eds. Sculley Bradley and Harold W. Blodgett. Rev. ed. New York: W.W. Norton and Co., Norton Critical Edition, 1973. P. lx, 1008. appendixes. illustrations. notes. index of titles. bibliography, 995-97. pa.

Whitman's hymn to life is regarded by some as the great American poem of male liberation. In particular, the "Calamus" and "Drum-Taps" sections contain celebrations of male comradeship that anticipate modern efforts to reestablish male emotional closeness. This edition contains textual variants, Whitman's critical writings, and literary studies.

MODERN LITERATURE

511. Butler, Samuel. **The Way of All Flesh**. London: Grant Richards, 1903. P. v, 423. Reprint. *Ernest Pontifex, or The Way of All Flesh: A Story of English Domestic Life.* Ed. Daniel F. Howard. Boston: Houghton Mifflin Co., Riverside Ed., 1964. P. xxviii, 365. appendixes. notes. bibliography, xxv-xxvi. pa.

This savagely ironic novel exposes the chasm that widened between British middle-class fathers and sons in late Victorian England. In Theobald Pontifex, Butler drew a memorable caricature of the authoritarian clergyman father whose son Ernest is predictably warped and rebellious. Howard uses Butler's manuscript for the text of his edition.

512.   Corman, Avery. **Kramer Versus Kramer.** New York: Random House, 1977. P. 234. Reprint. New York: New American Library, Signet, 1978. illustrations. pa.

This novel—and the Academy Award-winning film made from it—deeply touched a large segment of the American public, and thus became something of a cultural landmark indicating an altered attitude toward divorced fathers. From one point of view, the novel might be seen as a modern continuation of the story told in Henrik Ibsen's *A Doll's House* which closes with the middle-class wife walking out on husband and children. *Kramer Versus Kramer* centers upon Ted Kramer, a hustling advertising salesman, whose wife Joanna walks out on him and their four-year-old son, Billy. In the process of coping with the situation, Ted and Billy forge closer emotional bonds than would have been possible otherwise. But after eighteen months, Joanna returns, seeking custody of Billy. Following a wrenching trial, she wins custody because of traditional court prejudice favoring the mother as primary parent. The novel's ending, in which Joanna decides to relinquish Billy to Ted, may strike some readers as wishful thinking.

513.   Dickey, James. **Deliverance.** Boston: Houghton Mifflin Co., 1970. P. 278. Reprint. New York: Dell Publishing Co., 1971. pa.

When four suburban men escape from their tacky, banal lives for a weekend of whitewater canoeing and hunting in the wilds, the outing becomes a journey into the heart of male darkness. Set upon by two depraved mountain men, the four are swept into a maelstrom of violence that includes male rape and killings. Disturbingly, the novel suggests that at least some men, secretly bored with "feminized" civilization, yearn to light out for a wilder territory where they can engage in savage male-only rituals of challenge, death, and survival.

514.   Dreiser, Theodore. **An American Tragedy.** New York: Boni and Liveright, 1925. 2 vols. P. 429, 406. Reprint. New York: New American Library, Signet, 1973. pa.

In this large, richly detailed novel, the American male's dream of success becomes his downfall. Aspiring to the world of glittery wealth and ease, the poor boy Clyde Griffiths becomes entangled in a situation that destroys him. Arriving in a small upper New York state town after a brush with the law in Kansas, Clyde becomes caught between two women: the gentle factory worker, Roberta Alden, who shares his dreams of rising in the social scale, and the shallow socialite, Sondra Finchley, who personifies all the empty glamor that Clyde worships. Roberta becomes pregnant just as Clyde seems about to win Sondra. In his desperation he contemplates murdering Roberta, but when their boat overturns on a lake her drowning is partly contrived and partly accidental. Nevertheless, Clyde is convicted of murdering her and dies in the electric chair. Instead of a Horatio Alger success story, Dreiser depicts the plight of the young man destroyed by the American dream.

515. Duberman, Martin. **Male Armor: Selected Plays,** 1968-1974. New York: E.P. Dutton and Co., 1975. P. xv, 352. pa.

This collection contains seven plays: *Metaphors, The Colonial Dudes, The Guttman Ordinary Scale, The Recorder, The Electric Map, Payments,* and *Elagabalus.* As Duberman explains in the introduction, the plays reverberate with the question "What does it mean to be a 'man'?" and with the concept of male armor, i.e., the rigid shell of masculinity that some men construct to confront the world.

516. Fitzgerald, F. Scott. **The Great Gatsby.** New York: Charles Scribner's Sons, 1925. P. 182. pa.

For many readers Fitzgerald's enormously successful novel dramatizes how the American male has been destroyed by the American dream. Believing in all the Horatio Alger myths, young Jimmy Gatz transforms himself into Jay Gatsby and embodies his dream-vision of success in Daisy Fay. When she marries wealthy Tom Buchanan, Gatsby determines to win her back by accumulating his own wealth and by indulging in lavishly conspicuous consumption. Ironically, Gatsby's little-boy innocence remains untainted by the shady activities used to accumulate his money or by the motley crowd that frequents the glittering parties he stages in a mansion near Daisy's Long Island home. Although she yields to Gatsby's appeal, Daisy becomes uneasy about the questionable nature of his status and wealth. In the end she deserts Gatsby again, leaving him to be destroyed by the catastrophe that she and Tom have precipitated. Gatsby dies before he fully realizes that Daisy is as shallow as his dream of success, but the lesson is not lost on the novel's sharp-eyed narrator, Nick Carraway, nor on the thoughtful reader.

517. Fitzgerald, F. Scott. **Tender Is the Night.** New York: Charles Scribner's Sons, 1933. P. 315. pa. Reprint. Rev. ed. *Three Novels of F. Scott Fitzgerald.* Eds. Malcolm Cowley and Edmund Wilson. New York: Charles Scribner's Sons, 1953. appendix. notes. pa.

This Fitzgerald novel traces the rise and fall of Dick Diver, a likable and promising psychiatrist whose character and career are eroded by the emptiness of life among the wealthy people in Europe. Like Gatsby, Diver is destroyed by a fatal attraction for glamorous wealth, represented in this novel by the beautiful but mentally insecure Nicole Warren. Diver's story, which can also be read as an account of a man unsuccessfully negotiating a midlife crisis, is punctuated by insights into such matters as the ephemeral attraction between younger women and older men, the growing awareness of aging and death in midlife men, the destructive nature of many modern male-female relationships, and the greater survival skills of women. The 1953 edition incorporates Fitzgerald's considerable revisions of the earlier text.

518. Gold, Herbert. **Fathers: A Novel in the Form of a Memoir.** New York: Random House, 1966. P. 309. Reprint. New York: Random House, 1968. Reprint. Berkeley, Calif.: Creative Arts Book Co., 1980. pa. Reprint. New York: Arbor House, 1983. pa.

Telling the story of Sam Gold, a Jew who left Russia as a boy during the Czarist persecutions and who came to America early in this century, Herbert Gold not only brings to life his father's experiences but tells a story representative of many men's struggles to succeed in the new land. When the novel ends in the mid-1960s, Sam is a vigorous eighty-year-old survivor. As the divorced father of two daughters, his son

Herb has a deepened appreciation for Sam's achievement. The novel closes with an "Epilogue and a Beginning" which recalls the figure of The Crippler: to prevent their sons from being conscripted into the brutalities of the Czarist armies, nineteenth-century Russian Jews had them deliberately maimed by a "crippler." This story—and the novel-memoir itself—are parables of the price men must pay in order to survive.

519. Golding, William. **Lord of the Flies**. New York: Coward, McCann and Geoghegan, 1955. P. 243. Reprint. New York: G.P. Putnam's Sons, Capricorn Books, 1959. pa. Reprint. New York: Coward, McCann and Geoghegan, 1962. pa.

When a group of British boys is marooned on a tropical island, the scene seems to be set for an idyllic adventure story. Instead, the situation becomes a nightmare as the boys degenerate into brutal savagery. Golding's superb novel of suspense is also an electrifying parable of unchecked male aggression destroying civilized values and creating the threat of total annihilation. The 1959 reprint contains a biographical and critical note by E.L. Epstein. The 1962 reprint contains an introduction by E.M. Forster.

520. Goldman, William. **Father's Day**. New York: Harcourt Brace Jovanovich, 1971. P. 215.

In this funny-sad novel a divorced father (whose Walter Mitty-like imagination works overtime) attempts to reach out to his vulnerable six-year-old daughter, only to leave her scarred (literally and figuratively) by their encounter.

521. Gosse, Edmund. **Father and Son: A Study of Two Temperaments**. London: Heinemann, 1907. P. vi, 373. Reprint. Ed. William Irvine. Boston: Houghton Mifflin Co., Riverside Ed., 1965. pa.

In this famous autobiographical novel, Gosse crystallizes the plight of the mid-Victorian father who rejects science when he cannot reconcile it with faith, and the late-Victorian son who rejects his father's faith when he cannot reconcile it with life. Exacerbated by the conflict between Darwinian agnosticism and evangelical piety, the estrangement between well-meaning father and dutiful son is raised by Gosse's art to a representative and poignant tale of generational incompatibility.

522. Guest, Judith. **Ordinary People**. New York: Viking Press, 1976. P. 263. Reprint. New York: Ballantine Books, 1977. pa.

With an extraordinary ability to get inside her male characters, Guest writes a hymn to father-son bonding in this novel that served as the basis for a splendid film directed by Robert Redford. For young Conrad Jarrett the usual teenage problems are exacerbated by his older brother's accidental death by drowning and by his own attempted suicide. His parents reverse the usual role expectations: his mother Beth has locked herself away from feelings because they are too painful to cope with, while his father Calvin has begun to break out of the provider's usual detachment to establish emotional connections with those around him. Also influencing Conrad is a memorably frank and understanding psychiatrist named Berger. Guest's narrative conveys a vivid sense of "felt life" right up to what must be one of the most unusual and moving climactic love scenes in modern fiction, a scene in which father and son manage to say "I love you" to each other.

523. Heller, Joseph. **Something Happened**. New York: Alfred A. Knopf, 1974. P. 565. Reprint. New York: Ballantine Books, 1975. pa.

In a lengthy interior monologue, Bob Slocum explores the messy emotional upheavals of his midlife crisis. At work he is clawing his way through the corporate jungle. At home he has become alienated from his wife (who drinks during the day) and his teenage daughter (who alternately hates and loves him). One son is hopelessly retarded; the other is lovable but distressingly vulnerable. Slocum makes it through his various crises but only at the cost of destroying the little boy within himself, an act dramatized when he smothers his vulnerable little boy to end his suffering. Drawing together Slocum's memories, his fantasies, his participation in the callous pettiness of the office and the emotional sparring at home, the novel provides lightning glimpses into the lives and experiences of many modern men.

524. Hemingway, Ernest. **Men without Women**. New York: Charles Scribner's Sons, 1927. P. 232. pa.

According to Leslie Fiedler, all of Hemingway's fiction concerns men without women. In this collection of fourteen short stories, the Hemingway heroes struggle to affirm positive masculine values in the face of almost inevitable defeat. In addition to several Nick Adams stories, the selection includes "The Undefeated," "White Elephants," and "Fifty Grand."

525. Hemingway, Ernest. **The Nick Adams Stories**. New York: Charles Scribner's Sons, 1972. P. 268. pa. Reprint. New York: Bantam Books, 1973. pa.

Of the somewhat autobiographical Nick Adams, Philip Young has written: "Nick *is* the Hemingway hero, the first one." This collection brings together twenty-four short stories, including eight previously unpublished sketches, recounting Nick's early life. Although written and published at different times during the 1920s and 1930s, the stories are arranged here to provide a connected sequence. Nick is first seen as a frightened boy fishing with his father in the Michigan woods, then as a youth tramping around the country. Later he is seen as a young soldier wounded amid the carnage of World War I, as a shattered veteran returning home, as a young writer seeking to perfect his art, and finally as a father guiding his own son in the ways of men. Many of the earlier stories are initiation episodes in which Nick encounters fear and evil, the violence inherent in birth and death, the inhumanity of war, and the unsatisfactoriness of male-female relationships. Like many Hemingway heroes, Nick is left wounded—physically, psychically, emotionally. He becomes a lonely hero—stoically sensitive, serious, honest, courageous in his own way, and strangely vulnerable. Although he remains alienated from mainstream society and even from most women, he validates his manhood by performing capably such tasks as fishing, hunting, and (above all) writing honestly. This collection includes such celebrated stories as "The Killers," "Big Two Hearted River," and "Fathers and Sons."

526. Hemingway, Ernest. **The Old Man and the Sea**. New York: Charles Scribner's Sons, 1952. P. 140. pa.

In this hymn to courage and endurance, Hemingway's philosophy of manhood is exalted to the status of religion. The story's protagonist is an aging Cuban fisherman engaged in a life-and-death struggle with a marlin longer than the old man's

fishing skiff. Battling his failing bodily powers as dauntlessly as he battles the marlin and the sharks which appear on the scene, the old man states the book's theme
thusly: "A man can be destroyed but not defeated."

527. Kopit, Arthur L. **Oh Dad, Poor Dad, Mamma's Hung You in the Closet
and I'm Feeling So Sad: A Pseudoclassical Tragifarce in a Bastard French
Tradition.** New York: Hill and Wang, 1960. P. 89. illustrations. Reprint.
New York: Pocket Books, 1966. pa.

This bizarre tragifarce features the quintessential castrating mother, Madame Rose-
pettle, who travels about with the stuffed corpse of her late husband whom she did
to death. Also included in her entourage are two Venus flytraps, a piranha, and her
seventeen-year-old son Jonathan whom she has so smothered with her "love" that
he remains a stuttering child. When Jonathan literally smothers a young woman
who tries to make love to him, the mother-son legacy becomes all too clear. As the
title indicates, the play caricatures the plight of the American father and son.

528. Lawrence, D.H. **Sons and Lovers.** London: Duckworth, 1913. P. vii, 423.
Reprint. *Sons and Lovers: Text, Background, and Criticism.* Ed. Julian
Moynahan. The Viking Critical Library. New York: Viking Press, Penguin,
1968. P. xiii, 622. illustrations. appendixes. bibliography, 619-22. pa.

Set in a nineteenth-century Nottinghamshire mining town, this somewhat autobiographical novel contains important insights into the plight of working men in
industrial countries and into the psychosexual binds of young men who grow up
in a mother-dominated household. In part I, the drudgery of working in the mines
transforms the joyously spontaneous Walter Morel into an irritable, drink-soaked
authoritarian who is alienated from his family yet pitifully dependent upon wife
and home. Part II concentrates upon the son, Paul Morel, as he tries to break away
from his mother's possessive love. His task is complicated by his inability to
identify with his father and by his prolonged yet sexually inadequate affair with the
daughter of a neighboring farming family. Paul drifts into another affair with Clara
Dawes, an older and more dominating woman, but eventually he relinquishes her
to her estranged husband, who in many ways resembles Paul's father. Even though
Paul has symbolically resolved the oedipal tensions of his home life and even
though his mother dies, the question of whether Paul will ever be free of her
domination is left unresolved at novel's end. The Viking critical edition includes
a wealth of autobiographical and social background material, literary assessments,
and psychoanalytical studies, including Freud's "The Most Prevalent Form of
Degradation in Erotic Life."

529. Lawrence, D.H. **Women in Love.** New York: Privately printed for sub-
scribers only, 1920. P. 536. Reprint. London: M. Secker, 1921. Reprint.
New York: Penguin Books, 1976. pa.

This novel, which Lawrence considered his best, is "about" many things, including
men in love—with women and with other men. In the relationship between Rupert
Birkin and Gerald Crich, Lawrence portrays vividly men's hunger for—and resistance to—close male friendships that are not homosexual but that are a form of
love.

530. Lopate, Phillip. **Bachelorhood: Tales of the Metropolis**. Boston: Little, Brown and Co., 1981. P. xvi, 286.

This polished collection of personal essays, reminiscences, poems, anecdotes, and vignettes reflects numerous aspects of the author's bachelor life in New York City. Writing as a bachelor observer of life, Lopate offers wry and poignant "tales of the metropolis," including accounts of relationships that didn't work out, reflections on bachelorhood as a state of life, a recollection of Lionel Trilling in his last years at Columbia University, a poetic look at an extrovert couple making the most of a second marriage, a brief portrait of a gay couple, an assessment of pornography and the men who patronize Forty-second Street establishments, and an essay on the literature of bachelorhood.

531. Mailer, Norman. **An American Dream**. New York: Dial Press, 1965. P. 271. Reprint. Garden City, N.Y.: Doubleday and Co., 1983. pa.

In this outrageous pop classic, tough guy Steve Rojack murders his rich bitch of a wife, buggers the German maid, eludes police investigators, makes it with a singer named Cherry, faces off with a black pimp named Shago Martin, defeats his tycoon father-in-law, and escapes various forms of mayhem. Whatever it means, the novel seems quintessentially Maileresque, touching familiar themes, including the macho mystique, the blending of sex and violence, and black-white love-hate.

532. Maugham, W. Somerset. **The Moon and Sixpence**. New York: George H. Doran Co., 1919. P. 314. Reprint. New York: Penguin Books, 1944. pa.

Written in 1918-1919 when Maugham was forty-four and forty-five years old, this novel draws upon its author's recent stormy passage through midlife. Based somewhat loosely upon the life of Paul Gauguin, the novel's protagonist Charles Strickland at age forty violently breaks away from his stuffy life as a London businessman and runs off to Paris to be a painter. Refusing to feel guilt for deserting his wife and children, Strickland relentlessly pursues his new vocation, regardless of whom he hurts. Eventually he finds in Tahiti an environment more congenial to his art and self, but there he is consumed by leprosy, a disease as implacable as Strickland's monomania to create art. However one regards Strickland, Maugham has drawn a disturbing portrait of a man driven by furious impulses unleashed at midlife.

533. Michaels, Leonard. **The Men's Club**. New York: Farrar, Straus and Giroux, 1981. P. 181. Reprint. New York: Avon Books, 1982. pa.

In this crisply written novel, seven men meet in Berkeley to form a men's club as a counterpart to all the women's meetings going on around them. The evening turns into an intriguing rap session (with the men contributing "stories" from their lives) and ends in comic mayhem and a boozy reaffirmation of male bonding.

534. Miller, Arthur. **Death of a Salesman: Certain Private Conversations in Two Acts and a Requiem**. New York: Viking Press, 1949. P. 139. Reprint. New York: Penguin Books, 1976.

Since its first performance in 1949, Miller's *Death of a Salesman* has continued to move audiences powerfully, and it promises to become an enduring fixture of the American stage. Among other things, the play depicts a representative little man (a low-man) whose lot mirrors that of other ordinary American men. Its pathetic hero, Willy Loman, is typical in having once been filled with Horatio Alger-like dreams of success that are presented in imagined or real conversations between Willy and his older brother Ben who made his fortune in the jungles of ruthless business enterprise. But Willy himself has been unable to attain such success, and near the end of his career, in his early sixties, he feels himself a failure as a man. Although Willy has anxiously tried to raise his two sons with the proper formula for male success, his work and his values have deeply estranged him from both of them. When his older son Biff discovers his father's affair with The Woman (possibly representing the Bitch Goddess of Success), the break between father and son is irrevocable. Willy's wife Linda loves him deeply but is powerless to prevent his impending catastrophe. Having been used up and cast aside by his employer, Willy concludes that he is worth more dead than alive, and commits suicide in a last desperate effort to win an opportunity for his son. In brief, Willy kills himself trying to fulfill the masculine role of the provider who raises his family's social status. In the poignant Requiem that closes the play, Biff concludes sadly that Willy had all the wrong dreams and that "he never knew who he was."

535. Perlman, Jim, ed. **Brother Songs: A Male Anthology of Poetry.** Minneapolis, Minn.: Holy Cow! Press, 1979. P. xi, 118. illustrations. appendix.
Perleman has collected poems from fifty-five modern poets, arranged in sections about fathers, sons, brothers, and friends and lovers. The appendix contains information about the contributors. Graphics are by Randall W. Scholes.

536. Remarque, Erich Maria. **All Quiet on the Western Front.** Translated by A.W. Wheen. Boston: Little, Brown and Co., 1929. Reprint. New York: Fawcett Crest Books, 1979. P. 256. pa. Originally published as *Im Westen Nichts Neues* (N.p.: Ullstein A.G., 1928).
Perhaps more than any other novel, *All Quiet on the Western Front* captures the devastating effects upon men of the horror and futility of modern combat. Moved by the patriotic slogans of his teachers, young Paul Baumer enlists in the German army, only to be progressively dehumanized by military training and the nightmare of trench warfare. Although Paul is the central figure, the novel follows in some detail the grim plights of several other soldiers, as well prisoners and civilians. As the senseless carnage of battle continues, Paul's comrades are wounded or killed, and his own humanity is so irrevocably ravaged by the ordeal of combat that his death is likely to be perceived by the reader as a blessing and release.

537. Roth, Philip. **My Life as a Man.** New York: Holt, Rinehart and Winston, 1974. P. 330.
Trying to achieve a concept of manhood, author Peter Tarnopol involves himself in a wildly disastrous marriage from which he may never recover. The first sections of this novel consist of two Tarnopol stories in which he tries to exorcize his marital nightmares through fiction; in the longer second part of the book, he attempts to tell his "true story." Growing up in the fifties, Peter is told by society that it is "unmanly" and "immature" not to marry; it is men's duty to rescue women through marriage. "I wanted to be humanish: manly, a man," Peter reports—and so he succumbs to "the Prince Charming phenomenon." He marries Maureen, only to find himself in a cage with a wildcat. Peter discovers that in the sixties he cannot

divorce his wife without her consent, that the judge at the separation hearings regards women as victims and men as oppressors who ought to pay for their "misdeeds," and that alimony payments are rigged against him. After the separation, Peter begins an affair with Susan, who has her own emotional problems. After Maureen's death in a car accident, Peter must face the challenge of living with his own and Susan's battered psyches. In this novel, life as a man is nothing short of earthly damnation.

538.   Roth, Philip. **Portnoy's Complaint**. New York: Random House, 1969. P. iii, 274. Reprint. New York: Bantam Books, 1972. pa.

Portnoy's complaint is a disorder which many men will regard themselves as suffering from—a messed-up sex life traced primarily to a smothering mother-son relationship. With a schlemiel father and an extravagant guiltmongering "Jewish mother," Alex Portnoy finds his only relief in incessant masturbation and (later) kinky sex. When he finds a liberated but not-too-bright sex partner whom he calls The Monkey, Alex has trouble relating to her except in bed. The novel, consisting of Portnoy's primal-scream monologue to his psychotherapist, is by turns horrifying and hilarious.

539.   Schultz, Susan Polis, ed. **I Love You, Dad: A Collection of Poems**. Boulder, Colo.: Blue Mountain Press, 1983. P. 63. illustrations. pa.

Forty-five affectionate tributes to father from as many poets are attractively printed along with stylized color illustrations.

540.   Sherman, Martin. **Bent**. New York: Avon Books, Bard, 1979. P. 80. appendix. pa.

Depicting Nazi extermination of homosexuals, Sherman's play provides a metaphor for all persecution of gays.

541.   Trumbo, Dalton. **Johnny Got His Gun**. Philadelphia: J.B. Lippincott and Co., 1939. P. 309. Reprint. New York and Secaucus, N.J.: Lyle Stuart, 1959, 1970. pa. Reprint. New York: Bantam Books, 1970. pa.

This unsparing novel consists of the tortured ruminations of a World War I soldier whose wounds have left him a quadruple amputee, blind, deaf, dumb, and faceless. As such, Joe Bonham represents the millions of men who have died or been hideously wounded in battle. Bonham also imagines himself speaking for all the "little guys" of history who have been exploited, enslaved, tortured, and killed. Learning that the authorities prefer to ignore him in his present grotesque condition, Bonham envisions a time when victimized people will discover who their true enemies are and will turn their weapons on warmongering leaders.

542.   Updike, John. **Rabbit, Run**. New York: Alfred A. Knopf, 1960, 1970. P. 309. Reprint. New York: Fawcett World, Crest, 1962. pa. Reprint. New York: Ballantine Books, 1981. pa.

The plight of Updike's Harry (Rabbit) Angstrom has hit a nerve with many American men. After his high school years of basketball glory, Rabbit at twenty-six has settled into a life of thoroughgoing banality, including a second-rate marriage to Janice (complete with son Nelson and a baby on the way) and a deadening job as a a five-and-dime salesman in a drab small town. Unable to dispel the feeling that "somewhere there was something better for him than listening to babies cry and cheating people in used-car lots," Rabbit instinctively takes to flight—first into the arms of a prostitute Ruth, then back to Janice when she gives birth to their child, and then away from her again after she accidentally drowns it in the bathtub during a bout of daytime drinking. A final, futile attempt to reunite with Ruth ends in another of Rabbit's flights. Though often insensitive and feckless, Rabbit Angstrom also possesses considerable integrity and charm, and the ordinariness of his life and surroundings only magnifies their mystery and significance: "Why was he set down here, why is this town, a dull suburb of a third-rate city, for him the center and index of a universe that contains immense prairies, mountains, deserts, forests, cities, seas?" Perhaps in Rabbit Angstrom many American men have found the fictional representative of their feelings of being trapped in early adulthood, of their need for something more than meaningless jobs and second-rate marriages, and of their desire for flight from such life-sapping situations. (Rabbit's story is continued in a 1971 sequel, *Rabbit Redux*, where he appears as a thirty-six-year-old blue-collar reactionary unsettled by the social traumas of the late sixties and early seventies. In a 1981 book, *Rabbit Is Rich,* Angstrom is a successful Toyota dealer whose son Nelson exhibits a need to run from entrapment as his father did.)

543.   White, Edmund. **A Boy's Own Story**. New York: E.P. Dutton, 1982.
       P. 218. Reprint. New York: New American Library, Plume, 1983. pa.
This novel about growing up homosexual in America is laced with ironies, insights, and cynicism.

Cross references:

84.   Kafka, Franz. **Letter to His Father/Brief an Der Vater.**

182.   Swados, Harvey, ed. **The American Writer and the Great Depression.**

301.   Mullahy, Patrick. **Oedipus, Myth and Complex: A Review of Psycho-analytic Theory.**

352.   Galloway, David, and Christian Sabisch, eds. **Calamus: Male Homosexuality in Twentieth-Century Literature: An International Anthology.**

IMAGES OF MEN _____

544. Aymar, Brandt. **The Young Male Figure: In Paintings, Sculptures, and Drawings from Ancient Egypt to the Present.** New York: Crown Publishers, 1970. P. vii, 247. illustrations. index. bibliography, 245-47.
With the aid of numerous black-and-white photographs, Aymar traces the depiction of the young male body in classical antiquity, the Renaissance and mannerist periods, the seventeenth through the twentieth centuries in European art, and more exotic art.

545. Bamber, Linda. **Comic Women, Tragic Men: A Study of Gender and Genre in Shakespeare.** Stanford, Calif.: Standord University Press, 1982. P. 211. notes. index.
In contrast to critics who see Shakespeare as androgynous, Bamber argues that he often writes from a masculine viewpoint and sees women as "the other." Such a stance does not necessarily mean that Shakespeare is male chauvinist; the acceptance of "the other" may be positive. Bamber traces the Shakespearean heroine in the comedies, as well as in *Antony and Cleopatra, Hamlet, Macbeth,* and *Coriolanus.* In the final comedies, the "return of the feminine" can be seen as positive, although in *The Tempest* the mood is saddened by the failure of this return.

546. Davis, Robert Con, ed. **The Fictional Father: Lacanian Readings of the Text.** Amherst: University of Massachusetts Press, 1981. P. 206. notes. index.
Literary criticism, as well as the social sciences, has discovered the father. Utilizing the thought of Jacques Lacan (whose theories were fathered by Freud), the six critics represented in this collection search for literary fathers in such texts as *The Odyssey, Bleak House*, and Faulkner's novels.

547. Gloeden, Wilhelm, Baron von. **Photographs of the Classic Male Nude.** New York: Camera/Graphic Press, 1977. P. 105. illustrations. Originally published as *Taormina Debut du Siecle* (Paris: Editions du Chêne, 1975).
Living in Taormina in the early twentieth century, Baron von Gloeden photographed nude Sicilian youths, attempting to evoke a homoerotic Arcadia. Although

the preface by Jean-Claude Lemagny stresses their datedness, the photographs superbly reproduced in this volume represent a moving hymn to the young male body.

548. Hayes, Dannielle B., ed. **Women Photograph Men.** New York: William Morrow and Co., 1977. Unpaged. illustrations. pa.

Hayes brings together 118 photographs of males by seventy-one artists, including Dawn Mitchell Tress, Kathryn Abbe, Dianora Niccolini, Patt Blue, Arlene Alda, Ruth Breil, Karen Tweedy-Holmes, and Carolee Campbell. Happily, the photographers look at men as humans first, avoiding idealizations and caricatures. Although a few celebrities (e.g., Richard Burton) and a few pretty faces appear, the majority of men are remarkable for their ordinary humanity—a Vietnamese boy soldier with a pained smile and a missing leg, a pair of muddy oil riggers engaging in a ballet of work with their equipment, and an elderly roustabout wearily propped against a circus tent pole. Although some nudes appear, the photographers seem most fascinated by the men's hands and hairiness. Unfortunately, the introduction by Molly Haskell comes freighted with all the clichés about men that the photographers have avoided so splendidly.

549. Kahn, Coppélia. **Man's Estate: Masculine Identity in Shakespeare.** Berkeley: University of California Press, 1981. P. xiii, 238. notes. index.

In this scholarly blend of psychology and literary criticism, Kahn explores the recurring theme of masculine identity in Shakespearean drama. She focuses on the difficulties of various male characters to achieve gender identity in a culture that provides them with social dominance over females and yet makes them vulnerable to females for their masculine identity. Rather than studying the plays in chronological order, the author examines different themes as they appear in groups of works. In *Venus and Adonis* she sees the young hero's refusal to grow to sexual maturity as an adolescent rite of passage in reverse, resulting in a loss of identity. The history plays are fiercely masculine, almost excluding women; in them, male-male tensions run high. *Romeo and Juliet* shows adolescents trying to grow up but thwarted by adult enmity, while in *The Taming of the Shrew* Petruchio conquers Kate but in the process acknowledges that his identity is dependent upon her actions. Kahn traces the theme of cuckoldry through several plays, including *Hamlet* and *Othello*, and she sees in Macbeth and Coriolanus two half-grown men who are fatally dependent upon wife and mother. The final chapter examines male characters in the context of family, especially fathers who lose and then recover the feminine in daughter and wife. In *The Tempest*, however, Prospero does not rejoin with the feminine, but surrenders his daughter to her groom and proceeds to a solitary life. Kahn believes that Shakespeare questioned cultural definitions of manhood and knew how tenuous masculine identity could be.

550. Lee, M. Owen. **Fathers and Sons in Virgil's *Aeneid:* Tum Genitor Natum.** Albany: State University of New York Press, 1979. P. xi, 200. notes. index. pa.

This personal reading of Virgil's epic locates its prevailing sadness in the repeated failure of father-son relationships. Such failures are the touchstones of a tragic vision which is political, personal, and cosmic.

551.   Lynn, Kenneth S. **The Dream of Success: A Study of the Modern American Imagination.** Boston: Little, Brown and Co., 1955. P. 269. notes. index.

Lynn traces the theme of the American success dream in writers like Theodore Dreiser, Jack London, David Graham Phillips, Frank Norris, and Robert Herrick.

552.   Mellen, Joan. **Big Bad Wolves: Masculinity in the American Film.** New York: Pantheon Books, 1977. P. xvi, 367. illustrations. index.

Hollywood has not been kind to men, Mellen argues in this study of masculine images in American films. By manufacturing outsized screen images of males, it has made the ordinary male viewer feel insignificant while women have been made to feel inadequate: "An abiding malaise results in the male, victimized by this comparison between himself and the physical splendor of the hero with whom he has so passionately identified." Mellen's subject is not the comedians or musical stars but the "leading men" who have embodied cinema fantasies of masculinity. In the introduction the author describes how Hollywood manufactures its supermales on the screen, how American films have fostered competition between males and hostility toward women, and how the average working man has been virtually ignored by Hollywood's escapism. Politically, American films have encouraged men to support the status quo, fostering conformism, anti-intellectualism, and passive patriotism. Later chapters provide a decade-by-decade survey of American films, fitting in accounts of such stars as Tom Mix, Rudolph Valentino, Douglas Fairbanks, Gary Cooper, Clark Gable, Cary Grant, Humphrey Bogart, James Dean, and Marlon Brando. Mellen's severest strictures are reserved for John Wayne, Clint Eastwood as Dirty Harry, Sean Connery as James Bond, Charles Bronson, and other advocates of tight-lipped violence. The relationship between Bogart and Katherine Hepburn in *The African Queen* comes nearest to being Hollywood's depiction of male-female equality. Mellen is suspicious of male-bonding films, finding them laced with sinister misogyny. She is unimpressed by Paul Newman's liberal facade or Robert Redford's good looks. The author examines the image of black men in films, and she has positive words for the documentary *Men's Lives* by Josh Hanig and Will Roberts.

553.   Merriam, Sharan B. **Coping with Male Mid-Life: A Systematic Analysis Using Literature as a Data Source.** Washington, D.C.: University Press of America, 1980. P. vii, 129. index. bibliography, 118-25. pa.

Using twelve fictional works from twentieth-century American literature, Merriam explores their insights into male midlife transition, comparing her findings with psychosocial research. Midlife is marked by an awareness of aging, a search for meaning, a generation squeeze as the man finds himself neither young nor old, career malaise, and efforts at ego rejuvenation. Among the works examined are F. Scott Fitzgerald's *Tender Is the Night,* Arthur Miller's *Death of a Salesman,* Tennessee Williams' *Night of the Iguana,* Saul Bellow's *Herzog,* and Joseph Heller's *Something Happened.* "This study confirmed my belief," Merriam writes, "that literature offers the potential for uncovering significant insights into the process of adult development and aging."

554. Reich, Hanns, comp. **Children and Their Fathers.** Text by Eugen Roth. New York: Hill and Wang, 1962. P. 11, 74. illustrations. Originally published Munich: Hanns Reich Verlag, 1960.

Containing an unforgettable collection of photographs depicting fathers and children from around the world, this is a book to cherish.

555. Sadoff, Dianne F. **Monsters of Affection: Dickens, Eliot, and Brontë on Fatherhood.** Baltimore: The Johns Hopkins University Press, 1982. P. vii, 193. notes. index.

In this scholarly blend of Freudian, Lacanian, and feminist literary criticism, Sadoff traces the search for the father who engenders the action in Dickens's novels, the father-daughter seduction in George Eliot's novels, and the symbolic castration in Charlotte Brontë's novels.

556. Scavullo, Francesco, with Bob Colacello and Séan Byrnes. **Scavullo on Men.** New York: Random House, 1977. P. 186. illustrations.

This collection of photographs and interviews features fifty famous men. Scavullo quizzes the men on such topics as health, food, fatherhood, careers, drugs, and the women's movement. Memorable photographs include William F. Buckley Jr. with finger to lips, Truman Capote grinning like a possessed imp, Bruce Jenner and Christopher Reeve in barechested splendor, the serenity in Arthur Ashe's face and the intensity in Julian Bond's, the pain in Norman Mailer's eyes and the humane twinkle in Arthur Miller's, and the radiant smile and open arms of operatic tenor Luciano Pavarotti.

557. Spoto, David. **Camerado: Hollywood and the American Man.** New York: New American Library, Plume, 1978. P. xi, 238. illustrations. index. pa.

With the aid of numerous stills, Spoto describes dominant images of men in American films, including the Ordinary Guy, the sex symbols, the comedians, the heroes of suspense, and the strong men.

558. Todd, Janet, ed. **Men by Women.** Women and Literature, Vol. 2 (new series). New York: Holmes and Meier Publishers, 1981. P. 251. illustrations. notes. pa.

This collection of fifteen essays examines male characters and images of men created by female authors. The contributors examine such topics as men in the eighteenth-century feminine novel, male characters in female nineteenth-century British industrial novels, and the distinction between penis and phallus in the critical theories of Jacques Lacan. Individual essays are devoted to such concerns as the portrayal of men in Jane Austen's novels, the "feminization" of male characters in George Eliot's fiction, Emily Brontë's Heathcliff, Charlotte Brontë's Rochester, Emily Dickinson's poetry, the "spectacular spinelessness" of men in Dorothy Arzner's films, the biographical implications of Sylvia Plath's short fiction, and Iris Murdoch's male narrators.

559. Walters, Margaret. **The Nude Male: A New Perspective.** New York and London: Paddington Press, 1978. P. 352. illustrations. notes. index. bibliography, 339. Reprint. New York: Penguin Books, 1979. pa.

Calling the male nude "a forgotten subject," Walters surveys its history from classical Greece to modern pin-ups, focusing primarily on recognized paintings, sculptures, and other art forms. In contrast to the perfected glory of Greek nudes, Christian art used nudity to convey pathos and shame. Separate chapters are devoted to the Renaissance nude, Michelangelo, and each century from the sixteenth through the twentieth. After the "disappearing" male nudes of nineteenth-century art and the "disembodied" nudes of twentieth-century works, the newsstand pin-up and nude males depicted by women artists represent new departures in seeing men's bodies.

560. Wisse, Ruth R. **The Schlemiel as Modern Hero.** Chicago and London: University of Chicago Press, 1971. P. xi, 134. appendix. notes. index. bibliography, 127-30. Reprint. Chicago and London: University of Chicago Press, Phoenix, 1980. pa.

The wise fool of Jewish folklore and fiction, the schlemiel has emerged as the prototypical modern male hero, a preeminently weak man facing a hostile world. This perceptive and lucidly written study traces the history of the schlemiel, analyzes his humor, and follows his fortunes in such works as Sholom Aleichem's stories, Saul Bellow's *Herzog*, and Philip Roth's *Portnoy's Complaint.* Wisse goes beyond literary studies, however, to suggest the relevance of the schlemiel to the lot of modern men.

Cross references:

18. Young, Ian, comp. **The Male Homosexual in Literature: A Bibliography.**

197. Franklin, H. Bruce. **Prison Literature in America: The Victim as Criminal and Artist.**

266. Strage, Mark. **The Durable Fig Leaf: A Historical, Cultural, Medical, Social, Literary, and Iconographic Account of Man's Relations with His Penis.**

271. Cady, Edwin Harrison. **The Gentleman in America: A Literary Study in American Culture.**

337. Adams, Stephen. **The Homosexual as Hero in Contemporary Fiction.**

382. Sarotte, Georges-Michel. **Like a Brother, like a Lover: Male Homosexuality in the American Novel and Theater from Herman Melville to James Baldwin.**

MINORITIES

561. Barbeau, Arthur E., and Florette Henri. **The Unknown Soldiers: Black American Troops in World War I**. Philadelphia: Temple University Press, 1974. P. xvii, 279. illustrations. appendix. notes. index. bibliography, 249-70.

In a documented account, the authors vindicate the valor of black American soldiers during World War I. Despite racism, hostility, and humiliation that were all too often officially sanctioned, black troops served their country well. The narrative is enhanced by period photographs, extensive notes, and bibliography.

562. Gilder, George. **Visible Man: A True Story of Post-Racist America**. New York: Basic Books, 1978. P. xiii, 249.

On one level, this book recounts the story of Mitchell (Sam) Brewer, a black man accused of raping a white woman in Albany, New York. On another level, it is Gilder's representative tale of how black masculinity and the black family are being destroyed by welfare in "post-racist" America. Gilder pulls back from Sam's rape trial to depict life on Clinton Avenue, a region of black women on welfare, idle and often violent black men, fatherless children, winos, and white women— often welfare mothers and sometimes prostitutes, lesbians, or both. Because the men's earnings cannot compete with welfare benefits, they drift from one welfare woman to another, fathering children who will never know them for long as a father in the house. "Unlike virtually all human societies known to anthropologists," Gilder observes, "America does not offer virility rites. This society does not wish to acknowledge that boys have special problems of sexual passage. ... Without such opportunities, boys all too often resort to the lowest terms of masculinity: sexual violence." When Sam Brewer finds himself facing a rape charge from a white lesbian who apparently supports herself and her lover by occasional prostitution, the trial becomes a cause célèbre involving the Albany Rape Crisis Center, lesbian activists, and an overeager female Assistant District Attorney. Although Sam is acquitted of the rape charge, his future is hardly bright as he returns to Clinton Avenue to join the ranks of the violent male castoffs. "Poor black males," Gilder comments, "do not get brought up by fathers, socialized by marriage, or regulated by breadwinning." Unlike the "invisible" middle-class black males who help to hold their families together, these are the "visible men" whose masculinity has been eroded by well-meaning but shortsighted vendors of poverty "aid" and welfare "rights."

563. Howe, Irving, with Kenneth Libo. **World of Our Fathers.** New York and London: Harcourt Brace Jovanovich, 1976. P. xx, 714. illustrations. notes. index. bibliography, 685-93. Reprint. New York: Simon and Schuster, Touchstone, 1977. pa. Reprint. New York: Bantam Books, 1981. pa.

In this massive social and cultural history, Howe charts the journey of two million east European Jews who, starting in the 1880s, migrated to America, settled mostly in New York's East Side, established a rich Yiddish culture there, and then dispersed to other locales on the American landscape.

564. Kingston, Maxine Hong. **China Men.** New York: Alfred A. Knopf, 1980. P. 310. Reprint. New York: Ballantine Books, 1980. pa.

In impressionistic prose, Kingston recreates the stories of her male ancestors and other China Men who left their homeland to labor in Hawaiian cane fields, build railroads in the Sierra Nevada mountains, work the gold fields of Alaska, and establish families on the U.S. mainland. From thence sons issued forth to fight with American troops on World War II battlefields, in Korea, and in Vietnam. The initial tale of a man painfully transformed into a woman sounds a note of anti-male hostility that recurs in the book.

565. Liebow, Elliot. **Tally's Corner: A Study of Negro Streetcorner Men.** Boston: Little, Brown and Co., 1967. P. xvii, 260. appendix. bibliography, 257-60. pa.

A superbly written study, *Tally's Corner* recounts the activities of a group of black streetcorner men in inner-city Washington, D.C. By looking closely and humanely at their lives, Liebow is able to offer a rare glimpse of poor and marginally poor urban black males—the "losers" in our society. Such men have often been overlooked by scholars and social workers, the author contends, because it is assumed that "able-bodied" males neither need nor deserve social support. Liebow demonstrates the complex connection between men and work: the jobs available to them are sometimes beyond their physical capacity, the pay is often too low to support a family, and frequently the work is temporary. The men often lack hope for the future; in time they quit or drift away. The job fails the man, and the man fails the job. Liebow describes the range of father absence and presence in families, noting that fathers who feel they have failed their families drift away from them. Marriages and consensual unions are familiar in this world. Although the men frequently talk against marriage, they consider it a necessary rite of passage into manhood. The breakup of marriages is often attributed by the men to male sexual infidelity, but the man's inability to meet the demands of being head of the family is another likely cause. Similarly, the men talk about themselves as "exploiters" of women, but much of this talk may be crowing to cover up failure. An elaborate and shifting network of friends helps the men cope with the hardships of their lives. In a concluding chapter, the author discusses better employment as one of the needs to upgrade the lot of streetcorner men. The appendix describes how the white author conducted field work among black streetcorner men; like the rest of the book it is a fascinating human drama.

566. Rogosin, Donn. **Invisible Men: Life in Baseball's Negro Leagues.** New York: Atheneum, 1983. P. xiii, 284. illustrations. appendixes. index.

Rogosin recounts the history of black baseball greats in the days before the major leagues were integrated.

567.   Sochen, June, ed. **The Black Man and the American Dream: Negro Aspira-tions in America, 1900-1930.** Chicago: Quadrangle Books, 1971. P. ix, 373.

This collection of more than seventy contributions, both nonfiction and fiction, shows how much black men wanted to share in the Horatio Alger dream of success rather than subvert it. On occasion, it also suggests the repercussions to black masculinity of a dream deferred.

568.   Staples, Robert. **Black Masculinity: The Black Man's Role in American Society.** San Francisco: Black Scholar Press, 1982. P. 181. notes. pa.

Without denying the validity of women's grievances, Staples argues that "in the black community, it is the men who need attending to." Exploring the reality behind the image of the black male, Staples presents a disturbing picture of black men victimized by a virulent combination of racism and the masculine mystique. Shortchanged educationally and denied opportunities for life-sustaining and family-supporting work, the black man too often becomes a prey of exploitive capitalism, drugs, or suicide. Depicting the black community as an underdeveloped colony within the larger society, Staples explores the causes of high crime rates there and the socialization of young black males into numerous forms of violence. He discusses the "myth" of black sexual superiority, homosexuality, and the changing nature of male-female relations in recent times. The relationship between black men and white women is also reviewed. During the seventies the promises of civil rights legislation and black pride were fulfilled more for black women than for black men. "As it was," Staples remarks, "the decade's flowering of black manhood turned into a withering away of what little supremacy they had and consigned many black men into a prison of their gender." In the eighties, black men may prove to be the first and only casualty of the women's movement as affirmative action schemes increasingly benefit white women rather than black men. Although sympathetic with many feminist issues, Staples criticizes some black feminists for directing their anger indiscriminately against black men, who are not always the cause of their difficulties. In the final chapter Staples calls for a new unity between black men and women in order to forge their future together.

569.   Teague, Bob. **Letters to a Black Boy.** New York: Walker and Co., 1968. P. 211.

In a series of letters to his infant son, Teague captures the mood of black men in the late sixties. Touching upon the militants and the visionaries in the black movement, Teague offers an apologia for his own less-activist stance. He recounts episodes from his life, especially his career in television broadcasting. Everywhere in the letters—both explicitly and implicitly—is Teague's concept of what black masculinity should be.

570.   Wallace, Michele. **Black Macho and the Myth of the Superwoman.** New York: Dial Press, 1979. P. ix, 182. index. Reprint. New York: Warner Books, 1980. pa.

Wallace addresses what she perceives as an increasing hostility between black men and women. Attempting to assert their manhood in a racist society, black men have embraced a misogynist macho ethic; meanwhile, black women have been stereotyped as superwoman—capable and castrating. These antithetical roles have set black men and women on a collision course.

571. Whyte, William Foote. **Street Corner Society: The Social Structure of an Italian Slum**. 3d ed. Chicago and London: University of Chicago Press, 1981. P. xx, 386. illustrations. appendixes. bibliography, 376-80. pa.

In this classic study, Whyte describes the lives of men in the North Boston Italian slum during the late 1930s. He provides a history of the community, followed by a distinction between "corner boys" and "college boys," as well as an overview of racketeering and politics. Whyte focuses first upon the Nortons, a streetcorner gang of men mostly in their twenties, led by Doc. Next he examines the college boy Chick Morelli and his club, contrasting Chick and Doc as representative of upwardly mobile and nonmobile Italian men. Whyte then describes racketeering and its connection with the Social and Athletic Club, depicting the conflict between racketeer Tony Cataldo and corner boy Carlo Tedesco for control of the club. The interlinking of politics and streetcorner social structure is examined, and in the conclusion Whyte provides a survey of his findings, offering a vivid reminder of how ethnic prejudice hampered Italians in their efforts to enter the American mainstream. The first editions of *Street Corner Society* appeared in 1943 and 1955. The latest edition includes three appendixes. In the first, Whyte provides a detailed, personal account of his adventures while doing field work in North Boston; he describes his later relations with the corner boys and college boys of the study, and he tells of the book's rising and falling fortunes over the years. In the second appendix, Angelo Ralph Orlandella recounts how working with Whyte turned his life around. The third appendix contains a bibliography of Whyte's writings.

572. Wilkinson, Doris Y., and Ronald L. Taylor, eds. **The Black Male in America: Perspectives on His Status in Contemporary Society**. Chicago: Nelson-Hall, 1977. P. viii, 376. notes. author and subject index. bibliography, 361-69. pa.

The popular image of the black male as "emasculated" by white society and by his matrifocal upbringing, as immature, and as a poor husband and father is examined in twenty-four scholarly, readable articles. Contributions are grouped in four sections dealing with socialization to the black male role, stereotyping and stigmatization of black males, the issue of interracial mating, and the black male's roles in postindustrial society. Highlights include essays by Ronald L. Taylor and Ulf Hannerz on growing up as a black male, Robert Coles on black fathers, William H. Turner's account of "myths" and stereotypes of the African man in America, Harry Edwards's discussion of white fears of black athletes, Robert Staples's assault upon the "myth" of black matriarchy, Joan Downs's account of the political overtones of black-white dating, Nathan Caplan's description of the "new" ghetto male, and essays by Charles V. Willie and David A. Schulz on black fathers and black families. Many readers will see this book as a necessary introduction to any study of black men.

Cross references:

78. Brown, Claude. **Manchild in the Promised Land.**

99. Wright, Richard. **Black Boy: A Record of Childhood and Youth.**

518. Gold, Herbert. **Fathers: A Novel in the Form of a Memoir.**

RELIGION

573. Andelin, Aubrey P. **Man of Steel and Velvet.** Santa Barbara, Calif.: Pacific Press Santa Barbara, 1972. P. 316.

"This is a book which teaches men to be men," Andelin declares in his introduction. Because men have failed to be men, women have been forced to take the lead in too many areas of life. The results can be seen in dominant mothers, frustrated women, unruly children, juvenile delinquency, increasing homosexuality, and the stridency of women's liberation. Andelin's ideal man combines strength and gentleness, steel and velvet. The discussion is presented from a conservative Christian viewpoint.

574. Bakan, David. **And They Took Themselves Wives: The Emergence of Patriarchy in Western Civilization.** New York: Harper and Row, 1979. P. 186. illustration. notes. index.

Working closely with biblical texts, Bakan explores the centrality of paternity in the Bible, along with its traces of matrocentrism. After fixing the frames for interpreting the Bible, the author touches on such matters as ideas of divine impregnation and the meanings of circumcision, animal sacrifice, and male involvement in warfare. Among his conclusions is the idea that the Bible is associated with the reduction in sex role differences through its depiction of males "effeminized" toward greater child care.

575. Bianchi, Eugene C., and Rosemary R. Reuther. **From Machismo to Mutuality: Essays on Sexism and Woman-Man Liberation.** New York: Paulist Press, 1976. P. v, 142. appendix. notes.

Bianchi and Reuther alternate essays in this volume. A theologian influenced by radical feminism, Reuther reduces history to a tale of male oppression and female subjugation. A former Jesuit, Bianchi deplores the sexism inculcated by his church. "Mutuality" in this book seems to consist of indiscriminate female denunciations of men as evil accompanied by male recitations of mea culpa.

576. Bloesch, Donald G. **Is the Bible Sexist? Beyond Feminism and Patriarchalism.** Westchester, Ill.: Crossway Books, 1982. notes. scripture, name, and subject indexes. pa.

Rejecting both patriarchalism (that subordinates women to men) and feminism (that declares women's independence of men), Bloesch argues for a biblical alternative stressing the interdependence of men and women. Denouncing sexism as a sin, Bloesch nevertheless has reservations about some feminist goals and attitudes. In particular, he questions feminist efforts to alter biblical language, contending that in some cases the proposed changes create distortions. Bloesch is critical of societies like modern Sweden where he sees neopaganism and feminism allied to create a situation that dignifies neither women nor men.

577.   Eller, Vernard. **The Language of Canaan and the Grammar of Feminism.** Grand Rapids, Mich.: William B. Eerdmans Publishing Co., 1982. P. xiv, 56. pa.

In this brief book Eller takes issue with feminist critics who denounce biblical language as sexist. In particular, he argues that "man," like most words, has several levels of meaning depending upon usage; its use as a generic term comes closer to biblical meanings than do modern substitutes like "humanity" or "humankind." Likewise, the masculine pronoun "he" at one level is "sexually ignorant," that is, it does not call attention to sexual differences. The modern "he or she," however, forces gender differences into grammatical situations where they are unwanted. Eller argues that the biblical imagery of God as masculine is not sexist, nor is the imagery designating God and Israel, Christ and Church, as lover and beloved. In their zeal to have women recognized in language, feminists have inadvertently distorted biblical meanings.

578.   Johnson, James L. **What Every Woman Should Know about a Man.** Grand Rapids, Mich.: Zondervan Publishing House, 1977. P. 176. notes. bibliography, 176. pa.

For the more liberated Christian woman, Johnson attempts to explain what is often going on beneath the silent facade of the man—or men—in her life. Although many men find the armor of masculinity confining, they still wear it assiduously. The author cautions women to look beyond "myths" or images of men perpetuated by society and fostered by the media. He urges women to avoid the manipulative "total woman" role recommended by some female advocates; such a role he finds insulting to men and demeaning to women. Arguing for "equal but different" roles in the male-female relationship, Johnson discusses love, sex, striving, feelings, communication, the middle years, and the Christian man.

Cross references:

9.   Horner, Tom, comp. **Homosexuality and the Judeo-Christian Tradition: An Annotated Bibliography.**

50.   Greene, Thayer A. **Modern Man in Search of Manhood.**

55.   Kilgore, James E. **The Intimate Male.**

64.   Olson, Richard P. **Changing Male Roles in Today's World: A Christian Perspective for Men—and the Women Who Care about Them.**

307. Wellisch, E. **Isaac and Oedipus: A Study in Biblical Psychology of the Sacrifice of Isaac** *The Akedah.*

339. Bahsen, Greg L. **Homosexuality: A Biblical View.**

340. Barnhouse, Ruth Tiffany. **Homosexuality: A Symbolic Confusion.**

342. Boswell, John. **Christianity, Social Tolerance, and Homosexuality: Gay People in Western Europe from the Beginning of the Christian Era to the Fourteenth Century.**

353. Goodich, Michael. **The Unmentionable Vice: Homosexuality in the Later Medieval Period.**

369. McNaught, Brian. **A Disturbed Peace: Selected Writings of an Irish Catholic Homosexual.**

370. McNeill, John J. **The Church and the Homosexual.**

375. Oraison, Marc. **The Homosexual Question.**

399. Dobson, James C. **Straight Talk to Men and Their Wives.**

403. Grant, Wilson Wayne. **The Caring Father.**

407. Heidebrecht, Paul, and Jerry Rohrbach. **Fathering a Son.**

414. Leenhouts, Keith J. **A Father ... A Son ... and a Three-Mile Run.**

417. Lockerbie, D. Bruce. **Fatherlove: Learning to Give the Best You've Got.**

420. MacDonald, Gordon. **The Effective Father.**

423. Miller, Ted, ed. **The Christian Book on Being a Caring Father.**

433. Shedd, Charlie. **The Best Dad Is a Good Lover.**

434. Shedd, Charlie. **A Dad Is for Spending Time With.**

435. Shedd, Charlie. **Smart Dads I Know.**

436. Stanley, Charles F. **A Man's Touch.**

469. Benson, Dan. **The Total Man.**

476. Shedd, Charlie W. **Letters to Philip: On How to Treat a Woman.**

HUMOR _____

579. Berman, Edgar. **The Compleat Chauvinist: A Survival Guide for the Bedeviled Male.** New York: Macmillan Co., 1982. P. x, 219.

In prose laced with quips and puns, Berman twits militant feminist views on such matters as work outside the home, menstruation, spouse battering, women in sports and politics, affirmative action, and the ERA (which Berman supports enthusiastically as a boon to male chauvinists). Insisting that he is only antifeminist and not misogynist, Berman (an M.D.) believes that hormones are destiny, and he praises the "feminine" woman. Readers will have to decide for themselves if Berman's book represents an exercise in witty wisdom or ridiculous reactionism.

580. Bishop, Beata, with Pat McNeill. **Eggshell Ego: An Irreverant [sic] Look at Today's Male.** Short Hills, N.J.: Enslow Publishers, 1979. P. 140. pa. Originally published as *Below the Belt: An Irreverent Analysis of the Male Ego* (London: Coventure, 1977).

Arguing that some men are just being sullen because women have toppled them from their position of dominance in society, the authors conclude that the way to improve male-female relationships is for women to take a hatchet to men's fragile egos. Though some readers may doubt the wisdom of this tactic (to say nothing of the authors' hatchet imagery), Bishop and McNeill offer a series of gibes at men concerning such topics as sex, the strong silent (and dumb) male, and male dependence upon women. The authors insist that they are neither "doormat ladies" nor "bitter Amazons." Readers who can accept their belief that most men enjoy the privileges and powers of an Oriental potentate may see *Eggshell Ego* as witty and "with it." Others holding a less-exalted vision of the average man's lot may see the book as a tedious exercise in misguided man-baiting.

581. Charles, Claudia, ed. **Why I Hate Men.** Bayside, N.Y.: Planet Books, 1983. P. 128. illustrations. pa.

This potpourri of anecdotes, interviews, quick essays, quizzes, and so on will amuse some readers as a send-up of prevailing male insensitivities. Other readers may find in the book's straining for laughs only additional evidence that feminist self-righteousness and humor are mutually exclusive terms.

582.   Everitt, David, and Harold Schecter. **The Manly Handbook**. New York:
         Berkley Books, 1982. P. 134. illustrations. pa.
Written so that a real man can understand it, the text of this hilarious spoof of
American machismo is supplemented by wickedly funny photographs featuring
the likes of Humphrey Bogart, John Wayne, and (of course) George C. Scott as
General Patton.

583.   Feirstein, Bruce. **Real Men Don't Eat Quiche**. New York: Pocket Books,
         1982. P. 93. illustrations. pa.
A bestseller which has spawned a host of spin-offs, this "guidebook to all that is
truly masculine" parodies the macho pose, both working-class and corporate
style. Cartoons by Lee Lorenz punctuate brief chapters on such matters as the
Real Man's vocabulary, great moments in Real Men's history, and so on. Like many
parodies *Real Men* hovers between ridicule of and affection for its subject.

584.   Friedman, Bruce Jay. **The Lonely Guy's Book of Life**. New York:
         McGraw-Hill Book Co., 1978. P. xiv, 206. illustrations.
The walking wounded of modern life, the lonely guys are here provided with whim-
sical advice on such matters as apartment living, cooking, grooming ("clothes left
overnight in Woolite tend to rot away when you're wearing them at parties"),
running, eating alone in restaurants, illness, psychiatric counseling, and sex. Victor
Juhasz supplies comic illustrations.

585.   Gardner, Jani. **Three Hundred Sixty-five Ways to Seduce Your Very Own
         Husband**. New York: Hawthorn Books, 1972. unpaged. illustrations.
Guaranteed to make a memorable year, Gardner's exuberant suggestions reflect
the joy of love and sex. Dale Diesel's drawings are appropriately lighthearted.

586.   Jones, Julia Runk, and Milo Trump. **Livingston's Field Guide to North
         American Males**. Garden City, N.Y.: Doubleday and Co., Dolphin, 1984.
         P. 124. illustrations. notes. index. pa.
In this daffy guide to North American males, the authors provide species and sub-
species descriptions, including accounts of plumage (clothing), feathering (hairstyles), songs (identifying comments), habitat, range, nest, courtship and mating
practices, and track ("little tell-tale signs males leave behind, such as cigarette
butts, beer cans, business cards and dandruff"). Species include The Machoman
(homo hardhat), The Good Ol' Boy (homo buddy), The Slob (homo porkus),
The Jock (homo sweatsocks), the Golden Throated Tanner (homo coke), and The
Sweet Young Thing (homo cookie). The comical photographs of the species "in
their natural habitats" are by Alan Rabold. Not to be overlooked are the zany
footnotes.

587.   King, Florence. **He: An Irreverent Look at the American Male**. New
         York: Stein and Day, 1978. P. x, 204.
King describes herself as neither a Total Woman nor a women's liberationist.
(The most readable section of *Ms.* magazine, she notes, is the No Comment department.) With a sharp eye and ear, King skewers the foibles of American males—and
females—in recent times. After regaling readers with salty recollections of her
teenage sexual experiments in the fifties, King goes on to characterize various male

types in the seventies. Not to be missed is her send-up of the male feminist whom she dubs Jonathan Stuart Mill. Ever trendy, Jonathan has lost interest in black causes and is now (he explains with a straight face) "into women." King also exposes the literary sins of recent male writers, and she portrays the new misogynists, who got that way (she confesses) partly from too many encounters with strident feminists. Although she professes a passion for the polished Alistair Cooke types, one suspects that in reality they would be too tepid for her. Despite her "irreverent look at the American male," many readers will sense King's delight in him, foibles and all.

588.   Mead, Shepherd. **Free the Male Man! The Manifesto of the Men's Liberation Movement, Examining the Urgent Need to Free Malekind and Reestablish the Equality, Both Economic and Sexual, of the Two Sexes, Containing Explicit Sexual Instructions, Diagrams and Battle Plans for the Coming Masculist Revolution**. New York: Simon and Schuster, 1972. P. 155. illustrations.
Examining the comic side of the hazards of being male, Mead provides both laughter and consciousness raising about men's issues. John Huehnergarth's cartoons add to the fun.

589.   Myer, Andy. **The Liberated Father's Handbook**. New York: St. Martin's Press, 1983. P. vii, 87. illustrations. pa.
Myer provided the text and the illustrations—both hilarious—for this comic guide for the pregnant father. Chapters cover such topics as visiting the gynecologist ("No Man's Land"), surviving the baby shower, assembling the crib, handling labor and delivery, late-night feedings, the diaper dilemma ("Winning the Poo"), and traveling with baby ("The Longest Mile").

590.   Schoenstein, Ralph. **Yes, My Darling Daughters: Adventures in Fathering**. New York: Farrar, Straus and Giroux, 1976. P. 133. Reprint. New York: Avon Books, 1977. pa.
In comic style that will remind some readers of Jean Kerr's early family writings, Schoenstein recounts his wacky adventures as the father of two daughters.

591.   Stewart, D.L. **Fathers Are People Too**. Dayton, Ohio: Journal Herald, 1980. P. 122. illustrations. pa. Reprint. Indianapolis, Ind.: Bobbs-Merrill, 1983. pa.
One of the funniest writers in America today, Stewart recounts fourteen of his hilarious misadventures as the father of four. Lovers of laughter should not miss Stewart's account of chaperoning a cub scout troop around New York City, taking a son fishing (and actually catching a fish), a night with the kids at a roller-skating rink, and the ordeal of having a teen party in the basement. Illustrations are by Ted Pitts.

Cross references:

83.   Greenburg, Dan. **Scoring: A Sexual Memoir.**

AUTHOR INDEX

References are to bibliography entry number.

TITLE INDEX

References are to bibliography entry number.

DATE DUE